Death of an Insurance Salesman?

Death of an Insurance Salesman?

By
ROBERT D. ORR

A division of Squire Publishers, Inc.
4500 College Blvd.
Leawood, KS 66211
Phone: 1/888/888-7696

ISBN: 1-58597-037-9

Library of Congress Catalog Card No. 00-133111

A division of Squire Publishers, Inc.
4500 College Blvd.
Leawood, KS 66211
Phone: 1/888/888-7696

ACKNOWLEDGMENTS

Thanks to all of my Brooke Corporation colleagues for their inspiration and support during development of the Agent Entrepreneur and Master Agent concepts. A special thanks to Leland Orr and Mike Hess for many years of friendship and listening to my "tirades" on this subject.

I hesitate to list all of those who should be individually recognized because I may inadvertently miss someone who deserves mention. However, I do want to specifically recognize Brooke Corporation's management team because I feed off their youthful enthusiasm and ambition. They, not me, will make the Agent Entrepreneur and Master Agent concepts revolutionary forces in the sale of insurance and financial services.

And because I don't say it enough, thanks to Kimba, Kaley, Casey and Kelsey for keeping the Orr home fires burning.

Rob Orr

DEATH OF AN INSURANCE SALESMAN?

Overview
- Agent Distribution
- Business Ownership
- Book Organization

PART I.........FOOD FOR THOUGHT

OVERVIEW

The impact of the Internet Age rivals the economic transformation caused by the industrial revolution of the late 19th century. Although telegraph and cable communications played an important supporting role in the industrial revolution, Internet communication is the foundation of the current revolution. However, the Internet Age encompasses much more than Internet communication. Technological advances made the Internet accessible, and social changes made it acceptable. Perhaps the Internet is not the cause of a revolution but the result.

This book is targeted to an audience primarily interested in the impact of the Internet Age on the distribution of financial services. The author's basic premise is that financial services will be dominated by Internet distribution of financial "commodities" with the distribution of more complicated *non-commodities* by local agents. Distribution systems characterized by multiple management layers and expensive facilities are probably too expensive to survive in the Internet Age.

AGENT DISTRIBUTION

Using a military analogy, agents represent the "guerrilla" infantry of the Internet Age because they know the local population, travel light and require little artillery support.

The agency system that is currently used to distribute insurance provides a good starting point for developing an agent distribution system to compliment Internet distribution, although significant changes are required to improve efficiency.

Agents are important because they provide the local customer contact that is sometimes required to sell more complicated insurance and financial services. Any agent activities that do not involve customer contact must be delegated to more efficient providers. Accordingly, the author introduces the Master Agent concept to: 1) process non-customer contact activities, 2) consolidate agent purchasing power, and 3) develop a collective brand name.

BUSINESS OWNERSHIP

Eliminating layers of management and reducing overhead expense with agent distribution requires a motivated agent force and performance-based rewards. Business ownership is the ultimate tool for rewarding performance and motivating agents. As such, business ownership is an important part of developing an efficient agent distribution system. A Master Agent makes business ownership more attractive by facilitating: 1) ownership transfers, 2) credit extensions to buyers, and 3) the matching of buyers with sellers.

BOOK ORGANIZATION

This book is divided into three parts. The first part provides "Food for Thought" by presenting the author's various viewpoints on agent distribution. This material is organized into chapters on specific areas of interest beginning with a discussion of the changes required for insurance salesmen to become agent entrepreneurs. These discussions include comments on how the Master Agent concept is an integral part of the required changes.

The second part of this book describes the specific "Standards" that the author believes are necessary to fully implement the Master Agent concept.

The final section specifically demonstrates the "Implementation" of those ideas and concepts discussed in the previous two parts of the book. Included are the actual legal agreements and applications used by Brooke Corporation, pioneer of the Master Agent concept.

Part I

FOOD FOR THOUGHT

C H A P T E R

The Insurance Salesman

DEAD OR ALIVE?

The insurance salesman that does not adapt will eventually be a professional victim of the Internet Age. This also holds true for other "middlemen" such as securities brokers, real estate brokers, loan brokers and bankers.

Although the Internet plays an important role in insurance sales, there remain circumstances where personal contact is required, or preferred, to complete a sale, which demonstrates that insurance salesmen are needed. The following summarizes how an insurance salesman can survive by:

1) Possessing a survivor's personality
2) Adding value to products with expertise, persuasion, confidence or convenience
3) Focusing exclusively on customer contact and sales
4) Purchasing access, processing and protection from a Master Agent
5) Remaining independent from companies and customs

PERSONALITY

The personality of an insurance salesman is probably the single most important survivability factor. It is not a coincidence that the personality traits that characterize insurance salesman survivors also personify successful entrepreneurs. The following is a subjective and over-simplified comparison of personality traits for survivors and victims.

Survivors	Victims
Aggressive	Passive
Intense	Easygoing
Persistent	Order Taker
Ambitious	Paper Pusher
Competitive	Saver
Risk Taker	Averts Risk
Spender	Conservative
Progressive	Practical
Dreamer	

ADD PRODUCT VALUE

Survivors must also provide something of value to their customers that is not already or better provided by the Internet or an insurance company. If additional benefits are not provided, then an insurance salesman is useless and will not survive.

Expertise

For more complicated insurance, such as business insurance, customers often require advice to ensure the purchase of adequate and proper insurance. An insurance salesman provides customers with the benefit of his expertise in these circumstances.

Persuasion

Customers may be misinformed or ignorant of their need for insurance. An insurance salesman provides significant value by persuading customers to purchase the required insurance.

Confidence

"Peace of mind" is a benefit that customers receive when they purchase insurance from a source that they trust. A personal relationship and a trustworthy brand name are two ways that an insurance salesman provides this benefit.

Convenience

The convenience of purchasing insurance from a local insurance salesman is an additional benefit that is valuable to many customers.

FOCUS

Customer Focus

Virtually every additional benefit that an insurance salesman has to offer is centered on personal contact with the customer. It seems to follow that an insurance salesman should make customer contact a top priority.

Sales Focus

As a result of being compensated by a commission on sales, an insurance salesman is rewarded for providing additional customer benefits when a sale is made. Therefore, it also follows that an insurance agent should focus on customer contact for the specific purpose of selling.

MASTER AGENT

Processing

Survivors focus exclusively on customer contact, so an insurance salesman's processing-type activities that do not involve customer contact are outsourced to a Master Agent with processing expertise. By employing economies of scale and Internet Age technology, a Master Agent provides an insurance salesman with universal access to customer information at any time from any place.

Insurance Company Access

A Master Agent also provides an insurance salesman with an expanded "inventory" of insurance policies for sale to customers. A Master Agent's purchasing power ensures that insurance salesmen receive more reliable access to insurance companies.

Brand Marketing

Due to the unregulated nature of the Internet, developing a national brand name is critical for successful Internet marketing. A Master Agent develops a collective brand name by coordinating and monitoring the marketing activities of individual insurance salesmen from many locations throughout the nation.

Internet Marketing

An insurance salesman is valuable to customers because personal contact from a local representative is sometimes required to sell insurance. Internet marketing of insurance provides for a "hand off" of the customer from an Internet Web site to an insurance salesman when local representation is required to make the sale. Because Internet marketing is not restricted by geographical boundaries, a national network of insurance salesmen is required for the successful sale of insurance over the Internet. A Master Agent coordinates the policies and the actions of individual insurance salesmen to protect the brand names of the Internet site and the collective insurance salesmen.

INDEPENDENCE

Insurance Companies

Survivors do not purchase all of their insurance policies from one insurance company because such dependence is professionally dangerous. Survivors also create a marketing identity that is not closely associated with any one insurance company.

Convention

Survivors are unafraid to break with conventional wisdom. As might be expected of someone with a survivor's personality, experimentation and flexibility characterize their actions.

C H A P T E R

Agent Entrepreneurs

The Internet Age has brought renewed attention to entrepreneurs and the fortunes they've amassed from technological innovations. The Internet Age will create many more fortunes as new and courageous entrepreneurs make their mark in the business world. The following begins the discussions of how insurance salesmen can share the prosperity of the Internet Age as agent entrepreneurs.

ENTREPRENEURS
Schumpeter

Economist Joseph Schumpeter (1883-1950) foresaw the role of entrepreneurs in the Internet Age. Schumpeter noted that entrepreneurs interrupt the "circular flow" of mature economic systems with new perspectives on the economic system and new ideas about how to combine existing resources to create more valuable products.

Of significance to the following discussions on personal wealth is Schumpeter's view that entrepreneurial activity is "the foundation of material progress in capitalistic economies." Schumpeter's views are revisited several times throughout this book and are the intellectual foundation for the agent entrepreneur concept. (Please note that the author is not an economist and that any misinterpretations or distortions of Dr. Schumpeter's viewpoint are inadvertent.)

Entrepreneurial Spirit

Although the creation of material wealth is very important to entrepreneurs, a sense of accomplishment and a desire to control destiny combine to help form the psyche of successful entrepreneurs. This spirit is found in old clichés such as "being my own boss" or "owning my own business."

Personal Wealth

Successful entrepreneurs are usually rewarded with significant personal wealth. The richest of the rich listed in Forbes' magazine are entrepreneurs such as Bill Gates. In this Internet Age, entrepreneurs from the most humble beginnings can achieve their dreams of fortune and fame.

Schumpeter noted that successful entrepreneurs are helped by a certain amount of luck. However, these entrepreneurs put themselves in a position to become lucky with hard work, innovation and persistence.

Business Owners

Most of the wealth in our country is created by business ownership, and most successful entrepreneurs are business owners. Entrepreneurs would not be entrepreneurs if they did not take an active role in running and managing their businesses. Ownership provides a direct and proportional reward for an entrepreneur's business achievements.

AGENT PROSPERITY
Insurance Salesman or Agent Entrepreneur?

To prosper in the Internet Age, insurance salesmen must be reborn as agent entrepreneurs. The term "insurance salesman" denotes a professional person, and "agent entrepreneur" denotes a businessman. The remaining chapters of this book are devoted to creating personal wealth through business ownership, so the term agent entrepreneur shall be substituted for insurance salesman in the chapters that follow.

By definition, the product line of an insurance salesman is limited to insurance. However, as a businessman, the product line of an agent entrepreneur extends to financial services beyond insurance. Accordingly, references to insurance will be minimized in the remaining chapters of this book. For example, insurance companies will typically be referred to using the more generic term of "supplier."

Business Opportunity

Agent entrepreneurs create a valuable business enterprise as a distributor of insurance and financial services for insurance companies and other suppliers. "Ownership" of customer relationships is the primary, and most valuable, asset of an agent's business.

Customer relationships and, therefore, business value may be created by agent entrepreneurs from little more than hard work and persistence. With the assistance of a Master Agent, a ready market exists for the purchase and sale of customer relationships. This creates a tremendous opportunity for ambitious entrepreneurs to create significant personal wealth with limited capital.

Local Entrepreneur

The term "local entrepreneur" was recently used by a Daimler Chrysler executive to describe the distribution of automobiles by local business owners with personal customer relationships. This term can also be used to accurately describe agent entrepreneurs.

Development of long-distance customer relationships is a primary focus of Internet companies. However, there remain circumstances in this age of the Internet when local customer relationships are required; and local relationships are the forte of agent entrepreneurs. As such, agent entrepreneurs have an opportunity to compete with computer programmers for a slice of the wealth created by today's Internet Age.

MASTER AGENT

A primary role of a Master Agent is to help agent entrepreneurs realize or "cash in" the wealth created by the value of their customer relationships. The following lists some of the ways that a Master Agent facilitates the sale of an agent's business.

Buyers Pool

Business value cannot be realized until an agent entrepreneur finds a willing and capable buyer. A Master Agent maintains a database of potential buyers to help match sellers with buyers.

Acquisition Loans

Credit availability increases the pool of capable buyers and, therefore, increases the value of an agent's business. A Master Agent protects lenders' collateral interests by "safekeeping" commissions, which strengthens collateral values and makes credit more available. In many instances, a Master Agent makes loans directly to buyers through a finance company subsidiary.

Legal Standards

Standardized and comprehensive purchase agreements, agent agreements and subagent agreements have been developed by the Master Agent to help ensure that a buyer is getting what is paid for. Increasing buyer confidence also increases business value.

Ownership Transfers

Transferring customer relationships from sellers to buyers without alarming or inconveniencing those customers increases business value. A Master Agent makes an ownership transfer mostly transparent to the customer because the name and address information on the insurance policy or other financial instrument is that of the Master Agent and does not change when ownership transfers. Additionally, the insurance company or supplier issuing the insurance policy or other financial instrument does not change.

The Master Agent also gathers all customer information and stores it in an electronic format that is available anytime from anywhere; so the transfer of customer information is immediate and complete, which permits uninterrupted service.

C H A P T E R

Product Selection

Agents must select products to distribute that are less likely to be monopolized by Internet distribution. Economist Joseph Schumpeter noted that, in addition to price, factors such as sales effort (persuasion) and quality (expertise) must be considered in any discussion of monopolies. Although perhaps not entirely relevant, Schumpeter's observation on monopolies summarizes the basis for the following comments about product selection.

REGULATORY RELIEF

Recent financial services legislation demonstrates that market forces have prevailed, and the regulatory walls between various insurance and financial products are falling. This increases the products available for sale by agent entrepreneurs and permits selection of products based on their suitability for agents and their customers. Expanding the products available to agent entrepreneurs facilitates a transition toward selling more and different financial services through local agents.

COMMODITIES

Commoditization

Commodities are products that have the same, or nearly the same, features as competing products; so price comparisons are easy.

The process of commoditization is the conversion of insurance and financial services with similar features into commodities, primarily by providing customers with easy delivery of products and universal access to pricing information using the Internet and telephone. Examples include personal insurance (GIECO), securities (E-Trade) and personal banking (Wingspanbank). Products that are easy to understand and easy to sell are likely to become commodities. Products that are more complicated, such as business insurance and financial services, are less likely to become commodities.

Internet Sales
Commodities are excellent Internet products because the entire sales process of prospecting, pricing, underwriting, presentation and closing can typically be performed over the Internet. Products that are not commodities, such as business-related financial services, are likely to be marketed, *but not sold*, over the Internet because assistance and expertise are often required when pricing, underwriting and presenting more complicated products.

AGENT ASSESSMENT
Adding Value
It will be difficult for local providers that sell commodities to compete with Internet sales unless an additional value is provided that is not available on the Internet. Local convenience and a trustworthy brand name are two values that local agents can add to all of their products.

Customers are oftentimes unaware or uninterested in purchasing very important products such as life insurance. Even though this type of product is often a commodity, agents can add value by persuading customers to purchase. Perhaps most importantly, agents can add value by providing customers with access to their expertise when purchasing more complicated products.

Agent Qualifications
An agent's personality and experience are important factors to consider when selecting products to sell. Some agents may be

more comfortable and more skilled at selling products that require more persuasion and less expertise. On the other hand,
agents that have developed an expertise should probably select
products that capitalize on that expertise.

MARKET ASSESSMENT
Market Viability
The selection of products that are not likely to become obsolete
is an important selection criterion. Product obsolescence can result from disappearance of customers (such as fewer buggy whip
manufacturers because of fewer horse buggies) or the reduction
of the customer's need for a product (such as health care reform's
impact on health insurance).

Market Potential
Another important selection criterion requires an analysis of the
potential for additional product sales. An assessment of the future demand for a given product must account for economic and
demographic changes in an agent's geographical market area.
Competition from Internet sales or an entrenched local competitor must also be considered when selecting a product. If demand
for a product is not growing rapidly, then increasing sales by
wrestling the market share from a savvy competitor may be difficult and expensive.

Market Niche
Products that offer opportunities for specialization allow agents
to add value with their expertise. Identifying viable market niches
with significant growth potential is an ideal starting point for the
process of selecting products.

Although a "chicken or egg"-type dilemma, identifying products for a promising market niche for which an agent must acquire the required expertise may be a better approach than identifying products for a less promising market niche in which the
agent already has an expertise.

Product Development

During the course of analyzing markets to assist in product selection, an agent may identify customer needs for which a product does not exist or is inadequate. As such, product selection may require the development of new and improved products based on an agent's analysis.

VALUE ASSESSMENT

Selecting products based on the above analysis of agents and markets is of primary importance. Of secondary importance when selecting products is an assessment of how much an agency increases in value for each commission dollar received from the sale of a particular product.

All other things being equal, a dollar of commissions from the sale of a product that is likely to generate additional commissions for years to come is greater than a dollar of commissions from the sale of a product that is less likely to generate future commissions. Additionally, commissions that are less expensive to produce usually result in greater agency value.

PRODUCT CATEGORIES

The following is a laundry list of financial product categories which may help organize product selection. Within each product category is an almost infinite number of product possibilities.

Insurance

These discussions are primarily directed to the insurance salesman because the distribution methods currently employed by the independent insurance salesman will be the alternative for inexpensive distribution of more complicated financial services that are not easily sold over the Internet. As such, agent entrepreneurs are likely to have a preference for insurance products.

Insurance can be further segregated into property/casualty insurance sales and life/health insurance sales because a different sales approach is required for each. Property/casualty insurance sales generally create a more reliable and predictable commission stream which typically creates more business value than life/health insurance sales.

Securities
Equity and debt securities have historically been sold by commissioned salesmen. Internet sales of securities have soared, but there remains a place for agents that provide additional value with their expertise (research) or persuasiveness. Securities sales are a natural product line extension of life/heath insurance sales because of similar products and sales approaches.

Banking
Non-commissioned employees have historically sold deposit accounts and loans from impressive bank and branch offices. This method of distribution is expensive and is jeopardized by Internet sales of simple banking products and agent sales of more complicated products. Banks can become more competitive by separating their role as a distributor from their role as principals/investors and then choosing the distribution method best suited for each individual product.

Despite the erosion of the bank's share of the investment and loan markets, they remain a formidable force because of their local brand name and local convenience. Agents can provide banks with the local presence that has made them successful at a fraction of the cost.

Loan Brokerage
Non-bank lenders such as Countrywide Mortgage have led the way in the use of commissioned loan brokers to distribute their product. Because non-bank lenders appear more comfortable with agent distribution than bank lenders, if an agent sells a lending product, it is more likely to be supplied by a non-bank lender.

Real Estate Brokerage
The sale of real estate may be a good choice for the extension of an agent's product line if real estate sales fit into the agent's area of expertise and are compatible with the agent's other products.

Consulting

A consulting product is a natural fit for agents with expertise. Many insurance salesmen have already included consulting in their product line. The sale of products from any one of the above product categories may create an expertise that can be converted into a consulting product. It is likely that consulting will become more popular in the Internet Age, as businesses become more virtual and personnel is used on a project basis. Consulting is unique because agents supply their own products to sell.

ONGOING SELECTION

Product selection is an ongoing reevaluation process to help ensure that an agent's products remain suitable for the agent and his customers.

C H A P T E R

Supplier Relationships

Applying Joseph Schumpeter's "creative destruction" concept, the Internet Age will force some principal/investors to cannibalize sales from established methods of distribution with new and innovative methods of distribution such as Internet sales and agent sales. Agent entrepreneurs provide principals, or suppliers, with an inexpensive way to distribute complicated products or grow in an agent's local market. The following discusses various aspects of supplier relationships from an agent's perspective.

DISTRIBUTION

As agent entrepreneurs search for ways to increase commissions and agency value, their product line will extend beyond the sale of insurance, and their suppliers will include more than insurance companies. Accordingly, in these discussions, the more universal term of "supplier" is used instead of the industry-specific term of "insurance company." Securities firms, investment companies, non-bank lenders and banks may also be included in a definition of suppliers.

Control

Agent entrepreneurs require that suppliers grant them control of distribution. Agents are effective because they are motivated by the prospect of creating wealth through business ownership. However, if agents do not control distribution, then they do not "own" their customer accounts and cannot create business value.

Flexibility and Efficiency
Agents are likely to enjoy increased competition among suppliers for relationships with agents because of the flexibility and efficiency of agent distribution for certain types of products. Some suppliers have expensive direct sales organizations with large investments in facilities and employed professionals. In addition to being expensive, direct distribution hampers the suppliers' ability to innovate. Agent sales allow suppliers to experiment with new products in new territories without making a significant investment in facilities or employees.

ACCESS
The agent's access to the suppliers' products is of paramount importance. If the agents have no products to sell, then there are no commissions to receive and no value to create. Even when agents have the required access to the suppliers' products, the type of agent access can significantly affect business value. One of the most important benefits provided by a Master Agent is providing agents with easy, reliable and high-level access to the suppliers' products.

Easy Access
Easy access that results from a Master Agent's purchasing power is desirable and makes an agent's business more valuable. However, easy access because a supplier makes its product universally available makes an agent's business less valuable because future commissions are less certain.

Reliable Access
Reliability of commissions, and, therefore, business value correlates directly to the reliability of the agent's access to the suppliers' products. The combined sales volume of the Master Agent makes access more certain than it would otherwise be.

High Level Access

Again using its purchasing power, a Master Agent helps the agents acquire access directly with suppliers without "buying" access through brokers or other middlemen.

UNDERWRITING

The suppliers' evaluation of a customer's application to purchase a product (usually insurance or loans) is commonly referred to as "underwriting." Consistent and prompt underwriting is important to agents because it is important to their customers.

Formula Underwriting

If the underwriting process is simple, or if no underwriting is required, then a product is easier to sell; and an agent is less likely to add product value. Underwriting formulas, such as credit scoring, automate the underwriting process and make the product more suited to direct sale by the supplier over the Internet.

Field Underwriting

For more complicated situations, suppliers rely on qualified agents to make a local evaluation to supplement the supplier's evaluation. This local evaluation is sometimes referred to as "field" underwriting and is a way for agents to use their expertise to provide additional value to a product.

STABILITY

Supplier stability makes the agents' access to products more certain and commissions more reliable.

Pricing

The supplier's price for a product is always an issue, but as noted in a previous chapter (See Product Selection chapter), agents are more likely to sell products, for which pricing is not the only issue. Suppliers with the pricing philosophy of discount stores which "will not be undersold" have adopted a commodity approach to pricing, which leaves agents with fewer alternatives for adding product value. Reasonable product pricing that provides for consistent supplier profits makes the supplier a more stable source for products.

Financial

Seasoned and proven managers are more apt to meet the investment community's performance expectations and, thereby, provide a more stable source for products. A supplier's poor financial or stock performance may result in unpredictable product changes from new management, new owners or corporate restructuring.

TRUST

The suppliers' commitment to respect the agents' ownership of their customer accounts is a fundamental tenant of the supplier relationship. Suppliers that circumvent an agent to access the agent's customer directly, or provide the means for others to do so, violate the spirit of the supplier relationship.

The extent of the suppliers' relationship with the agent's customers must be specifically defined (see Technology and Operations chapter) because too much control by the supplier impacts the value of the agent's business.

C H A P T E R

Recruitment and Networking

Revenues are the primary determinant of agency value, so increasing revenues is a primary focus of agent entrepreneurs. Revenues grow to greater levels at faster speeds when agents leverage their time and resources by building a sales organization which makes selling easier (networking) and increases sales without the agent's direct involvement (recruitment).

Agency value also increases when sales are not directly dependent on one individual or concentrated in one industry. Building a sales organization permits diversification by generating sales from a variety of sources and reduces dependence on any one individual or industry.

MASTER AGENT

Agents must have maximum flexibility, so they can build their sales organization in the manner they choose. A Master Agent's role is to provide the structure or framework to assist agents in recruiting and networking while permitting the required flexibility.

Information Flow

One of the most important contributions that a Master Agent makes to an agent's sales organization is providing customer account information on a timely basis to those that need it and are entitled to it. By delivering customer account information over the Internet, a Master Agent can provide immediate access from anywhere in the world. However, an agent can also limit Internet access to customer accounts based on individual circumstances through the assignment of access security codes.

The Master Agent's centralized electronic filing requirements consolidate all information, so that it can be delivered and controlled by the agent. Accounting information is organized by the Master Agent; commissions may be "sliced and diced" by agents, and they have control of their individual compensation requirements.

Clearinghouse

A Master Agent provides valuable assistance as a clearinghouse for information about agent expertise or supplier access, so an agent can match up with other agents to share or broker sales. Because an agent may need information regarding a specific expertise infrequently, it is difficult for the agent to find the right networking connection unless the Master Agent keeps a database of this type of information.

As an extension of the clearinghouse concept, expert agents are encouraged to apply for the Master Agent's endorsement. If an agent's application is approved after a thorough investigation, then a Master Agent endorses and promotes expert agents to other agents.

Trickle Down

The added value that a Master Agent provides to an agent trickles down to those in an agent's sales organization. Supplier access, brand identity and even credit access are examples of Master Agent services that agents can offer to those in their organization.

GROWTH THROUGH RECRUITMENT

Recruitment of others to sell exclusively for an agent is an effective and proven way to increase commissions and, therefore, agency value. Building an organization that increases sales without an agent's direct involvement, as with recruitment, is another important ingredient for increasing agency value.

Adding Value

In addition to the benefits that trickle down from the Master Agent, agents must provide value to those that they recruit in the form of sales assistance such as training, prospecting, product expertise, social contacts or office facilities. If agents do not provide assistance to their recruits, then the additional expense for agent compensation is unwarranted, and the relationship will be eventually discontinued.

Hierarchical Structure

Recruits are directly supervised by and strictly accountable to an agent. Although agent recruitment results in some of the advantages of a multi-level sales organization such as Amway, agents are selling professional services and not Amway soap; so a greater degree of professional and ethical accountability is required. To promote control and accountability, the number of levels in an agent's sales organization is never more than three (Master Agent, agent and recruits); although sponsorships and networking alliances may result in additional commission splits.

The following discussion of recruitment has been separated into: 1) subagent recruitment where customer account ownership is granted to the subagent and 2) producer recruitment where customer account ownership is retained by the agent.

RECRUITMENT OF SUBAGENTS
Subagent Entrepreneurs

An agent will probably be most successful when recruiting subagents with entrepreneurial personalities because the same characteristics that make an agent successful will make a subagent successful. An ambitious and progressive subagent generates growth much faster, providing value to both the agent and subagent.

Customer Account Ownership

Subagent entrepreneurs want to create value from owning and running their own business in the same manner as agent entrepreneurs. Therefore, an agent provides subagents with ownership of their customer accounts in the same manner as a Master Agent provides agents with ownership. Subagents add to the pool of prospective agency buyers and, as a result, increase the value and liquidity of an agent's business.

Agent Sponsor

For the reasons outlined above, subagents may not recruit other subagents and, thereby, create an additional level in an agent's sales organization. However, subagents may sponsor other subagents for recruitment directly by an agent and receive a share of the recruit's commissions for his efforts.

RECRUITMENT OF PRODUCERS

Producer Entrepreneurs

It may be more difficult to recruit entrepreneurs into a producer relationship than a subagent relationship because producers are not granted any ownership in their customer accounts. Producers generally require more supervision and more support than subagents; however, a producer's commissions are more valuable to an agent because the agent retains full customer account ownership. For this reason, many agents prefer producer recruits despite the additional headaches.

To compensate for the absence of actual account ownership, agents can sometimes satisfy a producer's entrepreneurial needs with phantom ownership where the producer shares in the increased agency value resulting from the producer's sales. Independence is also an important issue to entrepreneurs, so agents can sometimes substitute for account ownership with a flexible and independent work schedule allowing the producer to feel as if he is running his own business.

Producer Sales

Subagent ownership is customer account oriented, and producer sales are product or policy oriented. Accordingly, producers are typically paid a share of commissions generated from the sale of individual products or policies and do not receive a share of commissions on all policies that comprise the customer's account.

Protecting Agent

The increased value resulting from a producer's commissions must survive the agent-producer relationship. If the commissions leave with the producer, then the agent does not realize any increase in value for his investment. To avoid this, producers agree to not solicit sales from an agent's customer accounts when a producer relationship is terminated. Although laws vary from state to state, generally a carefully worded non-solicitation clause in the producer's agreement will provide the necessary protection.

Much of a producer's time is invested in prospecting for new customers. Records of prospecting activities can be very valuable for making future prospecting more productive. Therefore, requiring producers to document all prospecting activity creates value which would otherwise be wasted when a producer relationship is discontinued.

GROWTH THROUGH NETWORKING

Adding Value

Networking with others creates more commission opportunities for agents and their recruits. From the perspective of an agent with customer access but without product expertise or supplier access, networking provides access to expertise and suppliers. From the opposite perspective of an agent with product expertise or supplier access but without customer access, networking provides access to customers.

Flexibility

Networking provides access on a customer-by-customer basis, so networking relationships are flexible and temporary. Agents can expand their product line, expert staff or customer contacts without much expense and without a significant commitment. The result of extensive networking is a "virtual" organization where alliances are formed on a project basis and give the sales organization access to resources that it could not otherwise afford.

Peer to Peer

Although customer account ownership is retained by the agent with the initial or primary customer access, networking is a relationship between professional peers. The flexible nature of networking alliances permits immediate exclusion of agents that are not professionally courteous or capable.

Networking is generally one of two types: 1) shared sales networking or 2) brokered sales networking.

NETWORKING WITH SHARED SALES

A shared sale means that both (all) agents have direct customer contact and share responsibility for selling and servicing the shared customer account. Agents that share sales are best described as teams. Because both agents have direct customer contact, customer account ownership must be specifically identified and protected by a commission sharing agreement. The agent with customer account ownership retains primary liability for professional errors and omissions and is responsible for compensation of the other team members.

NETWORKING WITH BROKERED SALES

Broker agents have a special relationship with suppliers that does not require direct customer contact. Most agents prefer to access expertise and suppliers through brokerage sales instead of shared sales because customer contact is not shared and customer account ownership is, therefore, more secure. As with shared sales, the agent with customer account ownership retains primary liability for professional errors and omissions; however, contrary to shared sales, the broker agent is responsible for agent compensation.

C H A P T E R

Margins

Respected economist Joseph Schumpeter observed that margins tend to shrink as more entrepreneurs apply innovation to business processes. Although Schumpeter made this observation many decades ago, it is a defining characteristic of the Internet Age.

An agent's share of sales (commission margin) has consistently and rapidly decreased. As additional innovation is applied to the distribution process, it is reasonable to assume that commission margins will continue to shrink. However, the margin or rate of commissions is much less important to agents than the actual amount of commissions received. As such, entrepreneurial agents must innovate to increase sales sufficiently to offset the anticipated decline of commission margins. This entire book is primarily devoted to a discussion about applying innovations to increase the amount of commissions and subsequently increase value. This chapter is limited to a discussion of the amount of commissions remaining after paying normal expenses (operating profit margin).

OPERATING PROFIT COMPONENTS

For analysis purposes, operating profits have been split into the following five components.

Commission Income

Commission income represents the agent's share of sales. As noted in the above and throughout this book, commission income is the most important ingredient to an agent's success and a primary topic of this book.

Processing Expenses

Processing expenses are related to "back room" operations such as the agent accounting and document processing. Processing activities do not include any customer contact and are more easily outsourced than other types of activities.

Servicing Expenses

Servicing refers to customer assistance and generally includes expenses relating to all customer contacts other than contacts for sales and prospecting. This component also includes office expenses such as rent, telephone and utilities.

MAP Expenses

MAP is an acronym for marketing, advertising and promotional-related expenses which are referred to as MAP expenses.

Commission Expense

That portion of an agent's commission income paid to subagents, producers, broker agents and others as compensation for their sales efforts shall be referred to as commission expense.

OPERATING PROFIT MEASUREMENT

Operating profits can be extracted from the agent's income statements by calculating earnings before interest, taxes, depreciation and amortization (EBITDA). Also excluded from operating profits are extraordinary or non-recurring income and expenses. By including only those expenses that are typical and not affected by financial variables, the operating profit calculation provides a consistent and reliable yardstick for measuring business performance. The consistent measurement of business performance permits an "apples to apples" comparison with previous and future periods. Reliable measurement of business performance is important, so the agents can make informed decisions regarding expansion.

The calculation of operating profits is useful for internal analysis of an agent's performance because actual amounts are the basis for comparison. However, it is also helpful to compare an agent's performance with other agents. External comparisons require a measurement that eliminates size differences by converting operating profits to a ratio. The operating profit ratio is calculated by dividing operating profits by commission income.

Operating profits are the performance measurement tool preferred by lenders. Reliable analysis can be made of the amount of commissions historically available for loan payments after the payment of typical expenses. Reasonable predictions regarding future loan payments can be made on the basis of this historical analysis.

IMPROVING OPERATING PROFITS

Measuring operating profits is relatively easy compared to improving operating profits. The following discussion briefly describes some of the more significant suggestions made elsewhere in this book.

Selling Innovations

Agent entrepreneurs constantly innovate in their quest for more commissions. The nature of those innovations depends on an individual agent's circumstances such as personality, location, competition and resources. Although selling innovation is primarily the domain of agent entrepreneurs, a Master Agent can also assist by using its purchasing power to provide better supplier access and negotiate for an additional share of commissions.

Servicing Innovations

Agent entrepreneurs' sales and organizational philosophy determine their approach to servicing innovations. Some agents may rely on ubiquitous Internet access and a virtual office to reduce servicing expenses. Alternatively, agents may choose to share expenses of a more traditional office with other agents to reduce servicing expenses. Regardless of approach, entrepreneurial agents use operating profits to measure the effectiveness of their servicing innovations.

Processing Innovations

It is mission critical for agents to remain focused on customers and avoid distraction by administrative or processing-type activities that do not require any customer contact. Outsourcing of processing activities to a Master Agent permits an agent to share in the Master Agent's economies of scale and distribute the cost of technology innovation over a large number of agents.

VALUE COMPARISON

Increasing operating profits is generally desirable; but if operating profits decrease due to funding an expansion of the agent's business, an agent may ultimately create more wealth. Comparing the decrease in operating profits resulting from expansion expenses to the increase in the agency's fair market value resulting from additional commission growth (after discounting for time value) provides an agent with a mechanism for making disciplined decisions regarding expansion. This approach is currently evident when Internet companies are managed for significant revenue growth with little regard for operating profits because the business's market value increases much more than operating profits decline.

True to their nature, entrepreneurs sometimes choose to grow without sufficient regard for the consequences to operating profits. Agent entrepreneurs must be disciplined when making expansion decisions because an agent's business will be jeopardized if operating expenses exceed operating income for an extended period of time.

C H A P T E R

Capitalization

The following discussion of capitalization is organized by sources of expansion capital and is not a discussion of capital or equity as defined by general accepted accounting principles. An agent entrepreneur's most important source of expansion capital is long-term debt. Economist Joseph Schumpeter long ago noted the primary importance of long-term debt to entrepreneurs. Additional sources of capital to be discussed include contributed capital from external sources, retained capital from internal sources and sweat equity from an agent's hard work.

It is generally faster and less expensive to expand by purchasing an existing commission stream than by creating a new commission stream, which makes expansion capital a significant issue to agent entrepreneurs.

LONG-TERM DEBT

Ownership is of paramount importance to agent entrepreneurs because it is their nature to risk more to reap more. Therefore, the availability of long-term credit to fund agency acquisitions is also of paramount importance to the agent entrepreneurs because it permits immediate expansion with less ownership dilution.

CONTRIBUTED CAPITAL

Agent entrepreneurs are more likely to use debt than equity to fund acquisitions because the potential return on their investment is much greater. However, lenders generally require a certain level of collateral margin for agents to qualify for long-term credit. If agents have not built sufficient sweat equity to meet the lenders' requirements, then they must contribute capital from personal resources or from outside investors.

Although capital contributions from outside investors dilute an agent's ownership position, an agent sometimes has little choice but to solicit outside investment. As might be expected, agent entrepreneurs prefer issuing a class of stock to outside investors that is characterized by a redemption or call feature. Attracting capital in these circumstances is more difficult and requires investor inducements such as a preferred liquidation position, a generous fixed rate of return or a put feature.

RETAINED CAPITAL

It is not typical for agent entrepreneurs to delay an acquisition until accumulating sufficient cash to pay the entire purchase price. As noted above, agent entrepreneurs prefer to use debt; so they can make acquisitions sooner and increase their returns. As such, it is very typical for agents to meet a lender's down payment requirements by accumulating cash from operating profits.

SWEAT EQUITY CAPITAL

Agent entrepreneurs create additional business value by producing new commission streams and retaining acquired commission streams while generating sufficient operating profits to pay off acquisition loans. Using innovation, hard work and long-term debt, agent entrepreneurs have the ability to create a business of significant value with little contributed capital.

The additional business value created by "sweat equity" is not accurately represented on accountant-prepared balance sheets until the commission stream is sold and the sale proceeds are recorded. Sweat equity is more accurately represented on a modified balance sheet, which substitutes the estimated market value of a commission stream for the book value of a commission stream.

Business value is impacted by factors such as industry conditions and credit availability that are not directly related to an agent's efforts. However, agent innovation and hard work are the most significant factors effecting business value. Therefore, for the purposes of this discussion, sweat equity is roughly estimated to be the difference between the book value equity on an accountant-prepared balance sheet and the market value equity on a balance sheet, as modified as in the above. Sweat equity is similar to the "intellectual capital" of software companies where book value equity does not accurately reflect business value created by the companies' innovations.

Sweat equity is frequently used as a source of expansion capital when mortgaged to meet a lender's equity requirements for an acquisition loan. Although sweat equity is a very real and valuable asset, it is not liquid; and the value is generally not realized until mortgaged for a loan or until the business is sold.

Sweat equity is a great equalizer because those without capital can create it!

MASTER AGENT
A Master Agent cannot build sweat equity on behalf of an agent. However, a Master Agent can provide access to the tools required by agents for building and eventually liquidating their sweat equity.

Accessing Long-Term Debt
The Master Agent's role in making credit available to agents is discussed in this book's chapter on Loans and Credit Availability.

Accessing Contributed Capital
Although not specifically addressed elsewhere in this book, the Master Agent consults with agents regarding outside investors and may assist agents by locating and soliciting outside investors.

Increasing Retained Capital

The Master Agent helps to increase an agent's operating profits by providing services such as the outsourcing of processing activities. Additional information about a Master Agent's processing role is discussed in this book's Processing chapter.

Liquidating Sweat Equity

The Master Agent assists agents in the sale of their business by matching buyers to sellers (see Value of an Agent's Business chapter) and making ownership transfers easier (see Legal Issues chapter).

C H A P T E R

Management and Organization

Successful agents are more likely to possess the aptitude and talents of entrepreneurs, and Master Agents are more likely to possess the aptitude and talents of professional managers. Correspondingly, an agent's management style and sales organization are likely to exhibit entrepreneurial characteristics such as flexibility and innovation rather than professional managerial characteristics of conformity and structure.

The following is not intended to be a comprehensive set of management principals such as those provided in any one of several best-selling business books devoted exclusively to the subject. The entrepreneurial nature of successful agents makes them rebel against the prescription of specific guidelines for managing and organizing the sales process. As such, agent entrepreneurs will "do it their own way" but are encouraged to take into consideration the following comments that are tailored for agents.

SALES PLANNING

Agent entrepreneurs know instinctively that execution is more important than planning. Although an agent's bias for action is desirable, it will result in more mistakes and misfires. An ongoing planning process will help an agent stay focused and perhaps reduce the number of misfires.

Sales Objectives

Planning is the process of identifying how to accomplish objectives; therefore, the first planning step is setting general objectives to accomplish within general time frames. General objectives should be broken down into more specific objectives with more specific time frames, so planning is limited to short-action cycles.

Short Attention Span

Another reason for an agent entrepreneur's success is a bias for *immediate* action. Planning in short-action cycles for the immediate future is most useful to agents because their tendency to innovate and adapt makes long planning cycles less relevant.

Pay Attention

Setting objectives and making plans is the easy part of the planning process. Squeezing time from each day to implement plans is more difficult. Constant reinforcement of the significance of sales plans makes implementation more likely. For instance, summarizing plans and objectives on a small card and posting in a conspicuous place will help remind busy agents to focus on their sales agenda.

SALES ORGANIZATION
"Hands-On" Management

"Hands-on" management fits with an entrepreneurial personality and is well suited for an organization that is sales oriented. A sales organization must be very proactive, and a hands-on manager is more likely to incite action.

Hands-on management means that more individuals report directly to an agent manager, which limits sales organization size. However, a smaller organization makes a better sales organization because it is more innovative and responsive. Perhaps most importantly from a sales perspective, a smaller organization makes it harder for poor performers to hide.

Staffing

Sales performance is the focus of an agent entrepreneur's organization, which requires the hiring and recruitment of more motivated and ambitious individuals. As a result, less direct supervision is needed; and the office environment is more aggressive and competitive. Middle managers are primarily information conduits and hands-on management and communication tools such as e-mail.

In a sales organization, everyone has direct customer contact responsibilities for either making sales to customers or servicing customers after the sale has been made. The processing of non-customer contact activities is outsourced to a more efficient provider with an organization more suited to processing than sales. However, clerical and administrative tasks that are integral to the customer-contact process cannot be easily outsourced. Instead, customer-contact personnel must be technologically savvy and use voice recognition, document imaging, voice-mail and e-mail to be more efficient. The use of technology for customer-contact activities is more fully discussed in the chapter on Technology and Operations.

ACCOUNTABILITY
An organizational focus on performance requires absolute accountability from each individual within the organization for their contributions. Absolute accountability is predicated on: 1) accurate measuring of performance, 2) setting reasonable performance expectations, 3) regular discussions of expectations and results, and 4) defined consequences of results.

Accurate Measurement
Individual performance is most often measured by calculating increases in commissions. Keeping measurements simple helps ensure accuracy and makes data accumulation less expensive. Simplicity also makes the measurement easier to understand and more trustworthy.

Setting Expectations
Setting individual expectations or objectives is a joint effort between the individual and agent manager, so that all parties "buy

in" to the expectations that have been set. To limit misunderstandings, expectations must be specific and in writing.

Regular Discussions

Regular analysis and discussion of results helps individuals change course or take other remedial actions when necessary. Sharing results with everyone in the organization motivates the performance driven through peer pressure and competition.

Defined Consequences

The consequences of meeting expectations must be reward and recognition. When compensation is based on sales, then the consequence is a big paycheck. The consequences of not meeting expectations must be fair and, as a result of regular discussions, predetermined. Manipulating results to change the consequences does great harm to morale and limits the usefulness of accountability as a management tool.

Commission Accountability

Since commissions are the primary determinant of business value, measuring individual contributions to commission growth is of primary importance to agents. Using an organization's commission "pulse" is a simple and inexpensive way to measure results. Commission pulse is the total of monthly commissions recorded on third-party (supplier/company) statements during a specific period. Because this information is captured during regular agent statement processing, no additional data entry is required.

Operating Profits Accountability

Despite an organizational focus on sales performance, the expense associated with increasing commissions must be reasonable, or agents may not be able to meet their financial obligations (see Margins chapter). However, making everyone in the organization accountable for operating profits is not practical because a hands-on manager has more control of expenses than others. Accountability for operating profits is, therefore, limited to those that control expenses.

C H A P T E R

Technology and Operations

Many years before the Internet Age, Joseph Schumpeter described the entrepreneurial process of combining inventions into innovations for commercial advantage. This process is just as relevant today as agent entrepreneurs find ways to transform technological inventions into operational innovations to become more efficient.

Although there have been many amazing technological inventions during the last several years, the following discussion is limited to those practical inventions that can immediately and directly affect an agent's operations. These discussions include an analysis of the two sources of customer information (documents and data) used in three separate areas of operations (agent sales, agent service and Master Agent processing).

CUSTOMER DOCUMENTS
Document Foundation
The written word, as recorded on documents, has been the foundation of business and commerce for centuries and is sure to be the foundation for future commerce. As a result, documents are the foundation for an agent's operations.

Electronic Documents

Because old-fashioned paper documents are increasingly being replaced by Internet Age electronic documents, an agent's operations focus on electronic documents. Electronic documents are typically created by: 1) converting paper documents to electronic documents using a "scanning" process or 2) direct entry of information into an electronic format using a word processing program.

Scanning is the process of converting a paper document into an electronic picture or "image." Although scanning is an inefficient process, it converts paper documents into a format that can be delivered electronically and is compatible with Internet browsers. As a result, images can be universally accessible. Fax machines, which combine the processes of scanning, electronic delivery and printing, are widely used communication tools.

Creating electronic documents directly using keyboard entry or voice entry is more efficient than converting paper documents and will eventually replace paper documents when the legal and security issues are worked out. However, the inertia of using paper documents will require conversion by scanning for many years.

Documents as Data

In the November 1999 issue of Imaging and Document Solutions magazine, an article drew several conclusions from a research study (The State of the Document Technologies Market 1997-2003) which are relevant to these discussions. Perhaps the most important conclusion was that the word "document" has been redefined to be "......*both the repository of information and data, as well as a presentation metaphor.*" Expanding on this conclusion, the article stated that "*Advances in 'processability' are expected to emerge as an important trend through year-end 2002. This relates to the computer's ability to perform functions by operating on document information as data.....This would enable the creation of overarching applications that combine the legacy data center with document technologies which would drive further business-process innovation and automation. For in-*

stance, document-enabled processing could bridge the gap between the front and back office in most customer relationship management applications."

The above conclusions support the use of documents as the foundation for an agent's operations because, in addition to business communication and codification of legal relationships, electronic documents can be used as data sources. Although gathering data from electronic documents may not be sufficiently reliable for financial transactions, it can provide data that is sufficient for marketing and customer service.

Document Access
Universal Internet access of documents by agents, customers and suppliers gives agents the flexibility to structure their customer service operations according to individual agent preferences. For instance, document access using an Internet browser permits shared servicing and virtual office arrangements. Agents may even grant customers access to electronic documents to reduce customer service calls.

The November 1999 issue of Imaging and Document Solutions supports this perspective by stating that, *"Expanding their relevance beyond paper-conversion and departmental parameters, the Web is helping to reposition document technologies as pivotal to organizational efforts to funnel heterogeneous formats into business processes."*

CUSTOMER DATA
Although an agents' operations are document based, the operations of most suppliers are data based; so agents are involved in the submission of customer data to suppliers and receipt of customer data from suppliers.

Submitting Data to Supplier
Although most suppliers accept submission of customer data on paper documents, it is not efficient because the information is first created as a document by the agent and then recreated (input) as data by the supplier. The extra cost to the supplier makes

it likely that this method of data submission will eventually be eliminated.

Many suppliers encourage the submission of customer data by agent input directly to a proprietary computer system. This reduces the cost to the supplier but increases the cost to the agent because the data is usually first created as a document by the agent and then recreated (input) by the agent as data. An additional cost to the agent is the training time required to learn each proprietary system. As alternatives become available, the agents are likely to avoid suppliers that require use of proprietary systems.

Suppliers will gradually develop methods for gathering customer data over the Internet using a friendly interface which allows agents (or customers) to submit data directly to the supplier's computer from any place at any time.

Receiving Data from Supplier

Most customer data is presented by the suppliers to the agents as paper documents in the form of contracts, letters or billings, which are scanned and converted into electronic documents. A logical next step is for suppliers to present data to agents as electronic documents, so scanning is not required.

Although an agent's operations are document based, the customer name and address information that is critical for filing and finding electronic documents is stored as data. Validation by agents of their customer name and address information is made from the data presented by the supplier. Commission data received by the agent from the supplier is presented as a paper document; but because accuracy is critical, it is recreated (input) as data.

It may be most efficient for agents to access customer documents and data directly from a supplier's computer over the Internet. However, agent entrepreneurs prefer to remain independent of their suppliers and maintain independent control of their customer information.

SALES BY AGENT

Agent entrepreneurs sell products that require expertise and persuasion which requires a spontaneous and unique approach to each sale. Therefore, agent operations associated with selling are mostly unstructured. Those sales that can be made from a defined and orderly process are good candidates for Internet sales without agent intervention. The following discussion suggests ideas which may improve agent productivity but do not prescribe any specific procedures.

Time Management

Voice recognition software, voice mail, electronic address books and e-mail can help agents make better use of their time if agents make a commitment to learn and habitually use these tools. Less commitment and training is required when agents use paper documents to record contacts, phone numbers and customer discussions, which can be scanned, electronically filed and made available for access over the Internet. Recording customer information makes agents and their staff more productive. If recording of this information is as easy and convenient as scribbling a note on a paper napkin, then agents are more likely to do it.

Prospecting

Recording contacts made with prospective customers allows prospecting results to be analyzed and reused. An agent's investment in prospecting is often wasted if not recorded. Using paper documents to record contacts is easy and, when converted to electronic documents, allows for automated analysis.

Applications

Application is the process of submitting customer information to a supplier for pricing and qualification (underwriting). Third parties and suppliers provide software to assist in the application preparation and electronic submission. Although it is efficient to enter data directly to the supplier's computer, preserving this information as an electronic document allows agents ready access to all previous applications for reference when completing future applications for other suppliers.

Sales Quotes

Supplier pricing (rating) is sometimes complicated and difficult. Agent productivity is increased significantly when supplier or third-party rating software is used. However, for an agent's reference in future prospecting and applications, all rating information should also be scanned.

SERVICE BY AGENT

Operations associated with agent servicing are more structured than the selling process. An agent's servicing philosophy determines the level of contact that the suppliers will have with their customers. As noted in the above, agent entrepreneurs prefer to remain independent of their suppliers and are reluctant to cede too much customer contact to suppliers. On the other hand, it is less expensive if some customer service is outsourced to suppliers; and resources are freed up for the agent's sales activities. The following comments are offered for agent consideration when developing servicing procedures.

Gathering Customer Information

The process of gathering customer information and submitting it to suppliers is a servicing function that does not typically require agent intervention. Examples include the supplier requests for additional customer information, customer reporting of insurance claims, customer billing inquiries and customer requests to change insurance coverage. Using telephone call centers and Internet sites, these types of servicing functions are relatively easy to perform by either the customer or agent. An agent's servicing philosophy determines the degree to which agents assist customers in submitting information to suppliers.

Advising Customer

Providing expertise is one of the ways that agents add value to customer relationships. As such, agents are less likely to outsource this servicing function except for the smallest of accounts. When consulting with customers, agents can also prospect for more sales opportunities. Consulting situations are usually unique, so developing procedures to improve productivity is difficult.

Customer Billing

Customer billing is a servicing function that is almost always delegated to the supplier. Decreasing commission margins leaves no room for bad debts and other collection expenses. Additionally, the collection process can disrupt the agents' relationship with their customers.

Professional Liability

Although professional liability is a very important consideration in developing agent procedures, it should not be the primary consideration; or the agent's operations will be unnecessarily cumbersome. The degree of professional liability risk that is acceptable is determined by the agent's servicing philosophy and the Master Agent's requirements.

Shared Servicing

Agents with common servicing philosophies often share customer service representatives and other servicing expenses to free up resources for sales activities.

PROCESSING BY MASTER AGENT

Documents are the foundation of agent operations, and the Master Agent is responsible for processing all documents on behalf of the agents. The Master Agent also uses documents as the basis for agent accounting. Document and accounting processing standards have been established by the Master Agent to improve efficiency and reduce the agent's expense (see Processing chapter).

HARDWARE SELECTION

The pace of technological and manufacturing advances is such that performance improvements make computer hardware rapidly obsolete. The cost of hardware is an immediate expense and not a long-term investment despite accounting treatment to the contrary. Accordingly, hardware is considered disposable; so cost is a primary consideration and performance a secondary consideration when purchasing.

SOFTWARE SELECTION

In contrast to computer hardware purchases, computer programs for specialized and mission-critical applications are a long-term investment, which must be carefully selected. However, agents do not have any mission-critical applications because processing is outsourced to the Master Agent. The computer programs typically used by the agents are common applications such as browsers, word processing and e-mail, which are more easily replaced and are relatively inexpensive. It is likely that the cost of common software applications will decrease further as they become available to rent over the Internet.

CHAPTER

Marketing and Advertising

Brand marketing and Internet marketing require cooperation and commitment from all agents in the Master Agent organization and are, therefore, administered by the Master Agent for the benefit of its agents as discussed below. The following discussion also includes the marketing and advertising activities of individual agents.

BRAND MARKETING
Brand Confidence

Over one hundred years ago the Good Housekeeping seal of approval was developed by Good Housekeeping magazine to assist consumers with their purchases because little consumer protection was provided by regulatory agencies. Consumers confidently purchased products endorsed with Good Housekeeping's seal of approval. The absence of regulatory consumer protection at the turn of the last century is analogous to the unregulated nature of today's Internet. Associating products with a trusted brand name is much the same as endorsing products with a trusted seal of approval, both of which result in additional product sales.

Brand Name

The "wild and woolly" Internet Age makes development of a trusted brand name a necessity for Internet marketing. Agent entrepreneurs prefer to remain independent of their suppliers, so an agent's brand name must not be identified with suppliers. A brand name should not be associated with any particular geographical region because the Internet eliminates geographical marketing boundaries. Additionally, a brand name should not be associated with any particular person because brand value is then partially determined by that person. As illustrated by the success of brand names such as Xerox and Polaroid, a unique name that is not associated with other people, products or places is preferred.

Brand Value

Association with a trusted and well-known brand name makes an agent's business more valuable by increasing current and future sales. Increasing future sales means that the benefits of a brand name are transferred to future agency owners, and the value of an agent's business is increased as a result.

Brand Development

The Master Agent's cooperative advertising program, where approved advertising expense is shared with agents, is one of the primary methods of developing brand recognition. The Master Agent also advertises independently of its agents to promote brand awareness. An important part of brand development is brand protection. The Master Agent is caretaker of the brand name and is, therefore, responsible for ensuring the consistency of advertising and policing agent behavior.

INTERNET MARKETING

Agent Sales

Because of the complexity of business insurance and other business financial services, the assistance of a capable representative is usually required. As a result, marketing of these products over the Internet generally requires an agent to meet with the customer before making a sale. Internet marketing of less complicated products, such as personal auto insurance and checking accounts, can be sold directly over the Internet without meeting the customer.

National Presence

Because Internet marketing of business insurance and financial services generally requires a meeting with customers and because such marketing is not restricted by geographical boundaries, a national network of agents is required to consummate sales originated through Internet portals or links.

"Business-to-business" Internet marketing has recently received a lot of attention. Agent entrepreneurs with a common brand name and Master Agent support can be major players in business-to-business Internet sales of insurance and financial services.

Quality Control

The Master Agent's policing of its agents' action also protects the brand name of the Internet portal or link that initiates the sale. Inappropriate agent behavior must be immediately remedied by the Master Agent.

AGENT MARKETING

Target Marketing

Although agent entrepreneurs devise their own individual marketing strategies, it is likely that agent marketing will be narrowly focused on a targeted group of customers or products. Target marketing is more likely to employ direct mailing, telemarketing and similar approaches, which permit a narrow marketing focus. Mass marketing to a general audience is better suited for brand name development, which is coordinated by the Master Agent.

Referral Marketing

A more passive approach to agent marketing is waiting for sales opportunities from portal referrals or as a consequence of brand recognition.

AGENT ADVERTISING

The return on an agent's investment in advertising is often difficult to measure. Individual agents determine the nature of their advertising investment; however, agent advertising is likely to be focused on an agent's local trade territory.

Advertising Brand

Local advertising to promote brand awareness is typical. By sharing the cost with the Master Agent, this type of advertising is relatively inexpensive; and the cumulative effect of many agents advertising locally is a national brand awareness.

Advertising Product

Since local advertising of a specific product is expected to result in a sale, the benefit is more immediate and apparent. Probably an agent's most cost-effective advertising incorporates brand awareness into advertisements for a specific product, so the cost is shared with the Master Agent.

C H A P T E R

Business Practices

The beauty of the Internet is its unregulated nature because there are few government restrictions to stifle entrepreneurial innovation. Paradoxically, the unregulated nature of the Internet can also be ugly because, without government oversight, entrepreneurs sometimes misbehave; and consumers are sometimes foolish. Although the Master Agent is responsible for policing agents to preserve the collective brand name, agents must separately and individually develop local business practices for their sales organization which inspire customer confidence.

CONDUCT OF BUSINESS

Instead of abstract discussions of ethics and morality, decisions regarding proper business conduct can usually be made as business decisions. For instance, misleading customers will alienate them; so it is a bad business decision without regard for whether or not lying is immoral. Similarly, stealing from customers is wrong, but it also has the potential to destroy an agent's business; therefore, it is a bad business decision. Agent entrepreneurs are hands-on managers and directly responsible for the business conduct of those in the agent's sales organization.

WORKPLACE BEHAVIOR
Business First

Agent entrepreneurs are intensely committed to the success of their business and, as a result, may not be well liked by everyone in the workplace. However, an entrepreneur's workplace is not for satisfying social needs, so popularity is not an objective and probably not even desirable. Successful agents have high expectations of those in the workplace and hold them strictly accountable. As a result, agents must sometimes make unpopular decisions.

Agent Liability

The nature of the workplace has changed significantly, and employment-related litigation has become commonplace. Although litigation is a legitimate business concern, workplace behavior should not be primarily determined by lawsuit protection and political correctness. Treating others as you would like to be treated remains the best (and oldest) prescription for workplace interaction.

Those recruited into an agent's sales organization are likely to have aggressive personalities, and disagreements are likely to occur. As a matter of business, confrontations are sometimes healthy. However, disagreements in the workplace should be about professional, not personal, issues and soon forgotten. Employment litigation resulting from professional disagreements or unpopular business decisions is a risk that agents must take.

Under no circumstances can an agent tolerate personal behavior in the workplace that is dangerous, racially demeaning or sexually offensive.

COMMUNITY RELATIONS

An agent's business reputation in the local community is important for protecting a brand name. However, agents cannot always be popular in the workplace; and similarly, agents cannot always be popular with everyone in their communities. Agents are sales people, and the nature of their business sometimes alienates people.

Promoting a brand name, expanding prospecting contacts or satisfying personal needs are excellent reasons to participate in community organizations and events. However, participation for the purpose of "elevating" the sales profession is not necessary. An agent's business is a noble profession and a critical distribution link that creates the potential for significant personal wealth.

TRAINING AND EDUCATION

An agent is an important part of the distribution of insurance and financial services because of the expertise and advice provided to customers. As such, an agent's intellectual investment in training and education is more important than investments in office facilities and other tangible property. The extent of continuing professional education must be determined by the customer's needs, which may significantly exceed the minimum education requirements set by regulators for licensing.

CHAPTER

Financial Services
Modernization

Joseph Schumpeter observed that the freedom of innovation is the "foundation of material progress in capitalist economies." The recently enacted "Financial Services Modernization Act" provides agent entrepreneurs with more freedom to sell financial services than has been possible for more than sixty years. News stories have consistently proclaimed that the changes from financial services modernization "will be dramatic" and "are far reaching."

The regulatory walls between insurance, securities and banking have been lowered which creates tremendous opportunities for agent entrepreneurs as they expand their financial services product line. The legislation requires more coordination between insurance, securities and banking regulators which reduces the overall regulatory burden. Additionally, a requirement for more cooperation among state regulators will standardize licensing and also reduce the regulatory burden.

Part II

STANDARDS

C H A P T E R

Processing

STANDARDIZATION

Conformity and standardization make product distribution more efficient, which is one of the primary reasons that the Internet Age has a positive economic impact. However, conformity is the antithesis of entrepreneurship; and the prosperity of the agents depends on their entrepreneurial ability to innovate and change. Therefore, careful analysis is required before standardizing any agent operation.

The primary determinant of agency value is revenues; so it follows that the primary focus of agent entrepreneurs should be revenue development, and agents must have maximum flexibility in this regard. It also follows that standardization of an agent's operations must be restricted to support activities that are not directly related to sales. As such, developing standards for the non-sales activities can make agent entrepreneurs more efficient and, thereby, more profitable. On the other hand, encouraging agents to experiment with unique and innovative sales methods will increase sales and agency value. As a result, agents get the "best of both worlds."

MASTER AGENT

Agent entrepreneurs have long cursed paperwork and accounting as expensive time-robbers that steal their ability to sell more. With the development of standards, it is much easier to outsource these time-robbers to an outside processor such as a Master Agent. The development of standards also permits Master Agents to reduce processing costs with economies of scale resulting from job specialization, bulk purchasing and e-commerce. As a result, outsourcing of document processing and statement accounting to a Master Agent can reduce costs and save time.

The following demonstrates how Master Agents have improved agency processing with a dramatic re-engineering of outdated industry standards left over from the pre-Internet Age. This discussion on processing standards has been divided into three sections: 1) Company Statement Processing Standards, 2) Agent Statement Processing Standards, and 3) Document Processing Standards.

COMPANY STATEMENT PROCESSING STANDARDS

The standard for processing company statements is simply the allocation, or reconciliation, of every credit and debit entry on a company statement to a customer account. Each customer account has been coded to indicate agent ownership, which permits the company statement entry to be simultaneously recorded to the corresponding agent statement.

All entries on a company statement are passed through to a customer account, and ultimately to an agent statement, regardless of whether the company statement entry is right, wrong, early or late; and the agent bears the responsibility for reviewing company statement entries for accuracy. As indicated by the above, the two most important reconciliation steps are: 1) ensuring that the customer account ownership code is correct and 2) selecting the correct customer account for reconciliation.

Customer Account Coding

The policies or products sold by an agent are linked to customer accounts, and customer accounts are coded to indicate an agent's ownership. If the Master Agent's customer account data is accurate, then comparing name and address information is a very reliable and straightforward way to link policies or products to the correct customer account, as discussed in the document processing section. Because coding of customer account ownership determines which company statement entries are recorded to an agent's statement, it is critical that customer account setup and ownership coding changes are restricted as follows: New customer accounts are set up only in those instances when an application is received for which the Master Agent has no current customer account with corresponding customer name and address. In this instance, a new customer account is set up with an ownership code that correlates to the agent's signature on the application. Thereafter, the ownership code cannot be changed without the owner's written authorization to transfer ownership.

Customer Account Selection

Choosing the right customer account begins with document processing, as outlined in the following section. When processing a document of the type representing an agent sale, a temporary "transaction" is added to the corresponding customer account, which sufficiently describes the sale so that the temporary transaction may be matched to an entry on a company statement. Temporary transactions that are matched to entries on company statements become permanent records when recorded on the agent's statement.

If a company entry cannot be matched up with a temporary transaction, then the company entry is reconciled to an exception account for holding until researched. If research indicates that the Master Agent has not received an application, then the sale is considered orphaned until an application is received.

Balancing Company Transactions (Direct-Billed)

Direct company billing is efficient and the billing method generally required by the Master Agent. The primary balancing check for direct- billed company statements ensures that the total amount received from companies for direct-billed commissions is exactly the same as the total credit amount reconciled or allocated to customer accounts and ultimately an agent statement.

Secondarily, the total commissions/premiums listed on company statements are compared to the total reconciled commissions/premiums.

Balancing Company Transactions (Agent-Billed)

Although the Master Agent generally prohibits the use of agent billing, sometimes it is the only billing method available. When agents are responsible for collecting from their customers, then the agent-billed company statement charges the Master Agent for a net amount (total amount due from customer less sales commission). The primary balancing check for agent-billed company statements ensures that the total net amount charged to the Master Agent is exactly the same as the total debit amount reconciled or allocated to customer accounts and ultimately an agent statement. Secondarily, the total commissions/premiums listed on the company statements are compared to the total reconciled commissions/premiums.

AGENT STATEMENT PROCESSING STANDARDS

The agent statements are monthly listings of all credits (amounts due to the agents) and debits (amounts due to the Master Agent) and are the basis for monthly "settlement" of an agent's account balance with the Master Agent.

In addition to the company statement entries reconciled in accordance with the above standards, the following non-company statement entries are also recorded to the agent statements: 1) receipts from the agent's customers, 2) checks issued to an agent's customers and vendors, and 3) pass-through or journal entries for amounts due the Master Agent. These entries are reconciled to customer accounts coded with the agent's ownership in precisely the same manner as company statement entries.

Balancing Receipt Transactions

Agents are required to deposit all customer receipts into a local deposit account owned by the Master Agent. Agents are also required to immediately advise the Master Agent of all receipt amounts and identify the corresponding customer accounts, so temporary transactions can be added. Temporary transactions, based on information provided by the agent, are matched to a deposit entry on the Master Agent's checking account records and then permanently recorded to the agent statement. As a result, the receipt recorded on the agent's statement is balanced to the Master Agent's checking account statement.

Balancing Check Transactions

The Master Agent sometimes acts as an agent's banker by issuing checks to customers and vendors on behalf of the agent and extending short-term credit to help with the agent's revenue fluctuations. An agent's authorized representatives may request issuance of checks for these purposes, and temporary transactions are added using this information. Temporary transactions are matched to a check entry recorded on the Master Agent's checking account records and then permanently recorded to the agent statement. As a result, the check recorded on the agent's statement is also balanced to the Master Agent's checking account statement.

Balancing Pass-Through Transactions

Receipt transactions and check transactions are balanced to the Master Agent's checking account statement; however, pass-through transactions are generally initiated by the Master Agent and are not balanced to statements from independent third parties such as company statements or checking account statements. Pass-through transactions include the Master Agent fees, the agent reimbursements, deferred receipts (see below) and error corrections.

Agent Statement Preparation

Following rigid guidelines for cutoff of reconciliation or allocation to the agent statement, the Master Agent prints, reviews and distributes the agent statements. After allowing a few days for agent analysis, the Master Agent settles with the agent by electronically debiting or crediting the agent's checking account for the statement balance.

Because virtually all entries recorded to an agent statement have been balanced to statements provided by third parties, any additions, deletions or changes to the entries recorded on the agent statements may not be made until the correction is recorded on the third parties' statements. As an accommodation to its agents, the Master Agent will sometimes revise the monthly settlement amount in anticipation of corrections on future company statements or checking account statements but will never revise the agent statement until the corrections are recorded on the third parties' statements.

Customer Account Grouping

Because all entries are reconciled or allocated to the agent statements by first selecting a customer account, the grouping of the agent-billed transactions by customer account is an excellent tool for monitoring the balances of agent-billed customers. Actual receipts credited to an agent for a customer account are grouped with actual charges made to an agent for the same customer account and, when added together, provide the customer's balance.

If customer account grouping indicates that a balance is due from the agent to customer, then a refund is made to the customer unless the balance due results from customer's prepayment of his account. In the event of prepayment, the customer's receipt is held (deferred) by the Master Agent and is not available for the agent's use until a corresponding charge is made on the company statement and reconciled to the agent statement.

DOCUMENT PROCESSING STANDARDS

Agency management system providers and developers have a vested interest in making incremental changes to yesterday's systems despite the accelerated pace of business changes. A top-to-bottom analysis of today's agency businesses resulted in standards that are focused on Internet delivery of electronic documents, which is integrated with simplified and document-oriented accounting.

In the Internet Age, agents cannot afford to duplicate the accounting and data maintenance functions of companies and other suppliers; so that leaves document management as the primary function of agency management systems. Agents also cannot afford to devote significant capital to an agency management system, so document processing standards provide for outsourcing to a central processing location with sufficient volume to reduce processing costs per document.

Paper Documents Flow

Although the exchange and storage of information using electronic documents is steadily increasing, most business is still conducted using paper documents. After gathering paper documents in a central processing location, the next step is conversion of the paper documents into electronic documents by "scanning." After scanning, electronic documents are displayed on a computer monitor and are ready for electronic filing. Using customer account commissions as criteria, paper documents may be forwarded to the agents or retained by the processor and eventually destroyed.

Electronic Documents Flow

Documents are forwarded to a central processing location in an electronic image format via fax machines or e-mail attachments. Because scanning is not required, electronic documents are less expensive to process and are immediately ready for viewing and electronic filing.

Electronic Filing

Paper files must be organized if paper documents are to be easily located in filing cabinets. Similarly, electronic files must be organized if electronic documents are to be easily located in computer databases. Organization of electronic documents is provided through accurate indexing of electronic files. Indexing can be roughly compared to the process of inserting a paper document under the proper tab in the proper file folder in the proper filing cabinet drawer. Accurate and consistent labeling of tabs, folders and filing cabinet drawers makes locating paper documents easier; and the same applies to indexing of electronic documents.

Indexing

Associating documents with the correct customer account is the most important step in the indexing process because it is the primary basis for: 1) locating documents and 2) allocating accounting entries to the agent statements. Provided that customer account information is updated during indexing, documents may be easily and accurately associated with customer accounts by comparing name and address.

After associating documents with the correct customer accounts, the next level of indexing is to link documents with a specific product or policy that the agent has sold to the customer. Updating of product information during indexing is also important because this information provides additional description of temporary transactions so that they can be accurately matched with entries on company statements for allocation to the agent's statement.

The final indexing level provides specific document information for refining the document search even more. Document types are assigned for document sorting, and document descriptions are added for additional reference.

Temporary Transactions

If a document is assigned a document type during indexing which indicates an agent sale and the possibility of commissions payment, then a temporary transaction is automatically added so that it can be matched to a company statement entry and allocated to an agent's statement. Transactions are always associated with a specific document.

Action Document Distribution

If a document is assigned a document type during indexing that indicates immediate action is required, then the electronic document is made immediately available to the corresponding agent on the processor's Web site; and any related paper document is mailed to the agent. The action document concept helps eliminate some of the agent's administrative burden.

Marketing Document Distribution

If documents are assigned a document type during indexing that indicates the documents are marketing materials or company manuals, then these are made available on the processor's Web site. By separately listing all marketing-type documents, the agents may pick and choose which are worthwhile for reading without handling a lot of mail.

Document Distribution

Although action and marketing documents are listed separately because they are time-sensitive, all documents are available to the agents on the processor's Web site.

C H A P T E R

Legal Issues

Although agent entrepreneurs are successful because they are flexible and innovative, an agent's relationships with Master Agents, subagents, other agents, customers, buyers and sellers must be structured and well- defined, so that agency value is preserved by 1) assuring asset quality and 2) facilitating ownership transfer.

The stream of commissions which comprises the value of agency assets must be carefully protected by comprehensive legal agreements and disclosures in order for buyers and lenders to be reasonably confident that agency assets meet their expectations. As a result, agency values increase because buyers are willing to pay more and lenders are willing to lend more for agency assets of more predictable quality.

Ownership transfers that are relatively safe, easy and transparent increase the value of agency assets because the underlying commission stream is less likely to be disrupted. As such, using legal agreements that protect ownership and facilitate ownership transfers is crucial.

STANDARDIZATION
The most important element of facilitating ownership transfers and assuring asset quality is the use of standardized legal agreement forms which have passed the tests of time and logic.

For example, the transfer of residential real estate ownership has become relatively risk free because realtors use standardized purchase agreements that have been approved for use by a state real estate commission. The use of standard forms facilitates real estate transactions because the seller, buyer and lender are comfortable with an agreement that has been developed by experts in real estate law and has been used many times before with few problems. A realtor without legal experience can "fill in the blanks" of a standard form. In the event that real estate issues arise which cannot be addressed by filling in the blanks of a standard form, then a separate "free form" section or addendum may be completed by the realtor which is clearly identified as not being prepared by an expert or reviewed by a real estate commission. Applying this standardized form concept to the transfer of agency ownership is an excellent way to facilitate ownership transfer.

Standardized forms also promote asset quality. The intangible nature of agency assets makes any such assets particularly susceptible from problems which are not apparent or visible. An inspection of real property will readily reveal defects; whereas, an inspection of agency assets may not reveal defects, so protective written agreements must be in place to help prevent or remedy any such defects or problems.

The availability and widespread use of standardized forms makes it more likely that all agreements will be committed to writing. There are few if any legal pitfalls that are more dangerous than oral agreements. It is common and natural for agents to hear what they want to hear and not necessarily what the other party is saying, which leaves a lot of room for misunderstanding. Making agreements with a handshake is admirable and romantic, but supplementing the handshake with a full and complete written agreement is good business.

Now that the importance of standardized forms has been established, the substance of these forms will be discussed by organizing legal agreements into the following categories:

1) Master Agent Agreement Standards
2) Subagent Agreement Standards

3) Broker Agent Agreement Standards
4) Other Agent Agreement Standards
5) Consulting Agreement Standards
6) Agency Purchase Agreement Standards
7) Disclosure Standards

Please note that all agreement forms are tailored to the transfer of agency assets without any regard for the transfer of corporate stock or corporate assets other than agency assets.

MASTER AGENT AGREEMENT STANDARDS

To ensure a harmonious and mutually beneficial relationship, an agent must enter into a comprehensive agreement with the Master Agent that specifies in detail each party's responsibilities. (Note: If a franchise format is used for disclosure to agents, then the agent's agreement with the Master Agent is typically referred to as a "franchise agent agreement" or "franchise agreement.") The following discusses the more important provisions of a standard Master Agent agreement.

Obligations of Master Agent

The Master Agent's primary responsibility is accounting for: 1) direct-billed commissions received from suppliers (insurance companies) for agent's customers, 2) agency-billed amounts due suppliers for agent's customers, 3) agent's deposits to a trust account, 4) advances made by the Master Agent on behalf of an agent, and 5) charges made by the Master Agent for services provided to an agent. Correspondingly, the Master Agent is responsible for providing a detailed monthly statement of all such activity to agents.

Other important responsibilities of the Master Agent include: 1) acquiring an errors and omissions insurance policy which identifies each agent as an additional insured and 2) providing each agent with a unique list of the Master Agent's suppliers that are accessible by the agent. This supplier listing also indicates the level of supplier access permitted and the authority delegated by suppliers to agents.

Obligations of Agent

The Master Agent concept is premised on an agent's obligation to sell all insurance, investment, banking and credit services exclusively through the Master Agent. The Master Agent does not have any responsibilities for servicing agents' customers; therefore, agents are obligated to provide the required personnel or facilities.

Other significant obligations of the agent include: 1) billing customers directly through the supplier, 2) monitoring and controlling the activities of the agent's employees and subagents, 3) forwarding copies of all customer documents to the Master Agent, and 4) depositing all money received by the agent into a receipts trust account.

Protective and Restrictive Covenants

Agents have a 100% or fully-vested interest in the ownership of their customer accounts. This ownership interest is protected by the Master Agent's promises to: 1) code or otherwise identify the agent's customer accounts on the Master Agent's records for accounting and document management purposes, 2) not change any customer account coding without the agent's consent, and 3) not disclose any customer account information without the agent's consent. As agency owners solely responsible for the operation of their business, agents may not incur liabilities for the Master Agent and vice versa.

Representations and Warranties

Perhaps of most significance in this section of the agreement form is an acknowledgement that the Master Agent does not guarantee the accuracy or timeliness of any billings provided by suppliers (insurance companies) to the Master Agent or to an agent's customers.

Termination of Agreement

Although the agent can terminate his relationship with the Master Agent at any time, because of the adverse financial consequences to an agent, the Master Agent cannot terminate its relationship with an agent except for specific reasons such as: 1) breach of contract, 2) improper or inappropriate business practices, 3) inadequate qualifications of the agent's employees or subagents, 4) sale of part or all of the agent's business, and 5) bankruptcy of the agent.

If an agent's agreement with a Master Agent is terminated for any reason, then very specific provisions are made for unwinding the relationship. The Master Agent is required to provide to the agent all of the relevant customer information stored in its data processing system and request "agent of record" transfers from suppliers as directed by the agent. To limit the Master Agent's professional errors and omissions liability exposure, the Master Agent shall acquire ownership of any customer accounts for which the agent of record has not been transferred from the Master Agent by the policy or product expiration date after termination. When the Master Agent acquires ownership as a result of an abandoned customer account, then the Master Agent is responsible for customer service and may assign any such abandoned customer accounts to other agents.

Trust Arrangement

Sales commissions received by the Master Agent are the primary source of funds used to pay agents and comprise the revenue stream which provides value to agency assets. Agents are comforted by the surrendering of the Master Agent's control of sales commissions to an independent trustee. The Master Agent and all agents are required to deposit all receipts in a receipts trust account for distribution by a trustee in accordance with a trust agreement between the Master Agent and an independent trustee.

Subagent Arrangements

Customer account ownership is important to entrepreneurs, so recruitment of entrepreneurial subagents by agents requires provisions for granting subagents ownership in their customer accounts. Therefore, provisions are made to permit agents to grant or transfer ownership of customer accounts to subagents under certain specific circumstances. Perhaps most importantly, the agreement between agents and their subagents must be in the standard form specified by the Master Agent, so that ownership issues are clearly stated and subagents understand the Master Agent's role.

Miscellaneous Provisions

Although mostly legal housekeeping, this section of the standard agreement form also clarifies that an agent's account will not be credited for any commissions or other payments made to the Master Agent that are not associated with the sale of a specific product to a specific customer because any such bonus or profit sharing commissions belong to the Master Agent.

Guaranty of Agreement

If an agent is a corporation or limited liability company, then the principal agency owners are required to guaranty that the agent honors his obligations to the Master Agent.

Addenda to Agreement

Several standard forms have been developed which may be appended to the standard agent agreement to provide for: 1) additional commission-related payments to agent by the Master Agent, 2) purchase of additional services by agent from the Master Agent, 3) protection of the lender, or 4) a perpetuation plan obligating the Master Agent to purchase agency assets. Standardizing the forms used for common modifications to the agent agreement is just as important as standardizing the agent agreement.

SUBAGENT AGREEMENT STANDARDS

To ensure consistency between an agent's agreement with the Master Agent and the agents' agreements with their subagents, the standard subagent agreement closely resembles the standard agent agreement. Consistency and clarity is important because subagent ownership in customer accounts must be coordinated through the Master Agent who is agent of record for all policies and other products sold by agents and their subagents.

Sponsors

Subagents may not grant ownership in their customer accounts to others and, therefore, may not recruit other subagents. Allowing subagents to grant ownership to other subagents would result in the distancing of control and delegation of authority too far from the Master Agent and perhaps jeopardize the Master Agent's relationship with its suppliers. Agents always have responsibility to the Master Agent for the actions of their subagents and, therefore, have direct control of their subagent relationships.

Although subagents may not recruit other subagents, subagents may sponsor other subagents for recruitment by the agent. Sponsoring agents guarantee that prospective subagents will fulfill their obligations to the agent. Sponsoring agents are compensated for their recruitment role with a share of the prospective subagent's commissions.

BROKER AGENT AGREEMENT STANDARDS

Agents may apply for the approval and endorsement of the Master Agent to broker sales for a specific market niche through other agents. A broker agent agreement allows agents to leverage their special expertise or supplier relationship by granting them the authority to sell through other agents that may or may not be part of the Master Agent's network. Although agents in the Master Agent's network may be convenient customers for the broker agent's services, they are not obligated to purchase through broker agents.

As with subagent agreements, broker agent agreements resemble the standard agent agreement for consistency reasons. The standard broker agreement makes the broker agent fully responsible for commission payments to agents if direct billed and premium collection from agents if agent billed. Broker agents' ownership is limited to their relationship with other agents because customer accounts are owned by the agent or subagent. The Master Agent's obligations pursuant to the broker agent agreement are almost exactly the same as its obligations in the standard agent agreement.

OTHER AGENT AGREEMENT STANDARDS

As noted above, the Master Agent dictates the content of agent agreements and subagent agreements because these agreements define and control the foundational agent relationship. To accommodate the independent nature of entrepreneurs, agents and subagents may enter into other agreements with agents and subagents at any time without approval of the Master Agent as long as those agreements comply with the terms of the foundational agent and subagent agreements.

Lenders and purchasers are less concerned with agreements that do not directly affect ownership and ownership transfer, so standardization of the following agreements is less important. Note that the Master Agent is not a party to any of the following and is not responsible for administration, implementation or supervision.

Producer Arrangements

A standard producer arrangement provides for compensation based on commissions associated with the sale of a specified policy or other product. A producer arrangement is oriented to the sale of a specific product; whereas, subagent agreements are oriented to the total customer account. Because a producer does not have any policy or customer account ownership, producer arrangements may not be attractive to the more entrepreneurial agents.

Commissions Sharing Arrangements

Agents and subagents that make joint customer calls to sell a specific policy or other product should specifically define their relationship prior to making the sales call. All too often, commission sharing arrangements are oral and informal, which leads to misunderstandings and problems with suppliers. Issues addressed in a standard commission sharing agreement include ownership, professional liability, servicing responsibilities, commissions, confidentiality, termination and non-solicitation.

Brokerage Arrangements

The Master Agent sometimes authorizes its agents to broker policies or other products through other agents and subagents. The broker agent provides an agent or subagent with access to a supplier or expertise and generally does not have any customer contact. A brokerage agreement spells out the relationship between agents and specifically addresses issues such as agent/subagent authority, professional liability and commission splits.

Service Center Arrangements

Sharing of employees and facilities reduces expenses of individual agents and subagents. This type of relationship is a marriage of sorts, and a service center agreement is essential to head off the problems that are certain to result from office cohabitation. A service center agreement must not only outline services to be provided but also requires all parties to cooperate to make the workplace safe, enjoyable, uncluttered and non-offensive. Multiple agents and subagents working from the same office and using the same personnel raise legitimate issues regarding confidentiality, which are also addressed in a service center agreement.

CONSULTING AGREEMENT STANDARDS

In most instances, an agent's customer enters into an agreement directly with the agent's suppliers; and the agent acts as an intermediary. Typical examples include an insurance policy issued directly to an agent's customer by an insurance company or a certificate of deposit issued directly to an agent's customer by a commercial bank. However, if agents expand their product line into consulting and advisory services, then the agent is also the supplier and, therefore, enters into a consulting agreement directly with the customer.

Consulting Agreement

The standard consulting agreement provides for a fixed fee and is a much more comprehensive agreement than an hourly fee-based retainer agreement because performance and the conditions for payment must be more carefully defined. Issues addressed in a fixed-fee consulting agreement include: 1) specific conditions for payment of fees, 2) specific timetable for payment of fees, 3) the agent's responsibilities and accountability, and 4) payment of "out-of-pocket" expenses.

Retainer Agreement

Customers typically pay professionals such as attorneys and accountants on an hourly-fee basis. This type of consulting arrangement may be more suitable for agents and their customers when flexibility is required. Retainer agreements are generally less comprehensive and less structured than fixed-fee consulting agreements, so either the agents or their customers may change the term and scope of the relationship at any time.

AGENCY PURCHASE AGREEMENT STANDARDS

A well-drawn agency purchase agreement will result in the orderly transfer of agency assets with minimal disruption to the agency's commission stream and a short transition period. This standard purchase agreement should be designed to withstand the legal scrutiny of numerous attorneys representing sellers, purchasers and lenders. Use of the standard purchase agreement is of particular importance to agency lenders because it eliminates the need for a separate legal review of each loan applicant's purchase agreement. The following discusses some of the more important issues addressed in a standard agency purchase agreement.

Subject Matter of Agreement

A detailed description of the agency assets being sold helps reduce misunderstandings and heartache. Although the value of agency assets is usually concentrated in the intangible right to a commission stream, certain tangible assets incidental to agency operations may also be included in an agency sale. Any such, office equipment, inventory or files are specifically listed on a standard form exhibit attached to the purchase agreement.

Purchase Price

The seller can directly and indirectly impact an agency's commission stream and, therefore, the agency's value after closing. To ensure the seller's continued cooperation, it is very important to the purchaser that a portion of the purchase price is paid to the seller well after the closing date. A provision for future installment payments to the seller is, therefore, included.

Conveyance of Title and Delivery of Property

The specific steps for transferring agency assets on the closing date include the seller's delivery to purchaser of: 1) a bill of sale in the standard form provided as an exhibit to the purchase agreement, 2) transfer letters to all suppliers in the standard form provided as an exhibit to the purchase agreement, 3) all paper or electronic files for past, current and prospective customers, and 4) all office equipment, inventory or other tangible items included as part of the agency sale.

Closing

After the standard purchase agreement has been signed, then it is crucial that closing occurs as soon thereafter as prudently possible. Customers, suppliers, employees and subagents may become disenchanted or anxious after learning of the agency sale and cause sufficient disruption to "scare off" the purchaser. Although it is easiest to close on the first day of a month because most supplier (insurance company) statements are cycled on a monthly basis, the above concern may justify closing in the middle of a month.

Effective Date of Transfer of Business and Obligations

Transition period accounting can be irritating and frustrating unless the accounting rules are easy to understand and implement. The standard purchase agreement provides for transition period accounting that is relatively simple.

As a general rule, the seller shall be entitled to any sales commissions on insurance policies or other products with an inception date that is prior to the closing date. Correspondingly, the seller shall be responsible for payment of any amounts due suppliers for these insurance policies or products.

To simplify administration, the following exceptions are made to the general rule. The seller shall not be entitled to sales commissions resulting from installments, endorsements or audits on policies or products which are recorded on supplier statements dated after the closing date, even if the inception date is prior to the closing date. Correspondingly, the seller shall not be responsible for payment of any return commissions or customer refunds resulting from cancellation of these policies or products.

Sellers have sometimes refused to honor their obligations to suppliers or customers, which can cause problems for the purchaser. In these circumstances, the purchaser is authorized to pay the seller's obligations and then reduce the amount the purchaser owes to the seller for the balance of the purchase price.

Hold Harmless Guaranty

The standard purchase agreement allocates the professional errors and omissions liability to the party that created the exposure. Otherwise, to the justifiable consternation of the purchaser's insurance carrier, the purchaser could incur a claim against his errors and omissions insurance policy sometime after the closing date that was the result of the seller's operations prior to the closing date.

Contingencies

The purchaser is entitled to a refund of the earnest money deposit if the commission stream is threatened because the purchaser cannot access the seller's suppliers or if the sales commissions disclosed by the seller cannot be verified during the purchaser's due diligence inspection.

Covenants of Seller

The continued cooperation and support of the seller after closing is critical to preserving the flow of commissions. To help the purchaser preserve the commission stream, the seller is specifically required to: 1) enlist the cooperation of employees and subagents in transferring ownership and 2) enforce any non-so-licitation or non-compete agreements to which the seller is a party.

The commission stream is further protected by the seller's promise not to compete against the purchaser within a specified geographical area. More protection is provided by the seller's additional promise not to solicit from former customers even if outside of the specified geographical area. A portion of the purchase price is allocated to the seller's promises not to compete and not to solicit in order to demonstrate that the seller has been paid to keep these promises.

Warranties and Representations

When inspecting an agency for purchase prior to closing, the purchaser and lender rely a great deal on what the seller has said. The seller specifically guarantees or warrants to be true the statements or representations of most importance to the purchaser which include guarantees that the seller's: 1) statements regarding the amount of commissions received by the seller are true, 2) documents provided to verify seller's commissions are true, 3) disclosures to the purchaser of seller's agreements with employees and subagents are true and complete, 4) disclosures to the purchaser of all trade names used by seller are true and complete, 5) statements regarding the purchaser's errors and omissions insurance are true, and 6) information provided on the seller's survey form is true and complete.

Assignment of Purchaser's Interest

The Master Agent sometimes purchases agency assets to facilitate a transaction, provide for agency perpetuation or exercise a right-of-first-refusal. Because the Master Agent prefers not to compete with agents, the Master Agent typically sells any such agency assets to an agent soon after closing or assigns its rights in a purchase agreement to an agent prior to closing. Therefore, the purchase agreement permits assignment by the purchaser, provided the purchaser remains obligated to seller.

Miscellaneous Agreements

Purchasers typically assume some of the seller's obligations (i.e. Yellow Pages advertising). Any such assumed obligations are specifically listed on a standard form exhibit to the purchase agreement.

Entire Agreement

Typically, the only agreement between seller and purchaser that is signed prior to signing a purchase agreement is a confidentiality agreement. To ensure that there is nothing in a confidentiality agreement which may contradict or conflict with the purchase agreement, any such agreement is void upon closing. A listing of all purchase agreement exhibits is provided to help ensure that all of the required exhibit forms have been completed and are a part of the purchase agreement .

DISCLOSURE STANDARDS

Before serious legal discussions begin, it is expeditious for all parties to disclose sufficient information to determine if a relationship is likely to be mutually beneficial. The following summarizes those standard disclosures used as the first step in a process leading to execution of one of the above agreements.

Master Agent Franchise Disclosures

A Master Agent has many of the same business characteristics as traditional franchisors. As such, it makes some sense for a Master Agent to use the franchise disclosure format prescribed by regulators, even if a Master Agent does not consider itself a traditional franchisor. The franchise disclosure format provides an excellent framework for full and consistent disclosures by the Master Agent.

Because of some inconsistencies between federal and state laws and regulations, if franchise disclosures are used, then the Master Agent must pattern its disclosure on either the: 1) FTC (Federal Trade Commission) Disclosure Format, or 2) Uniform Franchise Offering Circular (UFOC) format drafted by the North American Securities Administrator Association. Most franchisors use the UFOC format because it is more likely to satisfy both state and federal regulatory requirements.

Even if a Master Agent chooses not to use a franchise disclosure format, then much of the same information regarding business history, principals, financials and legal agreements should still be provided to prospective agents in a logical and understandable format.

Agent Application

A prospective agent makes disclosure about his business, history and principals to the Master Agent in the form of an agent application. Additionally, a prospective agent discloses specific information about his current suppliers (insurance companies) and professional liability insurance. Perhaps most importantly, the Master Agent is given authorization by the prospective agent to independently verify the agent's disclosures and solicit information from others about the agent.

Subagent Application

A prospective subagent discloses to an agent much the same information and in much the same form as an agent discloses to the Master Agent. Agents are fully responsible for the actions of their subagents, so full disclosure is necessary for an agent to make an informed business decision. Master Agents have the absolute authority to veto an agent's proposed relationship with a subagent, so the information provided on a subagent application is analyzed by the Master Agent with the same degree of thoroughness as an agent application.

Broker Agent Application

Disclosures on broker agent applications are focused on agent qualifications, experience and expertise because when a Master Agent enters into a broker agreement, it is an endorsement of the broker agent to the Master Agent's network. The broker agent application also identifies the broker agent's niche and required supplier access.

Licensing Application

Disclosure of personal information on each of the individual directors, officers, employees and independent contractors proposed to represent the agent or subagent is an integral part of the overall agent and subagent disclosures. A standard licensing application is required for each individual.

Seller Survey

A seller survey begins the process of analyzing an agency purchase by organizing the seller's initial disclosure to the purchaser of general agency information including size, suppliers and customer types. A seller survey is the opening salvo in purchase negotiations, and organizing the seller's disclosures in a seller survey makes the disclosures more reliable.

CHAPTER

Loans and Credit Availability

Agents must be entrepreneurial to survive. Joseph Schumpeter, an economist with extraordinary insights about entrepreneurs, contended that access to affordable credit is essential to the entrepreneurial process. Additionally, basic business sense indicates that access to affordable credit increases the pool of serious and capable buyers which, in turn, increases the liquidity and market value of agencies.

A good example of the benefits provided by access to affordable credit is the role that residential home lending plays in improving our standard of living by providing affordable and ever more comfortable housing. Much as the housing industry prospers by reliable access to home loans, the agency industry can prosper by reliable access to agency loans.

Providing reliable access to credit for agency loans requires solutions to the collateral "challenges" associated with intangible agency assets. After many years of lending experience (including collection of agency loans gone sour) and significant investments in attorney fees, the following solutions are offered as a foundation for providing reliable agent access to credit.

MASTER AGENT

The primary collateral for agency loans is customer relationships, customer information, supplier (primarily insurance company) relationships and similar intangibles which provide a stream of revenues or commissions. Collateral values are largely determined by agency market values, and agency market values are largely determined by the likelihood of continued commission flow after the agent borrower is no longer associated with the agency.

Many lenders shy away from agency loans because of a well-founded concern that collateral values will be significantly diminished when the agent borrower is removed from the agency because the intangibles that make up the agency value are controlled by the borrower.

Collateral values become much more certain when an agent enters into an agreement to protect the lender by relinquishing agent control of certain responsibilities and activities to a Master Agent for "safekeeping." Using residential home loans as an analogy, the Master Agent could be considered the rough equivalent of an escrow agent.

To minimize the impact of an agent borrower's removal from an agency and to facilitate ownership transfer to a lender, a Master Agent arrangement offers the following advantages:

1) The Master Agent's control of relationships with suppliers (insurance companies) which facilitates ownership transfer to the lender.

2) The Master Agent's buying power makes agent's access to suppliers more reliable and results in more stable collateral values.

3) The Master Agent is "agent of record," so ownership transfer to the lender is mostly transparent to customer.

4) The supplier (insurance company) approval is typically not required for ownership transfer because Master Agent is agent of record.

5) The Master Agent gathers customer information (including customer documents) for immediate transfer to the lender.

6) Third-party control of all receipts (analogous to lockbox arrangements) which facilitates transfer of funds to the lender.

7) Marketing identity that is separate from agent, so that agency is more portable.

8) Verification of commissions data by the Master Agent through reconciliation of all commission statements.

9) Continuous insurance coverage for professional errors and omissions claims is ensured because coverage is provided by Master Agent's policy.

As a result of the Master Agent's expertise, the lender has access to invaluable advice and assistance in the operation of an agency. Additionally, as a result of the Master Agent's industry contacts, the lender has access to a larger pool of prospective buyers.

Although lender liability issues are always a concern, with the expanded powers of the Financial Services Modernization Act it is possible that banks and other lenders with insurance expertise will assume the additional role of Master Agent; so the lender can generate additional non-interest fees as a Master Agent.

Successful agents often have personalities that are fiercely independent, and granting additional control to a lender through a Master Agent relationship may be distasteful. However, widespread implementation of the Master Agent concept will benefit the agency industry as the lenders become more certain of collateral values and expand agency lending.

STANDARDIZATION

Although an imprecise comparison, it appears that many of the lessons learned from the success of residential home lending can be applied to agency lending. The Congress created the Federal National Mortgage Association (Fannie Mae) during the Great Depression to enhance the availability of mortgage credit. Since then, Fannie Mae has taken the lead in standardizing the residential home lending process; whereby, home loans can be readily bought and sold by loan originators to investors in a secondary market. Creating investor demand for residential home loans required standards for ensuring that the corresponding legal documents were uniformly enforceable and the credit analysis uniformly reliable. Standardization makes residential home lending an "assembly line" which churns out loans in sufficient volume to attract many competing investors. The net result is a tremendous appetite for home loans that makes credit inexpensive and readily available to home buyers. In turn, credit availability creates a growing pool of potential home buyers and increasing home values.

If the lessons of residential home lending are applied to agency lending, then standardization of legal documents and credit analysis is of primary importance to creating a viable investor market; therefore, loan originators can sell their agency loans. As with home loans, this process creates a capacity to make more agency loans at lesser interest rates.

The impact of standardization on agency values can be significant. Credit availability increases the number of prospective agency buyers which stimulates demand for agencies and increases agency values.

Lower interest rates make agencies more affordable which also increases agency values.

LEGAL LENDING STANDARDS

The foundation for all lending relationships are the written legal documents, which fully inform and obligate all of the parties. Accordingly, the development of legal lending standards is the starting point for standardization of the agency lending process.

Despite the significant benefits of the Master Agent concept, the introduction of a Master Agent as a protective "buffer" into the borrower/lender relationship expands the required legal documents so that the Master Agent's relationship to the borrower and the Master Agent's relationship to the lender are carefully defined. The following lists and explains those legal documents which are proposed as standards for agency lending.

Agreement for Advancement of Loan

After credit approval, the lender's commitment to extend credit is made to the agent borrower in an Agreement for Advancement of Loan. This legal document is the first agreement entered into by the lender with the borrower and very specifically defines the terms under which the lender is willing to extend credit. The Agreement for Advancement of Loan contains those terms and conditions which are unique to agency loans.

General Legal Documents

Those documents that are required to obligate the agent borrower and protect the lender's collateral interest are referred to as General Legal Documents. General Legal Documents are usually standard or boilerplate forms purchased from a reputable and established vendor. These forms typically include promissory notes, security agreements, financing statements and guaranties.

Purchasing standard forms from a reputable and established vendor makes it likely that the General Legal Documents conform with individual state laws and regulations. Nevertheless, before lending in another state, it is an excellent investment for the lender to retain local legal counsel to review these forms and provide comments on state legal peculiarities such as financing statement filings.

After the agent borrower has agreed to the terms of the Agreement for Advancement of Loan, then the lender typically prepares the General Legal Documents and forwards for the borrower's signature and subsequent review by the borrower's counsel prior to the lender's execution of the documents.

Opinion of Borrower's Counsel

It is a legitimate lender concern that borrower's obligations may not be fully enforceable if the borrower has been rushed or coerced into incurring obligations that are not adequately understood. However, a full review of all legal documents by the borrower's attorney is assured with the lender's requirement for an Opinion of Borrower's Counsel.

After review of all legal documents and before loan closing, the borrower's attorney is required to provide an opinion regarding the enforceability of the borrower's obligations to the lender. In the event of default, this opinion of the borrower's attorney that the obligation is enforceable bolsters the lender's position.

Loan Closing Documents

Loan Closing Documents are miscellaneous authorizations and acknowledgements required by the lender before funding a loan. Included are documents such as a loan closing statement and affidavit regarding financial status.

The Agreement for Advancement of Loan and the General Legal Documents are the most essential of all legal documents. The Agreement for Advancement of Loan is typically executed by the lender and the borrower as the first legal step, so this agreement is not part of the Loan Closing Documents. The original General Legal Documents are typically signed by the borrower, reviewed by the borrower's attorney and forwarded to the lender with the Opinion of Borrower's Counsel prior to loan closing. These agreements are also not a part of the Loan Closing Documents although copies will be distributed at closing.

Lender's Protection Addendum

An agent agreement is negotiated between the Master Agent and the agent. (Note: If a franchise format is used for disclosure to agents, the agent agreement is referred to as a "franchise agreement"; however, the relationship is that of a Master Agent to an agent.) Because the lender is not a party to the agent agreement, the lender must require, as a condition of credit, modification of the agent agreement with a "Lender's Protection Addendum" to incorporate those issues of importance to the lender.

For instance, regardless of the other terms of the agent agreement negotiated between the Master Agent and the agent, it is important to the lender that the Master Agent: 1) control all supplier (insurance company) relationships, 2) be identified as agent of record, 3) provide errors and omissions insurance, 4) require direct billing, and 5) require agent exclusivity. Therefore, these are some of the primary issues addressed in the Lender's Protection Addendum.

Collateral Preservation Agreement

The importance of a Master Agent in preserving the lender's collateral interest has been demonstrated. The Master Agent's legal responsibilities in preserving the lender's collateral interest are specifically defined in a Collateral Preservation Agreement. Although the borrower acknowledges that the Master Agent will be entering into a Collateral Preservation Agreement with the lender, the borrower is not a party to this agreement.

The most important part of collateral preservation is retaining a knowledgeable and capable Master Agent. It is equally important that the Collateral Preservation Agreement provide for the removal of a Master Agent that is insolvent or has acted improperly. The Collateral Preservation Agreement also outlines the manner in which the Master Agent will assist the lender in the operation of an agency which the lender acquires as result of borrower default.

Receipts Trust Agreement

As an additional layer of protection for the lender, the Master Agent and its agents are required to deposit all receipts into a trust account. Distribution from the trust account is controlled by a trustee. In some ways, the Receipts Trust Agreement resembles a lockbox arrangement used by many lenders to control receipts.

A Receipts Trust Agreement provides the lender with an additional layer of protection from Master Agent misconduct. Sales commissions are distributed to the Master Agent when the corresponding amounts are credited to its agents. In the event of borrower default, then the trustee pays directly to the lender any amounts that would have been due to the agent borrower. The Receipts Trust Agreement may not be amended without the lender's approval.

CREDIT ANALYSIS STANDARDS

The lender's analysis of the financial information provided by the borrower or the borrower's accountant is an integral part of both the initial credit approval and ongoing credit-review processes. Agency loan analysis is a three-legged credit stool, supported by debt service analysis, collateral analysis and financial condition analysis.

Financial Information

Before analysis can begin, the lender must gather financial information from the borrower, guarantors and Master Agent. The borrower supplies annual income statements, year-end balance sheets, current net worth statements and income tax returns. Current net worth statements and income tax returns are required from all guarantors. The Master Agent provides commission data categorized by: 1) customer type, 2) supplier (insurance company), 3) account size, and 4) billing type.

The borrower's income statement is used for debt service analysis, and the Master Agent's commission data is used for collateral analysis. The net worth statements and balance sheets are used for financial condition analysis.

Debt Service Analysis

Debt service analysis measures and forecasts the borrower's ability to make the lender's payments. This analysis is accomplished primarily by comparing current and projected operating earnings or EBITDA (Earnings Before Interest, Taxes, Depreciation and Amortization) to the borrower's total annual payments. Projected operating expenses are tested for reasonableness against the lender's database for similar agencies. The results of this analysis are usually summarized as a percentage which is calculated by dividing operating profits by annual payments.

Debt service analysis is typically the primary tool used by many lenders for credit analysis. However, in the case of agency lending, it is inappropriate to assign greater importance to debt service analysis than collateral analysis. The two must be analyzed in tandem because agents often invest much of their operating earnings in building agency (and collateral) value by incurring additional expenses such as hiring more subagents or increasing advertising expense. Conversely, if agents choose to maximize operating earnings by cutting essential expenses, then value decreases.

It is not unusual for successful entrepreneurs to be "cash poor" but "asset rich" as they plow cash back into growing their business. This business approach is popular with agents because value is largely determined by the amount and reliability of revenues. Contrary to business property such as inventory or real estate, agency values are almost entirely dependent on reliable revenue streams with little salvage value if revenues disappear. Although an oversimplification, if a decline in operating earnings is less than the increase in agency value, then borrower performance is satisfactory and vice versa.

Collateral Analysis

Collateral analysis is performed primarily by analyzing commission data provided by the Master Agent because collateral for agency loans is usually the agency business, the value of which results from a reliable stream of commissions. This analysis is usually summarized as a percentage which is calculated by dividing the collateral values by the loan balances.

A detailed explanation of the appraisal process for agency businesses is provided in a separate chapter. However, generally speaking, the appraisal process analyzes recent sales prices of agencies with commission characteristics comparable to the subject agency to estimate the subject agency's market value. Commission characteristics used to determine if agencies are comparable include: 1) customer type, 2) supplier (insurance company) suitability, 3) account size, and 4) billing type. The resulting estimation is then adjusted for more subjective criteria such as agent personality, community size, local competition and industry conditions to determine a final market value estimation.

Financial Condition Analysis

Analysis of the net worth statements and balance sheets provided by the borrower/guarantor does not provide specific indication of agency performance. Instead, this analysis provides a general indication of the resources available to the borrower for agency expansion or to fall back on if the agency has problems. Traditional methods of measuring financial condition include comparison of current assets to current liabilities and comparison of debt to capital. The primary measurement used in agency loan analysis is the ratio of total borrower/guarantor debt to total borrower/guarantor net worth.

Credit Memorandum

Debt service analysis, collateral analysis and financial condition analysis are summarized by the lender in a credit memorandum for use during the credit approval and credit review processes. Credit memorandums incorporate the borrower's comments into the lender's analysis, so a telephone interview with the borrower is required.

CREDIT APPROVAL STANDARDS

"An ounce of prevention is worth a pound of cure." In other words, preventing problems with a well-defined and standardized credit approval process is much better than identifying and fixing problems during the credit review process. Accordingly, the credit approval process requires analysis and investigation that goes well beyond the credit review process.

Credit Application

The process begins with the borrower's completion of a comprehensive and standardized written application for credit. Agent biographical information, agency historical information and agency marketing plans are part of the required information. In addition, the borrower provides the financial information required for the lender's credit analysis as listed above. The reliability of the financial information is substantiated by accessing Dun and Bradstreet reporting, accessing consumer credit reports, contacting references listed in the application and other sources of financial information not listed in the application.

Credit Commitment

The lender or lender's loan committee reviews the credit application and credit memorandum and then approves (or denies) credit, subject to further investigation during the lender's due diligence inspection. The following four guidelines provide the lender with well-defined and standardized loan approval criteria that is based on credit analysis. However, if the borrower/ guarantor's financial condition warrants, then compliance with one or more of the guidelines may be waived by the lender. On the other hand, compliance with all four guidelines does not result in automatic credit approval:

1) Projected EBITDA/Annual Interest and Principal Payments > 115%
2) Agency Long-Term Debt/Projected EBITDA < 450%
3) Estimated Collateral Value/Loan Ratio > 110%
4) Agency Long-Term Debt/Borrower & Guarantors Combined Net Worth < 400%

If credit is approved, then the lender executes and forwards to the borrower an Agreement for Advancement of Loan that is subject to a due diligence inspection and provides for loan repayment over a term of not more than ten years if an agency acquisition loan and not more than one year if a working capital loan.

Due Diligence Inspection

If the borrower accepts the terms of the lender's Agreement for Advancement of Loan, then a due diligence inspection is scheduled. A due diligence inspection is the lender's investigation of the borrower, guarantors and any related transactions to find circumstances or issues which may concern the lender. A partial list of the required investigative activities includes:

1) Verify commissions from an independent source such as supplier (insurance company) statements. Categorize verified commissions by customer type, supplier, account size and billing type.
2) Assess agent's personality, sales skills and management skills (Use personality or skills testing if necessary).
3) Identify loss ratio problems from insurance company production reports. Review profit sharing commissions paid during the last twelve months.
4) Assess efficiency and courtesy of office staff. Evaluate orderliness and completeness of customer files. Review office procedures and personnel policies. Evaluate office appearance and cleanliness.

5) Assess productivity of subagents and producers. Review all subagent and producer agreements. Review all non-compete and non-solicitation agreements with current and former subagents or producers.

6) Research circumstances of all professional errors and omissions claims filed against anyone in the agency. Review errors and omissions insurance policy. Review all past, present and pending litigation.

Once a loan has been approved for agency acquisition, it is imperative that the due diligence inspection be completed without delay to minimize the effect on agency values resulting from the actions of opportunistic competitors, anxious customers and insurance companies during the crucial period of time from when word leaks out of the proposed acquisition until the acquisition is consummated and the borrower acquires possession.

After the due diligence inspection, a memorandum is prepared which summarizes the result of the lender's investigation.

Loan Funding

Before the loan closing is scheduled, funding is specifically approved by the lender or the lender's loan committee, after review of the due diligence memorandum, the opinion of the borrower's counsel and the proposed closing statement. If all goes as expected, then funding is approved; and the loan is closed.

CREDIT REVIEW STANDARDS

The credit approval process is designed to underwrite loan applicants in a manner which minimizes problems. Nevertheless, problems do occur; and a credit review process is required to identify problems before they become unmanageable.

Credit Review

On an annual basis, a full credit analysis is performed and the resulting credit memorandum reviewed by the lender or the lender's loan committee. This information is used to identify credit problems, so the lender can work with the borrower to correct.

Collateral Review

On a monthly basis, a partial credit analysis of collateral values is performed; and the resulting collateral worksheet is reviewed by the lender or the lender's loan committee. Although collateral analysis is a partial review, it is sufficient to identify unfavorable trends and trigger a full credit review.

C H A P T E R 16

Value of Agent's Business

The basic premise of "Death of an Insurance Salesman" is that insurance salesmen must be entrepreneurial to prosper in the Internet Age. By definition, entrepreneurs are motivated by the creation of personal wealth through business ownership; so creating a valuable agency business is the ultimate goal of successful agents. The following summarizes: 1) how agency value is created, 2) how agency value is measured, and 3) how agent entrepreneurs "cash in their chips" and collect agency value.

CREATING AGENCY VALUE

The following summarizes the conclusions of previous discussions on the primary issues that agent entrepreneurs confront when creating agency value. For the most part, these agency-value issues may be controlled by the agent entrepreneur and must be aggressively managed to create value.

Product Selection

Selecting the right product line may require the agent entrepreneurs to sell products that are not traditionally identified as "insurance related." From this perspective, the title "Death of an Insurance Salesman" is very appropriate because the agents must not limit themselves to the sale of insurance products.

Agent entrepreneurs must avoid products that are easily "commoditized" because the product's features are standardized and quantified, which makes price competition likely. Avoiding commoditized products requires the agents to focus on products to which value may be added through less standard and quantifiable features such as: 1) providing product expertise to the customer, 2) persuading customers of need for product, 3) inspiring customer confidence through brand awareness, and 4) providing customer convenience through agency location or method of operation.

As measured in the following section on agency valuation, the selected product must provide a reliable future stream of commissions to create more agency value.

Customer Selection

Selecting customers, or identifying the agent's "market," is integrated with the product selection process summarized above. Adding value to a product usually requires focusing on a specific market segment which may be defined in terms of age, geography, profession, industry or other similar criteria. On the other hand, selling to the masses typically results in product standardization and commoditization which adversely impacts agency value. An agent's marketing efforts will probably be more effective and brand identification more likely if the agent's market is specifically defined.

Commissions are more reliable if the selected market has sufficient potential for an agent to grow, is viable and not likely to become obsolete, and is a market with which the agent is comfortable.

Selecting customers who buy for reasons other than price helps agents retain customers for longer periods of time, which increases commissions reliability and is one of the primary criteria used in the agency valuation process described below.

Supplier Selection

Agent entrepreneurs must have access to suppliers (insurance companies for insurance products) who can provide the selected product for sale to the selected customers. However, to generate reliable commissions, access to insurance companies must also be reliable. As a result, the selection of suppliers is critical and may impact the product selection and customer selection processes outlined above.

Supplier selection is a primary criteria used in the agency valuation process. As such, agents must be willing and able to change suppliers as circumstances dictate.

Recruitment

Although contrary to the instincts of hard-charging entrepreneurs, more value is created if the success of an agent's business is not entirely dependent on the agent entrepreneur. An agency has more value if an organization of subagents is primarily responsible for sales, provided that the subagent relationship is properly structured.

Recruitment of subagents permits agent entrepreneurs to grow much larger by leveraging their time, expertise and investment. The amount of commissions is unquestionably the most important ingredient in calculating agency value, so incorporating a consistent and orderly recruitment process is fundamental to creating agency value.

Networking

Agents can further leverage their expertise by assisting other agents on a project basis. Correspondingly, agents can leverage their contacts by soliciting specialized assistance from other agents on a project basis. Networking with other agents can increase commissions and thereby increase agency value, provided the sharing of commissions or brokerage arrangement is well defined.

Marketing, Advertising and Prospecting

An agent's investment in marketing, advertising and prospecting is usually justified if the result is an immediate sale that has an obvious impact on agency value. However, the return on this investment can be significantly increased if the benefits from an agent's marketing, advertising and prospecting result in additional sales for future owners.

Using marketing and advertising to create a brand identity that is separate and distinct from the agent owner creates a brand that is easily transferable to a new owner and provides a long-term benefit to the new owner. It is also beneficial to new owners to analyze an agent's prospecting failures. Therefore, well-organized and well-documented prospecting files can make new owners more productive and create additional value.

Margins

Operating profit margin (earnings before interest, taxes, depreciation and amortization) is an important measurement of agency success and the primary credit-analysis tool used by lenders. As such, increasing operating profit margins generally increases the relative value of a commission stream. Accordingly, agent entrepreneurs who keep operational expenses such as rent and support staff at optimal levels create additional value. This requires innovative approaches such as service centers to share support staff expense and office sharing or office elimination. On the other hand, if operating profit margins are adversely impacted by sales-related expenses such as subagent commissions or marketing expenses, then agency value resulting from increased commissions may offset any reduction in value resulting from decreased operating profit margins.

Capitalization

By definition, entrepreneurs are ambitious and therefore have a tremendous opportunity to create value from sweat equity. Businesses such as car manufacturers require a large investment of real capital in factories, equipment and inventory. However, agent entrepreneurs can create value with little more than hard work and persistence. Factories are valuable because it is obvious that the facilities may be used to manufacture and therefore generate revenues for many years to come. To create value, agents must also demonstrate that their business will generate revenues even though their "factory" is not visible. This is the essence of the agency valuation process.

Management and Organization

The Internet Age has ushered in a management style and philosophy that is especially applicable to agent entrepreneurs as they dodge the Internet bullet. Agents must be nimble and responsive to changes in suppliers and customers. Although business planning is essential to creating agency value, the accelerating pace of change requires that the time frames used for planning and implementation be significantly shortened.

Technology and Operations

As noted in the previous discussions on operating profit margins, the value of a commission stream increases when operating expenses are at the minimum optimal levels. Using technology to reduce operating expenses by improving productivity has fueled recent general economic performance and will improve an individual agency's operating profits. The most promising technology for improving agent productivity is document imaging.

Less chic than technology, but just as important, is the implementation of operational procedures that improve workflow and eliminate redundancy. One of the most obvious examples are procedures which require the use of direct billing by suppliers/insurance companies.

Business Practices

The business of agent entrepreneurs is intangible, which increases the impact that business practices can have on an agency's value. An agent who conducts business in an unethical manner will be punished in the market place, and agency value will suffer. Similarly, agents who permit inappropriate workplace behavior will find recruitment more difficult, and agency value will suffer.

CALCULATING AGENCY VALUE

The following provides a unique perspective on agency valuation and inserts more objectivity and consistency into the valuation process. The entire discussion on calculating agency value focuses on the fair market value estimation of intangible agency assets and agency goodwill without regard for the value of other tangible assets and any agency debt or other liabilities.

Account Durability

As outlined in the above, agency value is primarily determined by the amount and reliability of commissions received. "Account durability" measures the desirability of those commission revenues based on certain selected characteristics.

Suppliers such as insurance companies typically use "policy retention" to analyze the reliability of policy premiums. As a matter of convenience, agents may also be tempted to use policy retention for analysis of commission reliability. However, measurement of policy retention is geared to insurance companies' analysis requirements. Account durability focuses on the agent's perspective, which does not necessarily correspond with an insurance company's perspective. The following illustrates the differing perspectives:

1) Agents tend to focus on customer accounts and insurance companies on policies because the agent may have a customer account for which multiple insurance companies are used.

2) Agents focus on commissions because it represents the amount of funds available to the agents; whereas, insurance companies have access to the entire premium and, therefore, focus on premiums.

3) Agents often transfer policies from one insurance company to another, which reduces policy retention but increases account durability if transferred to a more desirable insurance company.

4) If agent retains the smaller commission policies and does not retain the larger commission policies, then analysis of policy retention may not indicate the significance of impact on agency commissions.

Account durability predicts the likelihood with which various combinations of customers, suppliers and products criteria will result in continued commission revenues. Account durability is not intended to provide any predictions regarding an agent's effectiveness in attracting new customers and so may not be useful in predicting commissions growth. As its name implies, the term "account durability" refers to commissions received from an entire customer account without regard for individual policy premium.

Account durability takes the following criteria into consideration:

1) Because of fundamental marketing differences, a distinction is made between customers purchasing policies for business use and customers purchasing products for personal use when analyzing account durability.

2) The suitability of suppliers/insurance companies has significant impact on agency value and is, therefore, an important consideration.

3) The age of the account is an important consideration based on the logic that the longer the customer relationship, the more likely the relationship will continue.

4) If commissions are concentrated in fewer and larger accounts, then commissions are less reliable. Note that the servicing of more small accounts may have an adverse effect on operating margins if agents are not innovative in their servicing approach.

5) Direct billing by suppliers/insurance companies makes agents more efficient and the commissions more valuable. Therefore, billing is an important consideration in measuring account durability even though it has less to do with predicting commissions reliability than the above factors.

An excellent case can be made for considering additional criteria, but it should first be demonstrated that the added complexity significantly increases the measurement's predictive capabilities. Furthermore, additional care must be taken to ensure the integrity of the process of accumulating any additional data required as result of adding additional criteria.

Weighted Commissions

Incorporating account durability into a method for valuing agencies requires that commissions be "weighted" by applying an account durability factor to a specific category of commissions. Weighting of commissions promotes consistency and objectivity in making comparisons between agencies because unambiguous and a well-defined criterion is used to categorize and value each agency's commissions.

The first step in weighting commissions is to categorize all commissions using the above account durability criteria. The following lists the levels of durability criteria typically used by an appraiser of small-to-medium-sized agencies to categorize commissions:

1) Preferred Supplier or Regular Supplier
2) Commercial Customer or Personal Customer
3) Account Age More Than One Year or Account Age Less Than One Year
4) Account Size More Than $1,000 Or Account Size Less Than $1,000 (Annual Commissions)
5) Direct Billing or Agent Billing

Even limiting the commission categories to two levels for five durability criteria as in the above, all of the possible combinations result in splitting commissions into a large number of categories. To promote accuracy, the number of commission categories must be limited to a manageable number. Additionally, the commission categories should be limited to those that are easily measured and for which the source of most data is third-party (supplier) statements.

The second step in weighting commissions is to establish durability factors for each commissions category. Currently the durability factor amount is determined by the agent surveys and management experience. As more account-oriented data becomes available, then data will augment the information from agent surveys and management experience. To promote consistency, durability factors are established annually and applied without exception and without adjustment for all commissions-weighting calculations. Because durability factors are consistently applied and changed infrequently, then even if the durability factors are incorrect, the commissions have been categorized so that more accurate comparisons may be made between agencies.

The final step in weighting commissions is to calculate the weighted commissions amount for each commission category by multiplying the actual commission times the durability factor. The amount of weighted commissions bears little correlation to a projection of actual commissions and is intended for the primary purpose of making accurate comparisons. However, provided that the durability factors are reasonable, general assumptions regarding future commissions can be made by analyzing the durability ratio (total weighted commissions divided by total actual commissions). The lower the ratio, the less likely commissions will continue; and the higher the ratio, the more likely commissions will continue.

The result of commissions weighting is to provide an objective data-oriented tool for lenders, sellers and purchasers to use to compare agencies with no subjective assumptions or input by the appraiser. As a further result, commissions weighting provides a calculation that is virtually "untouched by human hands"; and for this reason does not account for differences between agencies that are not measured by one of the durability criteria.

Comparative Sales Method of Valuation

Commission weighting allows the appraisers to make "apples to apples" comparisons of agencies by categorizing and valuing annual commissions; therefore, it is an excellent tool to use with the Comparative Sales Method of Valuation.

When using annual commissions as the primary determinant of estimating fair market value, then the relative value of agencies must be expressed as a multiple of annual commissions. As such, an agency's "commissions multiple" is the fair market value (or sales price if comparable sale) divided by total annual commissions. Correspondingly, the weighted commissions multiple is fair market value divided by weighted total annual commissions.

The first step of comparative sales valuation provides a raw and unadjusted estimate of fair market value by valuing the subject agency after applying the weighted-commission multiple of all recent agency sales in the appraiser's database (after eliminating the highest 10% and lowest 10% of weighted-commission multiples to reduce effect of aberrations) to the subject agency's weighted commissions. This unadjusted valuation provides lenders, sellers and purchasers with a reasonable test of agency value before the appraiser begins making subjective adjustments.

The final step of comparative sales valuation allows appraisers to use their experience and expertise to make reasonable adjustments to preliminary unadjusted valuation. To limit the latitude provided to the appraiser, all issues that may result in an adjustment and the amount of any such adjustments are predefined and prioritized. Therefore, the appraiser's input is limited to scoring of these predefined issues and applying the resulting calculation to the preliminary unadjusted valuation.

The nature of the above valuation method permits an updated estimation of fair market value on a month or quarterly basis with an annual adjustment for changes in durability factors and the appraiser's scoring.

Alternative Methods of Valuation

Estimating fair market value by comparing the subject agency with actual sales of comparable agencies relies on the "invisible hand" of the marketplace to estimate values. Comparable sales analysis is the most popular method of valuation and is the approach most favored by lenders. The following demonstrates why alternative methods of valuation are less useful than the comparable sales method.

For small-to-medium-sized agencies, most alternative methods of valuation require that the appraiser recast earnings or cash flow (earnings before interest, taxes, depreciation and amortization) to adjust for the owner's compensation and other extraordinary expenses. This requires the appraiser to make assumptions that could significantly impact the results.

Alternative methods of valuation also require that the appraiser make assumptions regarding the projected level of commissions. Although a process such as commission weighting can be used to project commissions produced from existing accounts; the projection of commissions from new accounts is an assumption that is much less reliable because it depends on factors such as the agent's ambition, personality, plans, experience and skill which are difficult to measure. Projection of revenues in other industries may be more reliable if the projections depend less on intangible issues such as the agent's ambition and more on tangible issues such as location.

Alternative methods of valuation also require the appraiser to make assumptions regarding appropriate benchmarks for price-earnings multiples, cash flow multiples, discount rates or capitalization rates.

Projecting commissions, selecting benchmarks and recasting expenses requires a manipulation by the appraiser which makes alternative methods of valuation less reliable than comparative sales method of valuation which is market-based and depends less on the appraiser's judgment. Alternative methods of valuation are best used as a reality check to see if the marketplace is irrational.

COLLECTING AGENCY VALUE

The culmination of an agent's entrepreneurial endeavor and of this book is a discussion of those issues relating to "cashing in the chips." There is much ado in the agency industry about agency perpetuation plans; but the best perpetuation plan is a system that provides easy, transparent and risk-free transfer of ownership to a growing pool of capable buyers.

Credit Availability

Agent access to affordable credit increases the pool of serious and capable buyers which, in turn, increases the liquidity and market value of agencies. The two primary requirements for improving agent access to credit are: 1) a Master Agent relationship which protects the lender and 2) the development of standards for loan documents, credit analysis and credit approval.

Legal Issues

The liquidity and market values of agencies increase when the buyer (and lender) are reasonably sure that the purchased agency assets will meet the buyer's expectations, which is made more difficult as a result of the intangible nature of agency assets. Ensuring that the agency assets meet the buyer's expectations is facilitated by standardized and comprehensive purchase agreements, agent agreements and subagent agreements.

A Master Agent relationship makes ownership transfers relatively quick and easy, which also increases liquidity and market values. A Master Agent can transfer customer records, agent identity and suppliers (insurance companies) with minimal hassle or disruption.

Finding Buyers

The Master Agent typically plays an additional role when an agent decides to "cash in the chips," which includes matching buyers with sellers.

Agent entrepreneurs will create and enjoy personal wealth during the Internet Age because of their willingness to change and a commitment to provide additional value to their customers. Insurance salesmen without an entrepreneurial appetite for change and without a product line that extends beyond insurance will probably not survive.

Part III

IMPLEMENTATION

C H A P T E R

Agreements

The following agreements have been developed by Brooke Corporation, a pioneer of the Master Agent concept, over many years and at great expense. These agreements are provided to specifically demonstrate the manner in which the Master Agent standards outlined in the previous chapters have been adopted by Brooke Corporation and successfully used in its agent organization.

All of the agreements listed and described below represent proprietary information which may not be copied or otherwise used or distributed in whole or part without first purchasing a license from Brooke Corporation.

Agreement	Description
Master Agent Agreement	Agreement between agent and Master Agent (Brooke Corporation).
Receipts Trust Agreement	Agreement between trustee and Master Agent (Brooke Corporation).

Subagent Agreement	Agreement between agent and subagent. Exhibits referenced in agreement are not included.
Broker Agent Agreement	Agreement between Master Agent (The American Agency, Inc.) and agent which grants agent the authority to broker (indirectly sell).
Producer Agreement	Agreement between agent and agent's employee or independent contractor.
Commission Sharing Agreement	Agreement between agents to share commissions for customer account sold jointly.
Brokerage Agreement	Agreement between agents to share commissions for customer account brokered through broker agent.
Service Center Agreement	Agreement between agents to share office expenses and staff.
Consulting Agreement	Agreement between agent and customer to provide consulting or advisory services to customer.
Agency Purchase Agreement	Agreement between agency seller and agency buyer. Exhibits referenced in agreement are not included.
Agreement for Advancement of Loan	Agreement between agent borrower and lender (Brooke Credit Corporation). Exhibits referenced in agreement are not included.

Opinion of Borrower's Counsel	Opinion letter from agent borrower's attorney to lender (Brooke Credit Corporation).
Lender Protection Addendum	Addendum to agreement between agent and Master Agent that is required by lender (Brooke Credit Corporation).
Collateral Preservation Agreement	Agreement between Master Agent (Brooke Corporation) and lender (Brooke Credit Corporation). Exhibits referenced in agreement are not included.

FRANCHISE AGREEMENT

THIS AGREEMENT made and entered into this _____ day of _____, _____, (which with all addenda shall be referred to herein as the "Agreement") by and between Brooke Corporation, a Kansas Corporation, having its principal place of business at 205 F Street, Phillipsburg, Kansas referred to hereafter as "Brooke"; and, _____, by and through _____, its _____, whose offices and primary place of business is located at _____, _____.

The proprietorship, partnership, corporation or other Person referenced above is referred to hereafter as "Franchise Agent".

WITNESSETH:

WHEREAS, Franchise Agent is in or may enter the business of selling, servicing and/or delivering Policies from the agency offices referenced above; and

WHEREAS, Brooke is primarily in the business of providing certain services and assistance to businesses selling insurance; however, Brooke is in or may enter the business of selling, servicing and/or delivering other Policies and may provide certain services and assistance to businesses selling same; and

WHEREAS, Franchise Agent and Brooke desire to associate together effective _____, _____, for the purpose of Brooke providing certain services and assistance to Franchise Agent with respect to Franchise Agent's business;

NOW THEREFORE, in consideration of the mutual promises set forth herein and other good and valuable consideration, the receipt and sufficiency of which are hereby acknowledged, the parties agree as follows:

1. DEFINITIONS OF TERMS USED IN THIS AGREEMENT:

For purposes of this Agreement, the following terms shall have the following meanings unless the context clearly requires otherwise:

1.1 Agency Bill Policies: Any Policies for which a Franchise Agent is responsible for all or any part of premium or fee billing and collection.

1.2 Agent of Record: Person designated on Company's records as the agent or representative regarding a specific Policy and the owner of all Sales Commissions.

1.3 Company: A company issuing, brokering, selling or making a market for Policies and which has a contract with Brooke.

1.4 Company Billings: Statements or billings received by Brooke from Companies for amounts due Brooke from Companies and for amounts due Companies from Brooke.

1.5 Customer Account: A Person who has a Policy purchased from, serviced, renewed or delivered through Franchise Agent. Customer Accounts shall be owned by Franchise Agent or a Subagent.

1.6 Direct Bill Policies: Any Policies for which a Company is responsible for premium or fee billing and collection.

1.7 Franchise Agent Account: An account on Brooke's ledgers to which Brooke records amounts due Brooke from Franchise Agent and amounts due Franchise Agent from Brooke.

1.8 Gross Premiums: Total premium, fees or other amounts due from the sale, renewal, service or delivery of Policies including the corresponding Sales Commissions.

1.9 Insurance, Investment, Banking and/or Credit Services: Insurance services include but are not limited to the sale, renewal, service or delivery of insurance policies, annuities, insurance brokering services, insurance customer services, risk management services and insurance related consulting or advisory services. Investment services include, but are not limited to, the sale, renewal, service or delivery of mutual funds, stocks, bonds, notes, debentures, real estate services, investment customer services, and investment related consulting, and financial, investment, or economic advisory services. Banking services include any banking service Franchise Agent is allowed to perform under federal and/or state laws. Credit services include, but are not limited to, origination or brokerage of loans or mortgages, credit customer services, and credit related consulting or advisory services.   At any point in time, Insurance, Investment, Banking and Credit Services shall be limited to those services then offered by Brooke.

1.10 Net Premium: Gross Premiums on Agency Billed Policies less the corresponding Sales Commissions.

1.11 Other Receipts: Deposits made to the Receipts Trust Account that are not Sales Commissions. Such receipts may include but are not limited to: Profit Sharing Commissions; Net Premiums, advertising reimbursements, proceeds from sale of personal money orders; Gross Premiums for Direct Billed Policies (e.g. on line payments); loan proceeds; Company refunds; supplier refunds; and vendor refunds.

1.12 Person: Any individual, sole proprietorship, partnership, joint venture, trust, unincorporated organization, association, corporation, limited liability company, institution or other entity.

1.13 Policies: Any and all insurance services, policies, coverages or products sold, renewed, serviced or delivered through Franchise Agent to any Person. Policies include, but are not limited to, any and all Insurance, Investment, Banking or Credit Services, or policies, coverages or products associated therewith sold, renewed, serviced or delivered through Franchise Agent to any Person.

1.14 Profit Sharing Commissions: Commissions or fees which are not associated with the sale of a specific Policy through Franchise Agent. Profit Sharing Commissions are typically contingent upon factors such as sales volume, premium volume, profitability and other special concessions negotiated by Brooke. Profit Sharing Commissions include, but are not limited to, payments identified by the Companies as profit sharing commissions, contingency commissions, advertising allowances, prizes, override commissions, expense reimbursements and bonus commissions.

1.15 Receipts Trust Account: An account established and owned by Brooke, but controlled by a trustee, to which premiums, fees, Sales Commissions and Other Receipts received by Franchise Agent or Brooke from Companies or customers shall be deposited and from which Brooke, or its designee, makes regular withdrawals by Electronic Funds Transfer.

1.16 Return Commissions: Direct Bill Policy commissions that are unearned because Policy premium or fee was reduced or Policy canceled.

1.17 Sales Commissions: Commissions paid by Companies to Brooke or assigned by Franchise Agent to Brooke for the sale, renewal, service or delivery of a specific Policy through Franchise Agent. Sales Commissions are not normally contingent upon factors such as Brooke's loss ratio, premium volume, sales volume or special concessions negotiated by Brooke.   For the purposes of this Agreement, Sales Commissions shall specifically exclude Profit Sharing Commissions and other similar payments. However, Sales Commissions shall specifically include amounts paid by Brooke pursuant to a bonus plan, the terms of which are defined by Brooke in its sole discretion and for which Brooke makes no representation regarding future payments or Franchise Agent's eligibility. Sales Commissions shall also include any consulting fees, advisory fees, placement fees, service fees, renewal fees, or any similar payments paid on or related to any Customer Account by any Person.

1.18 Subagent: A Person which has entered or may enter into a Subagent Agreement with Franchise Agent.

1.19 Subagent Agreement. An agreement entered into by and between Subagent and Franchise Agent and approved by Brooke pursuant to which Subagent is allowed vested ownership rights in Customer Accounts coded to Subagent and Franchise Agent performs certain accounting and processing services for Subagent.

2. OBLIGATIONS TO BE PERFORMED BY BROOKE:

2.1 As of the effective date of this agreement, Brooke shall provide services with respect to accounting for and processing of Policies for Franchise Agent. Brooke may provide other services as may be agreed upon by Brooke and Franchise Agent from time to time. Furthermore, certain duties and obligations of Brooke set forth in this Agreement may be performed by a subsidiary or an affiliate of Brooke.

2.2 Brooke shall account for all Sales Commissions on Direct Bill Policies issued, renewed, endorsed, changed, serviced, delivered or canceled on behalf of Customer Accounts. Brooke shall credit Franchise Agent Account for Sales Commissions received by Brooke from Companies for Customer Accounts in the amounts indicated on the appropriate Company Billing. Brooke shall debit Franchise Agent Account for Return Commissions due to Companies by Brooke for Customer Accounts in the amounts indicated on the appropriate Company Billing.

2.3 (a) Brooke shall account for all Net Premiums on Agency Bill Policies issued, renewed, endorsed, changed, serviced, delivered or canceled on behalf of Customer Accounts. Brooke shall debit Franchise Agent Account for Net Premiums due to Companies by Brooke for Customer Accounts in the amounts indicated on the appropriate Company Billing. Brooke shall credit Franchise Agent Account for Net Premiums returned to Brooke from Companies for Customer Accounts in the amounts indicated on the appropriate Company Billing. Brooke has the absolute right to and is fully vested in all Net Premiums. Franchise Agent has no right, title or interest in such amounts. (b) Brooke shall credit Franchise Agent Account for Agent Billed Policy premiums received from any insured or other Person for a Customer Account. At Brooke's option, Brooke may defer any such credit for Agent Billed Policy premiums until a corresponding charge is made to Franchise Agent Account for Net Premiums in accordance with subparagraph 2.3 (a).

2.4 Brooke shall calculate and credit Franchise Agent Account monthly for amounts due Franchise Agent by Brooke. Amounts due Franchise Agent shall be Eighty-five percent (85%) of any Sales Commissions from Companies for Customer Accounts.

2.5 Subject to the prior approval of the insurance company involved, Brooke shall endorse Brooke's errors and omissions insurance policy to provide errors and omissions insurance coverage for Franchise Agent. Brooke shall calculate and debit Franchise Agent Account for Franchise Agent's share of the errors and omissions insurance policy premium. Brooke may adjust said policy premium to maintain a Franchise Agent deductible fund. Brooke shall calculate Franchise Agent' share of said errors and omissions insurance policy premium by dividing the estimated annual commissions received on Customer Accounts by the total estimated annual commissions received by Brooke from all Companies. However, Franchise Agent's share of Brooke's annual policy premium shall not be less than the minimum annual premium that is set from time to time by Brooke's Board of Directors. Franchise Agent has the responsibility to provide Brooke with copies of those documents which Brooke deems necessary for errors & omissions documentation.

2.6 Brooke will pay for 50% of advertising that is pre-approved by Brooke and shall be reimbursed by Franchise Agent for Franchise Agent's share of payments made to advertisers on behalf of Franchise Agent.

2.7 Brooke shall account for and debit Franchise Agent Account monthly for any other supplies or services provided by Brooke to Franchise Agent if previously agreed upon by Brooke and Franchise Agent.

Franchise Agent acknowledges that, pursuant to this paragraph, Brooke provides Franchise Agent with additional services and retains additional commissions when Policies are sold, renewed, serviced or delivered through Franchise Agent through a Brooke subsidiary which provides such Policies to agents on a brokerage or non-exclusive basis.

2.8 Brooke shall forward a record of Franchise Agent Account to Franchise Agent on or about the 15th day of each month. Upon written notice to Franchise Agent, Brooke may change the date on or about which statements are forwarded.

2.9 Brooke, or its designee, shall pay to Franchise Agent, by electronic funds transfer, the credit balance recorded on the Franchise Agent Account on or about the 20th day of each month. If Franchise Agent has not paid to Brooke, or its designee, the debit balance recorded on the Franchise Agent Account by the 20th day of each month, then Brooke, or its designee, shall withdraw the amount of any such debit balance from Franchise Agent's checking account using an electronic funds transfer. Upon written notice to Franchise Agent, Brooke may change the date on or about which Franchise Agent's account is credited or debited.

2.10 Brooke shall provide Franchise Agent with a rules and procedures manual that has been adopted by Brooke's Board of Directors and shall provide Franchise Agent with notice of any changes made by Brooke's Board of Directors to said manual from time to time.

2.11 Brooke shall provide Franchise Agent with a unique written list of Companies that have been approved for Franchise Agent use by Brooke's Board of Directors and shall provide Franchise Agent with notice of any changes made by Brooke's Board of Directors to said list from time to time. Franchise Agent acknowledges that changes to the list of Companies may be made by Brooke's Board of Directors at its sole and absolute discretion.

2.12 Brooke shall provide Franchise Agent with a unique written list specifying Franchise Agent authority for binding Companies to Policies or coverages and shall provide Franchise Agent with notice of any changes made by Brooke's Board of Directors to said list from time to time.

2.13 Unless otherwise agreed in writing by Brooke, Franchise Agent shall do business under the name "Brooke Financial Services" or "Brooke Insurance and Financial Services". Therefore Brooke permits the use of its trade names, trademarks, service marks, logotypes, commercial symbol and promotional materials for the purpose of advertising such relationship. Brooke does not represent or guarantee that Franchise Agent will have exclusive use of such name, that such name is available for use in Franchise Agent's market and/or that there are no competing names or uses. If such name is not available for use, Franchise Agent shall do business under a name mutually agreed upon by the parties.

2.14 Brooke shall provide Franchise Agent full and complete access to Brooke's records of Customer Accounts provided that it shall be upon reasonable advance request and during such times and upon such conditions as shall not unreasonably impair the operations of Brooke.

2.15 Brooke shall license Franchise Agent to use Brooke's proprietary Document Manager system provided that Franchise Agent purchase, license, install and maintain all software and hardware, other than Brooke's proprietary Document Manager programs, which may be required to use the Document Manager system and provided that Franchise Agent not sell, lease or authorize the use of the Document Manager programs to anyone else and provided that Franchise Agent not configure, program or change any Document Manager programs. Franchise Agent may access customer information through the Internet. Franchise Agent acknowledges that access to customer information through the Internet is provided by Brooke as a convenience to Franchise Agent and not as a required manner of access to such information. Accordingly, Franchise Agent, its owners, officers, directors, employees and independent contractors agree to release, indemnify and hold Brooke harmless for and from any and all claims, losses, liabilities, damages or expenses (including, but not limited to reasonable attorneys' fees, court costs, and costs of investigation) of any kind or nature whatsoever incurred by Franchise Agent, its owners, officers, directors, employees and independent contractors resulting from an interruption in Internet services or from any unauthorized use of or access to Customer Account information through the Internet. This release, indemnification and hold harmless shall survive the termination of this Agreement.

3. OBLIGATIONS TO BE PERFORMED BY FRANCHISE AGENT:

3.1 Upon the signing of this Agreement, Franchise Agent shall pay to Brooke an initial nonrecurring and nonrefundable set up fee of One Thousand Dollars ($1,000.00), the receipt of which is acknowledged, following which Franchise Agent shall do business under the name "Brooke Financial Services" or "Brooke Insurance and Financial Services", unless otherwise approved in writing by Brooke.

3.2 Franchise Agent shall provide competent and qualified personnel for the sale, renewal, service and delivery of Policies and to serve as liaison or contact with Customer Accounts.

3.3 On or before the effective date of this Agreement, Franchise Agent shall, subject to prior approval of the Companies involved, change the Agent of Record for all existing Customer Accounts to Brooke.

3.4 After the effective date of this Agreement, Franchise Agent shall process all applications for Policies exclusively through the facilities of Brooke.

3.5 Franchise Agent shall make Brooke (for the purposes of this subparagraph, "Brooke" shall include a subsidiary or affiliate of Brooke) the Agent of Record for all Policies sold, renewed, serviced or delivered through Franchise Agent with an effective date for coverage after the effective date of this agreement, unless prior written approval is obtained from Brooke. If a Company refuses to make Brooke the Agent of Record for all Policies sold, renewed, serviced or delivered through Franchise Agent, then Franchise Agent shall assign all Sales Commissions and Profit Sharing Commissions associated with such Policies to Brooke. Franchise Agent agrees and acknowledges that by making Brooke the Agent of Record, all Sales Commissions and Profit Sharing Commissions are assigned to Brooke for accounting and distribution to Franchise Agent Account pursuant to this Agreement. Franchise Agent appoints Brooke as its attorney in fact to endorse or deposit checks made payable to Franchise Agent by customers, Companies or master general agents. Franchise Agent also agrees to obtain from its producers or Sub Agents an appointment of Brooke as attorney in fact to endorse or deposit checks made payable to such producers or subagents by customers, Companies or master general agents.

3.6 Franchise Agent shall apply for issuance of Direct Bill Policies if payment of premiums in this manner is permitted by the Company providing coverages. Franchise Agent shall obtain specific approval of Brooke prior to submitting any application for issuance of an Agency Bill Policy.

3.7 Franchise Agent shall be solely responsible for the collection of all Agency Bill Policy premiums from Customer Accounts, which amounts shall be made payable to Brooke Corporation. Franchise Agent shall not have authority to endorse or deposit such payments to its own account. Franchise Agent appoints Brooke as its attorney in fact to endorse or deposit checks made payable to Franchise Agent by customers, Companies or master general agents. Franchise Agent also agrees to obtain from its producers or Sub Agents an appointment of Brooke as attorney in fact to endorse or deposit checks made payable to such producers or Sub Agents by customers, Companies or master general agents. Brooke shall establish a Receipts Trust Account to which all premiums, fees , Sales Commissions and Other Receipts from Companies or customers shall be deposited and from which Brooke, or its designee, makes regular withdrawals by Electronic Funds Transfer.

3.8 Franchise Agent shall be responsible for payment to Brooke of all Agency Bill Policy net premiums and Direct Bill Policy return commission resulting from Customers Accounts.

3.9 Franchise Agent authorizes Brooke to retain Fifteen percent (15%) of any Sales Commissions from Companies under contract with Brooke for Customer Accounts; Franchise Agent shall pay its share of errors and omissions insurance policy premiums; fees for ny other supplies and services provided by Brooke if previously agreed upon by Franchise Agent and Brooke.

3.10 If Franchise Agent has not paid to Brooke, or its designee, the debit balance recorded on the Franchise Agent Account by the 20th day of each month, then Franchise Agent authorizes Brooke, or its designee, to withdraw the amount of such debit balance from Franchise Agent's checking account using an electronic funds transfer.

3.11 Franchise Agent shall be responsible for providing to Brooke any information regarding Franchise Agent or Franchise Agent's owners, officers, employees and independent contractors that may be required from Brooke by any self regulatory organization, governmental agency or any Company. Franchise Agent shall be responsible for ensuring that Franchise Agent and Franchise Agent's owners, officers, employees and independent contractors comply with all federal, state and local requirements including but not limited to the sales practices, education and licensing requirements of all governmental agencies and any Company. Franchise Agent shall provide evidence satisfactory to Brooke that Franchise Agent and Franchise Agent owners, officers, employees and independent contractors have complied with such requirements. If Franchise Agent does not comply with the terms of this paragraph, it is cause for immediate termination of this Agreement without any liability on or against Brooke.

3.12 Franchise Agent shall abide by and conform to the rules and procedures adopted from time to time by Brooke's Board of Directors. Franchise Agent acknowledges that said rules and procedures include, among other requirements, a requirement that Franchise Agent provide Brooke with copies of all Policy applications and all other records or documents originated, received or processed by Franchise Agent which are related to Customer Accounts, Policies or Franchise Agent's business. Franchise Agent acknowledges the importance of complete and timely transmittal of all records and documents and agrees to submit in a timely manner to Brooke all such records and documents.

3.13 Franchise Agent shall apply for coverages only with the Companies that are authorized for Franchise Agent's use from time to time by Brooke's Board of Directors. Franchise Agent acknowledges that Brooke, in its sole and absolute discretion, shall decide which Companies Franchise Agent may use.

3.14 Franchise Agent shall abide by and conform to the conditions and limits of authority for binding Companies to insurance and other coverages which are set forth from time to time by Brooke's Board of Directors.

3.15 Franchise Agent shall obtain the prior written consent of Brooke before using Brooke's trade names, trademarks, service marks, logotypes or commercial symbols on any advertising literature, promotional materials, signs or business forms that are not provided by Brooke.

3.16 Immediately upon termination of this Agreement for whatever reason, Franchise Agent shall cease the dissemination of any advertising material containing any of Brooke's trade names, trademarks, service marks, logotypes or commercial symbols. Brooke shall have a cause of action against Franchise Agent for failure to immediately cease using the same upon any such termination.

3.17 Franchise Agent shall purchase a standard Business Owners Policy providing coverage for Franchise Agent's place of business with liability limits of not less than $1,000,000 / $1,000,000 unless such requirement is waived in writing by Brooke. Franchise Agent shall also purchase a Workers Compensation insurance policy with liability limits of not less than $500,000/$500,000 unless such requirement is waived in writing by Brooke.

3.18 Franchise Agent shall be responsible for payment of all defense and other claims expenses in amounts up to $2,500 per incident for any errors and omissions related claims made as a result of Franchise Agent's or its Subagent's actions or lack of actions.

3.19 Franchise Agent shall obtain Brooke's prior written approval of any agreement for Franchise Agent to purchase insurance or other agencies' assets.

3.20 Franchise Agent shall immediately and fully report to Brooke any policyholder related legal or regulatory issues such as errors and omissions claims, insurance department or other regulatory complaints, legal summons and subpoenas. Franchise Agent shall not make any written or verbal comments or responses regarding said issues to anyone until fully discussed with Brooke. Franchise Agent acknowledges that Brooke shall coordinate and control responses to any such issues.

3.21 Franchise Agent shall provide Brooke full and complete access to records of Customer Accounts and other records and documents deemed necessary by Brooke to perform an audit to determine compliance with the provisions of this Agreement; provided however, that access shall be upon reasonable advance request and during such times and upon such conditions as shall not unreasonably impair the operations of Franchise Agent.

4. PROTECTIVE AND RESTRICTIVE COVENANTS

4.1 Franchise Agent shall not transfer to Brooke any incident of ownership of the Customer Accounts. Customer lists, Policy expiration lists and other records shall remain Franchise Agent's (or its Subagent's, as applicable) exclusive property, and Franchise Agent (or Subagent) shall be fully vested in the ownership thereof.

4.2 All Customer Accounts shall be coded on Brooke's records to Franchise Agent. Brooke shall not be authorized or permitted to change the coding of Customer Accounts without the written consent of Franchise Agent.

4.3 Brooke and Franchise Agent acknowledge that all information with respect to Customer Accounts is confidential information constituting trade secrets and shall be treated as such. Brooke shall not divulge any such confidential information to anyone without the consent of Franchise Agent unless disclosure is compelled by law.

4.4 Franchise Agent shall not have any authority to incur any liability in the name of or on behalf of Brooke. Brooke and Franchise Agent agree that the relationship of Brooke to Franchise Agent shall be that of an independent contractor.

4.5 Brooke and Franchise Agent shall not assume any liability of the other, and any such liability shall remain the exclusive individual liabilities of each. In addition, Brooke and Franchise Agent each agree to release, indemnify, and hold each other harmless from any and all losses, damages and expenses, including legal expenses, attorneys fees, discovery expenses and costs which are suffered or incurred by the other by reason of the actions, omissions or liability of any kind created, caused or allowed by each indemnifying party, individually or in conjunction with any other Person.

4.6 Franchise Agent, its owners, officers, directors, employees and independent contractors release, indemnify and hold Brooke harmless for and from any and all claims, losses, liabilities, damages or expenses (including, but not limited to reasonable attorneys' fees, court costs, and costs of investigation) of any kind or nature whatsoever incurred by Franchise Agent, its owners, officers, directors, employees and independent contractors arising out of or in connection with interruptions of service caused by an act of God or any other event outside the direct control of Brooke. This release, indemnification and hold harmless shall survive the termination of this Agreement.

4.7 Franchise Agent, its owners, officers, directors, employees and independent contractors release, indemnify and hold Brooke harmless if Brooke permits Franchise Agent its owners, officers, directors, employees and independent contractors to use an insolvent Company and Franchise Agent, its owners, officers, directors, employees or independent contractors incur any claims, losses, liabilities, damages or expenses of any kind or nature whatsoever resulting therefrom. This release, indemnification and hold harmless shall survive the termination of this Agreement.

4.8 Franchise Agent agrees that Brooke may rely on statements, representations, requests, instructions, commitments and agreements (without verification or confirmation of same) of Franchise Agent's owners, officers, directors, employees or independent contractors as if same had been made or delivered to Brooke by Franchise Agent unless and until written instructions limiting Brooke's right to rely on such statements representations, requests, instructions, commitments and agreements have been provided by Franchise Agent and received by Brooke. Franchise Agent agrees to release, indemnify and hold harmless Brooke, its owners, officers, directors, employees, and independent contractors (for purposes of subparagraphs 4.8 and 4.9, collectively, "Brooke") for and from any and all claims, losses, liabilities, or damages or expenses (including, but not limited to reasonable attorneys' fees, court costs, and costs of investigation) of any kind or nature whatsoever arising out of or in connection with Brooke's reliance or which Franchise Agent, its owners, officers, directors, employees, and independent contractors may incur as a result of Brooke's reliance on same. This release, indemnification and hold harmless shall survive termination of the Agreement.

4.9 The duties and obligations of Franchise Agent set forth herein apply to Franchise Agent, its owners, officers, directors, employees and independent contractors. In as much as this Agreement is by and between Franchise Agent and Brooke, Franchise Agent is responsible for the compliance of its owners, officers, directors, employees and independent contractors with the terms of this Agreement and any rules and procedures adopted from time to time by Brooke's Board of Directors. Franchise Agent agrees that it is fully responsible for the acts and omissions of its owners, officers, directors, employees and independent contractors (for purposes of this subparagraph, collectively "Franchise Agent"). Accordingly, Franchise Agent agrees to release, indemnify and hold harmless Brooke for and from any and all claims, losses, liabilities, or damages or expenses (including, but not limited to reasonable attorneys' fees, court costs, and costs of investigation) of any kind or nature whatsoever arising out of or in connection with Franchise Agent's acts or omissions or which Brooke or Franchise Agent may incur as a result of Franchise Agent's acts or omissions. This release, indemnification and hold harmless shall survive termination of the Agreement.

5. REPRESENTATIONS AND WARRANTIES OF EACH PARTY:

5.1 Brooke warrants and represents that it is a corporation, duly organized, existing and in good standing under the laws of the state of Kansas. Franchise Agent, if a corporation, warrants and represents that it is duly organized, existing and in good standing under the laws of the state in which it was organized and incorporated.

5.2 Franchise Agent represents and warrants that all of Franchise Agent's owners, officers, directors, employees or independent contractors that are required to be duly and fully licensed by any self regulatory organization, governmental agency or any Company contracted with Brooke shall be, at all times during the term of this Agreement, duly and fully licensed as insurance agents or representatives under the auspices of Brooke and have all other requisite licenses, registrations, and authority to sell, renew, service or deliver Policies in any state in which Franchise Agent sells, renews, services or delivers such Policies.

5.3 Franchise Agent shall notify Brooke of any and all litigation to which Franchise Agent or any of Franchise Agent's owners, directors, officers, employees or independent contractors may become a party, whether as plaintiff or defendant, and represents and warrants that no such litigation is now pending.

5.4 Franchise Agent shall notify Brooke of any investigations of or hearings related to Franchise Agent or any of Franchise Agent's owners, directors, officers, employees or independent contractors by any self regulatory organization, governmental agency, or Company and represents and warrants that no such investigations or hearings are now pending.

5.5 Brooke has taken all necessary corporate action, including, but not limited to, binding resolutions of its directors to enter into this Agreement and to carry out the terms and conditions thereof. Franchise Agent, if represented in the beginning paragraph of this Agreement to be a corporation, has taken all necessary corporate action, including, but not limited to, binding resolutions/actions of all of its directors and/or shareholders to enter into this Agreement and to carry out the terms and conditions thereof.

5.6 Brooke does not warrant, guarantee or make any representations regarding the accuracy and/or timeliness of any billings provided by Companies.

6. TERMINATION OF AGREEMENT:

6.1 The term of this Agreement is for five years and is renewable at expiration.

6.2 Brooke shall have the right to terminate or refuse to renew this Agreement only upon good and sufficient cause which shall be defined as:

(a) material and substantial breach of the terms of this Agreement by Franchise Agent (unless otherwise agreed in writing, for the purposes of paragraph 6.2 and all its subparagraphs, "Franchise Agent" shall include Franchise Agent's owners, officers, directors, employees and independent contractors);

(b) refusal by the insurance company which provides errors and omissions insurance coverages to Brooke to endorse said insurance policy to provide errors and omissions insurance coverage for Franchise Agent;

(c) such public actions by Franchise Agent, which in the judgment of a majority of Brooke's Board of Directors, shall be materially injurious to the reputation of Brooke or the cumulative goodwill related to the use of Brooke's name, trademarks, service marks, logotypes or commercial symbols.

(d) insurance coverage or Policy underwriting practices by Franchise Agent, which in the opinion of a majority of Brooke's Board of Directors, may jeopardize Brooke's continued contractual agency relationship with any Company;

(e) the commission or omission of any act by Franchise Agent, which in the opinion of a majority of Brooke's Board of Directors, would be sufficient cause for the revocation of a license, registration, or other authority by any self regulatory organization, governmental agency or Company in any state in which Franchise Agent sells, renews, services or delivers Policies;

(f) legal proceedings involving Franchise Agent, which in the opinion of a majority of Brooke's Board of Directors, may impair Franchise Agent's capacity to perform Franchise Agent's obligations as set forth in this Agreement;

(g) business practices by Franchise Agent, which in the opinion of a majority of Brooke's Board of Directors are unethical or unacceptable to the general business community;

(h) inadequate qualifications of Franchise Agent, which in the opinion of a majority of Brooke's Board of Directors, may impair the ability of Franchise Agent to provide adequate assistance and service to Customer Accounts;

(i) the partial or total sale or transfer of Franchise Agent ownership or the partial or total sale or transfer of ownership of Customer Accounts without Brooke's prior written consent;

(j) the location or relocation of Franchise Agent's agency office to an address other than the address designated in the beginning paragraph of this Agreement without Brooke's prior written consent;

(k) the establishment by Franchise Agent of an additional agency office at an address other than the address designated in the beginning paragraph of this Agreement without Brooke's prior written consent;

(l) bankruptcy of Franchise Agent;

(m) dishonor of a draft or electronic funds transfer drawn by Brooke, or its designee, on Franchise Agent's checking account, if such draft is authorized by this Agreement;

(n) failure to provide proof of liability insurance as mandated by 3.17;

(o) the agreement (oral or written) of Franchise Agent to enter a brokerage, commission sharing, account sharing or service center agreement with any Person not on the company list described in paragraph 2.11 or obligated by contract (either through an agreement with Brooke or a Brooke franchise agent) to process all applications for Policies exclusively through the facilities of Brooke or a Brooke franchise agent.

(p) the refusal by Franchise Agent to provide a description of brokerage, commission sharing, account sharing or service center agreements Franchise Agent has entered into, and copies of the agreements memorializing same, within 30 days of entering any such agreement or after receipt of Brooke's written request for same, if sooner. Brooke's receipt of any such agreement shall not charge Brooke with actual or implied knowledge of its terms nor shall such agreement have any binding effect on Brooke unless Brooke is expressly a party thereto in a written document signed by Brooke.

6.3 In the event Brooke shall terminate or refuse to renew this Agreement for cause as aforesaid, it shall give Franchise Agent written notice of its intent to terminate or non-renew, which notice shall state all of the material facts upon which Brooke relies as grounds for termination. Such notice shall fix an effective date of termination which shall be not sooner than 30 days from the date of the notice.

6.4 Franchise Agent shall have the unilateral right to terminate this Agreement for any reason upon not less than 30 days advance notice to Brooke.

6.5 Upon termination of this Agreement, Brooke shall request the pertinent Companies involved to make the Franchise Agent the Agent of Record for all Customer Accounts. In the event that a Company refuses to make the Franchise Agent the Agent of Record for Customer Accounts , then Franchise Agent shall, on or before the next Policy term expiration date following termination of this Agreement, obtain replacement coverages for said Customer Accounts with another Company. Brooke shall continue to account for and process Customer Accounts until the Policy term expiration date following termination of this Agreement. Although Brooke shall not be obligated to assist Franchise Agent in obtaining replacement coverages for Customer Accounts, Brooke shall provide to Franchise Agent the Policy term expiration data and Customer Account data available through Brooke's Document Manager system. If the Franchise Agent does not obtain replacement coverages for Customer Accounts on or before the policy term expiration date following termination of this Agreement, then Brooke shall obtain coverages for said Customer Accounts and Franchise Agent thereby relinquishes to Brooke all ownership of, possession of, or other right to or interest in said Customer Accounts and any related files.

6.6 Upon termination of this Agreement and for as long as necessary thereafter, Brooke shall continue to account for all Sales Commissions on Direct Bill Policies audited, endorsed, changed, or canceled on behalf of Customer Accounts processed through the facilities of Brooke. Brooke shall continue to record Customer Account activity on Franchise Agent Account as set forth in paragraph 2.2 and 2.4 of this Agreement.

6.7 Upon termination of this Agreement and for as long as necessary thereafter, Brooke shall continue to account for all Net Premiums on Agency Bill Policies audited, endorsed, changed, renewed, serviced, or canceled on behalf of Customer Accounts processed through the facilities of Brooke. Brooke shall continue to record Customer Account activity on Franchise Agent Account as set forth in paragraph 2.3 and 2.4 of this Agreement.

6.8 After the termination of this Agreement, Franchise Agent shall remain responsible for payment to Brooke of all Agency Bill Policy net premiums and Direct Bill Policy return commissions incurred on behalf of Customer Accounts processed through the facilities of Brooke.

6.9 If entries are recorded to Franchise Agent Account in the month of or any month after the termination of this Agreement, Brooke shall forward a record of Franchise Agent Account to Franchise Agent on or about the 15th of said month. Franchise Agent shall pay Brooke, or its designee, on or about the 20th of each month any amount owed by Franchise Agent. Upon written notice to Franchise Agent, Brooke may change the date such records are forwarded to Franchise Agent and the date Franchise Agent shall pay Brooke amounts owed Brooke by Franchise Agent.

6.10 Upon termination of this Agreement, Brooke shall cease to provide errors and omissions insurance coverage for Franchise Agent and Franchise Agent shall not be entitled to any refund of errors and omissions insurance policy premiums.

6.11 Upon termination of this Agreement, Brooke shall be permitted to retain copies of any files and records with respect to Customer Accounts as it shall deem reasonably necessary to account for and process Customer Accounts and for any other legitimate business purposes including preparation of tax returns and audits thereof, defense of litigation, collection of Franchise Agent Account, or otherwise.

6.12 In the event Franchise Agent elects to sell some or all Customer Accounts owned by Franchise Agent, Brooke shall have the first right to purchase such assets at a price equal to the amount offered to or by any other bona fide purchaser. Brooke shall have a right to purchase Customer Accounts owned by Subagents second only to Franchise Agent's right to purchase same.

7. TRUST ARRANGEMENT:

7.1 Franchise Agent acknowledges that Brooke may enter into or has entered into a trust agreement (the "Trust Agreement") which among other terms provides for a trustee's control of all Sales Commissions. Accordingly, Franchise Agent agrees that all premiums, fees, Sales Commissions and Other Receipts received by Franchise Agent or Brooke from Companies or customers which are related in any way to the sale, renewal, service or delivery of Policies through Franchise Agent shall be promptly deposited in the Receipts Trust Account.

7.2 Franchise Agent agrees that said Receipts Trust Account shall be owned by Brooke, but controlled by the trustee. Trustee shall have sole right to withdraw funds from the Receipts Trust Account. Trustee shall distribute to Franchise Agent and/or Brooke Sales Commissions and Other Receipts in accordance with the terms of the Trust Agreement. However, unless otherwise agreed upon by the parties in writing, nothing in the Trust Agreement shall change amounts due Franchise Agent, as shown on the statement of Franchise Agent Account pursuant to the terms of this Agreement or amounts payable by Franchise Agent to Brooke as shown on the statement of Franchise Agent Account pursuant to the terms of this Agreement.

7.3 Franchise Agent acknowledges and agrees that Trustee (as an authorized designee of Brooke under paragraphs 2.9, 3.10 and 6.9 hereof) shall initiate an electronic deposit to Franchise Agent's business account of all amounts due to Franchise Agent by Brooke as shown on the statement of Franchise Agent Account and in accordance with Franchise Agent's pre-authorization, or that Trustee shall initiate an electronic withdrawal from Franchise Agents' business account of all amounts due to Brooke by Franchise Agent as shown on the statement of Franchise Agent Account and in accordance with Franchise Agent's pre-authorization.

7.4 Franchise Agent agrees to release, indemnify and hold harmless Brooke, its owners, officers, directors, employees, and independent contractors (for the purposes of this subparagraph, collectively "Brooke") for and from any and all claims, losses, liability, or damages or expenses (including, but not limited to reasonable attorneys' fees, court costs, and costs of investigation) of any kind or nature whatsoever arising out of or in connection with the Trust Agreement, the deposit or withdrawal of money from the Receipts Trust Account or which Franchise Agent, its owners, officers, directors, employees, and independent contractors may incur as a result of Brooke's performance of its rights, obligations or duties hereunder or under the terms of the Trust Agreement or in connection with the deposit or withdrawal of money from the Receipts Trust Account or Franchise Agent's business account. Provided, however, that this shall not relieve Brooke from liability for its breach of any of its agreements under this Agreement or for its own willful misconduct, recklessness, bad faith or gross negligence, nor for the gross negligence, recklessness, bad faith or willful misconduct of its owners, officers, directors, employees, or independent contractors. This release, indemnification and hold harmless shall survive termination of the Agreement.

7.5 Franchise Agent, its owners, officers, directors, employees and independent contractors agree to release, indemnify and hold harmless the trust, its trustee, its owners, officers, directors, employees, and independent contractors (collectively, "trust") for and from any and all claims, losses, liability, or damages or expenses (including, but not limited to reasonable attorneys' fees, court costs, and costs of investigation) of any kind or nature whatsoever arising out of or in connection with the Trust Agreement or which Franchise Agent, its owners, officers, directors, employees, and independent contractors may incur as a result of trust's performance of its rights, obligations or duties under the terms of the Trust Agreement. This release, indemnification and hold harmless shall survive termination of the Agreement. Upon Brooke's request, Franchise Agent agrees to sign a separate document (to which trustee may be a party) releasing, indemnifying and holding harmless the trust.

8. SUBAGENT ARRANGEMENTS:

8.1   Transfer of Customer Accounts may result in termination of this Agreement in accordance with paragraph 6.2(i).   However, Brooke authorizes Franchise Agent to enter into agreements ("Subagent Agreements") with qualified Subagents which provide for the vesting of ownership in Customer Account to Subagents. Said authorization is contingent upon the following:

(a) Franchise Agent agrees to provide a copy of this Agreement and Brooke's complete and current offering circular to all prospective Subagents. Franchise Agent acknowledges that said franchise offering circular has been prepared by Brooke for disclosure to prospective franchise agents and is provided to Subagent to disclose Franchise Agent's direct relationship with Brooke.

(b) Franchise Agent agrees not to make any oral agreements, modifications or representations with or to any Subagent or prospective Subagent with regard to the subject matter of this Agreement or any Subagent Agreement. All such agreements and representations must be in writing, true and complete, and without a tendency to mislead. Further, Franchise Agent agrees not to furnish any oral or written representations, information or projections concerning the actual or potential sales, costs, income profits or performance of any Subagent's or prospective Subagent's agency.   Any modifications to a Subagent Agreement must be in writing and are subject to the prior approval of Brooke. Such approval shall be at Brooke's sole discretion.

(c) Franchise Agent acknowledges that Brooke shall not be a party to any agreements between Franchise Agent and Subagent. Franchise Agent agrees to enforce for the benefit of Brooke all provisions in Subagent Agreements executed by Franchise Agent that pertain to or benefit Brooke and Franchise Agent agrees not to waive any provisions which pertain to or benefit Brooke.

(d) Franchise Agent agrees to submit to Brooke a Subagent Application, in a form approved by Brooke, at least five (5) business days prior to the proposed effective date of any Subagent Agreement. A fully completed, but not executed, Subagent Agreement must be attached to the Subagent Application. Franchise Agent shall not enter into a Subagent Agreement until Franchise Agent receives written approval from Brooke. Such approval shall be at Brooke's sole discretion. Brooke's approval of same shall not be deemed Brooke's warranty of such agreement's compliance with any laws, enforceability or suitability for Franchise Agent's purposes or any other purpose.

(e) Franchise Agent agrees to provide a fully completed, but not executed, Subagent Agreement to the Subagent at least five (5) business days prior to the proposed effective date of the Subagent Agreement.

(f) Subagent Agreements shall be executed in triplicate prior to the effective date of the Subagent Agreement and Franchise Agent shall deliver one fully executed original to Brooke.

(g) Franchise Agent agrees to identify Subagent ownership by assigning a specific Subagent sub code to all Customer Accounts owned by Subagent. Franchise Agent agrees to ensure that this Subagent sub code is recorded on all applications and to otherwise ensure that Brooke receives the information necessary to sub code those Customer Accounts for which ownership has been vested in a Subagent.

(h) Franchise Agent acknowledges that Brooke's accounting responsibilities to the Franchise Agent with regard to Subagents is limited to the recording of the Subagent sub coding information provided by the Franchise Agent and that the accuracy of said sub code information is the exclusive obligation of Franchise

Agent. Brooke agrees to record said sub code information in a manner which permits the separation of all entries to the Franchise Agent Account so that Franchise Agent can provide statements of Subagent's account with Franchise Agent. Franchise Agent acknowledges and agrees that Brooke may rely exclusively on sub coding instructions, statements and information provided to Brooke by Franchise Agent and Brooke is not required to verify or confirm same. Franchise Agent agrees to release , indemnify and hold harmless Brooke, its owners, officers, directors, employees and independent contractors for and from any and all claims, losses, liabilities, damages or expenses (including, but not limited to reasonable attorneys' fees, court costs, and costs of investigation) of any kind or nature whatsoever arising out of or in connection with Brooke's reliance on Franchise Agent's sub coding instructions, statements or information.

(i) Franchise Agent acknowledges that it is responsible for collection of all amounts due from Subagent and payment of all amounts due to Subagent pursuant to the Subagent Agreement. The Franchise Agent further acknowledges that the entire Franchise Agent Account balance shall be paid to Brooke when due, irrespective of whether the Franchise Agent has collected amounts due Franchise Agent from Subagent.

(j) Franchise Agent acknowledges that its Company list may be modified or restricted as a result of entering into a Subagent Agreement.

8.2 Subject to the approval of the insurance company involved, Brooke shall endorse Brooke's errors and omissions insurance policy to provide errors and omissions insurance coverage for Subagent. Upon termination of the Subagent Agreement, errors and omissions insurance coverage for Subagent shall no longer be provided to Subagent under Brooke's errors and omissions insurance policy.

8.3. Brooke shall provide Customer Account and document information to Franchise Agent pursuant to this Agreement. Such information may subsequently be made available by Franchise Agent to Subagent at Franchise Agent's discretion. At Franchise Agent's discretion, Franchise Agent may authorize Subagents to use Brooke's proprietary software under Franchise Agent's license; provided however, such authorization is subject to the same restrictions applied to Franchise Agent pursuant hereto.

8.4 Franchise Agent shall immediately notify Brooke when any Subagent Agreement is terminated and, upon Franchise Agent's written request, Brooke shall request the pertinent Companies involved to make Subagent the Agent of Record for all Customer Accounts identified by the sub code information provided by Franchise Agent.

9. MISCELLANEOUS PROVISIONS:

9.1 Brooke shall not be obligated to pay Franchise Agent any share of Profit Sharing Commissions.

9.2 Any notices required hereunder shall be deemed effective if in writing, and delivered by hand or mailed by United States Mail, postage prepaid, or mailed by certified mail, with return receipt requested or mailed by express courier with confirmed delivery date. The effective date of notice shall be the day of delivery by hand, and if mailed by regular mail, four days following the mailing thereof, and if by certified mail or express courier, the date of receipt thereof. A business day shall be deemed any day on which the United States Postal Service shall have regular mail deliveries to the address to which the notice is mailed.

9.3 This Agreement may not be modified, revised, altered, added to, or extended in any manner, or superseded other than by an instrument in writing signed by all of the parties hereto.

9.4 This Agreement may be executed in duplicate, each of which shall be deemed an original, but all of which together shall constitute one and the same instrument representing the agreement of the parties hereto.

9.5 The failure by an party to enforce any provision of this Agreement shall not be in any way construed as a waiver of any such provision nor prevent that party thereafter from enforcing each and every other provision of this Agreement.

9.6 The invalidity or non-enforceability of any particular provision of this Agreement shall not affect the other provisions hereof, and this Agreement shall be construed in all respects as if such invalid or unenforceable provisions were omitted.

9.7 This Agreement shall be binding upon and inure to the benefit of the parties hereto and their heirs and legal representatives but the rights and property interests hereunder shall not be assignable by any party except as set out herein.

9.8 This Agreement (including all Exhibits and Addenda hereto) contains the entire agreement between the parties hereto and shall supersede and take precedence over any and all prior agreements, arrangements or understandings between the parties relating to the subject matter hereof. No oral understandings, oral statements, oral promises or oral inducements exist. No representations, warranties, covenants or conditions, express or implied, whether by statute or otherwise, other than as set forth herein, have been made by the parties hereto.

9.9   Franchise Agent agrees to sign, acknowledge, deliver, and/or file any additional documents, certifications or statements that Brooke may deem necessary to carry out the intent of this Agreement.

9.10 This Agreement shall be construed and governed by the laws of the State of Kansas. At the option of Brooke, jurisdiction and venue for any dispute arising under or in relation to this Agreement will lie only in Kansas with the Phillips County District Court, Phillipsburg, Kansas or in the U.S. District Court having jurisdiction over Phillips County Kansas. In the event a lawsuit or litigation is brought with respect to this Agreement, the prevailing party shall be entitled to be reimbursed for and/or have judgment for all of their costs and expenses, including reasonable attorney's fees and legal expenses.

9.11 Timeliness and punctuality are essential elements of this Agreement.

IN WITNESS WHEREOF, Brooke Corporation and Franchise Agent have executed this Agreement as of the day and year first above written.

BROOKE: FRANCHISE AGENT:

By:_____   By:_____

Title:_____   Title:_____

GUARANTY AGREEMENT

If Franchise Agent is a corporation or limited liability company, we the undersigned, as individuals, jointly and severally guarantee the faithful performance of Franchise Agent to perform all duties and obligations set forth in the forgoing agreement including without limitation the duty to pay any sum which Franchise Agent may become liable to pay Brooke by virtue of the foregoing agreement.

IN WITNESS WHEREOF, the undersigned has executed this Guaranty Agreement as of the day and year first above written.

_____   _____

_____,individually   _____, individually

RECEIPTS TRUST AGREEMENT

This Receipts Trust Agreement ("Agreement") is entered into this _____ day of _____, _____, by and between _____ as Trustee ("Trustee") and Brooke Corporation ("Master Agent").

RECITALS

WHEREAS, Master Agent owns Sales Commissions and Other Receipts acquired during the course of operating its Insurance, Investment, Banking and Credit Services business.

WHEREAS, pursuant to separate Agent Agreements, Master Agent credits Agent's Accounts in amounts that are based on Sales Commission and, in some instances, Other Receipts.

WHEREAS, pursuant to separate Collateral Preservation Agreements, certain Lenders have represented to Master Agent that they hold a security interest in Agent's Accounts.

WHEREAS, Master Agent desires to appoint Trustee to control distribution of Sales Commissions to help ensure that the Master Agent credits amounts to Agent's Accounts if said amounts are based on Sales Commissions. Until such time as Trustee distributes Sales Commissions to Master Agent or Agent, Master Agent desires for Trustee to invest any balances in accordance with Master Agent's written instructions.

WHEREAS, Master Agent does not desire for Trustee to control distribution of Other Receipts that are not Sales Commissions. However, until such time as Trustee returns Other Receipts to Master Agent, Master Agent desires for Trustee to invest any balances in accordance with Master Agent's written instructions.

WHEREAS, in the event of Agent's default on its obligations to a Lender that has entered into a Collateral Preservation Agreement with Master Agent, this trust arrangement helps ensure that Agent's Account balances are paid directly to the Lender.

NOW, THEREFORE, in consideration of the terms and conditions set forth herein, and for other good and valuable consideration, the receipt and sufficiency of which are hereby acknowledged, Trustee and Master Agent agree as follows:

DEFINITIONS OF TERMS USED IN THIS AGREEMENT

For the purposes of this Agreement, the following terms shall have the following meanings unless the context clearly requires otherwise:

Agent. Person who has entered into an agreement with the Master Agent to sell, renew, service or deliver Policies exclusively through the Master Agent and whose agency assets are the subject of a Collateral Preservation Agreement. Further, Agent may include Persons who have entered into an agreement with Master Agent to sell, renew, service or deliver Policies exclusively through the Master Agent but whose agency assets are not the subject of a Collateral Preservation Agreement so long as a list of such Agents is provided to Trustee.

Agent's Account. An account on Master Agent's ledgers to which the Master Agent records amounts due Master Agent from Agent and amounts due Agent from Master Agent.

Agent Agreement. An agreement, which has been or will be executed, by and between Master Agent and Agent providing for Agent to sell, renew, service or deliver Policies exclusively through Master Agent.

Agent-Billed Policies. Any Policy for which Agent is responsible for all or any part of premium or fee billing and collection.

Agent Statements. A record of Agent's Account prepared by Master Agent listing all credit and debit entries made to Agent's Account by Master Agent for a specified period of time, or a summary report of Agent's Account for a specified period of time prepared by Master Agent and acceptable to Trustee. Such debit and credit entries may include, but are not limited to, Sales Commissions, Net Premiums and Master Agent advances to Agent.

Collateral Preservation Agreement. Agreement, as amended from time to time, between Master Agent and Lender which requires the Master Agent to help protect and preserve Lender's collateral interest in certain Agency Assets including, without limitation, Agent's Account and Customer Files.

Company. A company issuing, brokering, selling or making a market for Policies and which has a contract with Master Agent.

Company Billings. Statements or billings received by Master Agent from Companies for amounts due Master Agent from Companies and for amounts due Companies from Master Agent.

Customer Files. Documents, data and correspondence to or from customers, Agent, Master Agent, Companies or others regarding Policies.

Direct-Billed Policies. Any Policy for which a Company is responsible for premium or fee billing and collection.

Gross Premiums. Total premium, fees or other amounts due from the sale, renewal, service or delivery of Policies through Agent including the corresponding Sales Commissions.

Insurance, Investment, Banking and/or Credit Services. Insurance services include but are not limited to the sale, renewal, service or delivery of insurance policies, annuities, insurance brokering services, insurance customer services, risk management services and insurance related consulting or advisory services. Investment services include, but are not limited to, the sale, renewal, service or delivery of mutual funds, stocks, bonds, notes, debentures, real estate services, investment customer services, investment related consulting, and financial, investment, or economic advisory services. Banking services include any banking service Agent is allowed to perform under federal and/or state laws. Credit services include, but are not limited to, origination or brokerage of loans or mortgages, credit customer services, and credit related consulting or advisory services. At any point in time, Insurance, Investment, Banking and Credit Services shall be limited to those services then offered by Master Agent.

Lender. The Person extending credit to Agent and who is a party to a Collateral Preservation Agreement with Master Agent.

Net Premiums. Agent Billed Policies Gross Premiums less the corresponding Sales Commissions.

Other Receipts. Deposits made to the Receipts Trust Account that are not Sales Commissions. Such receipts may include but are not limited to: Profit Sharing Commissions; Net Premiums, advertising reimbursements, proceeds from sale of personal money orders; Gross Premiums for Direct Billed Policies (e.g. on line payments); loan proceeds; Company refunds; supplier refunds; and, vendor refunds.

Person. Any individual, sole proprietorship, partnership, joint venture, trust, unincorporated organization, association, corporation, limited liability company, institution or other entity.

Policies. Any and all insurance services, policies, coverages or products sold, renewed, serviced or delivered through Agent to any Person. Policies include, but are not limited to, any and all Insurance, Investment, Banking or Credit Services, or policies, coverages or products associated therewith sold, renewed, serviced or delivered through Agent to any Person.

Profit Sharing Commissions. Commissions or fees which are not associated with the sale of a specific Policy through Agent. Profit Sharing Commissions are typically contingent upon factors such as sales volume, premium volume, profitability and other special concessions negotiated by the Master Agent. Profit Sharing Commissions include, but are not limited to, payments identified by the Companies as profit sharing commissions, contingency commissions, advertising allowances, prizes, override commissions, expense reimbursements and bonus commissions.

Receipts Trust Account. One or more accounts owned exclusively by Master Agent to which Sales Commissions and Other Receipts are deposited by Master Agent or its Agents and controlled by Trustee under this Agreement.

Sales Commissions. Commissions paid by Companies to Master Agent or assigned by Agent to Master Agent for the sale, renewal, service or delivery of a specific Policy through Agent. Sales Commissions are not normally contingent upon factors such as Master Agent's loss ratio, premium volume, sales volume or special concessions negotiated by the Master Agent. For the purposes of this Agreement, Sales Commissions shall specifically exclude Profit Sharing Commissions and other similar payments. However, Sales Commissions shall specifically include amounts paid to Agent by the Master Agent pursuant to a bonus plan, the terms of which are defined by the Master Agent in its sole discretion and for which the Master Agent makes no representation regarding future payments or Agent eligibility. Sales Commissions shall also include any consulting fees, advisory fees, placement fees, service fees, renewal fees, or any similar payments paid on or related to any Customer Account by any Person.

OBLIGATIONS TO BE PERFORMED BY TRUSTEE

1) Safekeeping of Documents. Trustee shall be given copies of Collateral Preservation Agreements and Agent Agreements or have access to legible and complete copies of same via the Internet. The parties agree that Trustee has no rights or responsibilities under such agreements; Trustee is not a beneficiary of their terms and has no standing to seek enforcement thereof. Trustee acknowledges that said agreements are confidential and shall not copy or otherwise distribute information about or contained in said agreements without the prior written consent of Master Agent.

2) Gathering from Receipts Trust Accounts. Master Agent shall provide Trustee with exclusive pre-authorization to electronically withdraw the daily total of all deposits made to Receipts Trust Accounts for daily investment by Trustee in an account which designates Master Agent's ownership interest in such deposits. The Trustee shall initiate said electronic withdrawals immediately upon Master Agent's notification regarding the amounts of deposits to the Receipt Trust Account and the location of the Receipts Trust Account.

3) Settlement of Agent's Account. a) The Trustee shall, on the third banking business day immediately following the date Master Agent delivers Agent Statements to Trustee, initiate an electronic deposit to Agents' accounts of all amounts due to Agents by Master Agent as recorded on the Agent Statements and in accordance with Agents' pre-authorization unless such amounts have been adjusted as provided in paragraph 3(c) below. The total amount of any such electronic deposits made by Trustee to the Agents' accounts shall reduce the amount of distributions made by the Trustee to the Master Agent pursuant to the terms of this Agreement.

b) The Trustee shall, on the third banking business day immediately following the date Master Agent delivers Agent Statements to Trustee, initiate an electronic withdrawal from Agents' accounts of all amounts due to Master Agent by Agents as recorded on the Agent Statements and in accordance with Agent's pre-authorization unless such amounts have been adjusted as provided in paragraph 3(c) below. The total amount of any such electronic withdrawals made by Trustee shall be returned to the Master Agent in the same manner as an Other Receipt.

c) Notwithstanding the above, the Master Agent may adjust the amount of electronic deposit or withdrawal as provided in the above. In this event, Master Agent shall authorize any such adjustment and forward written authorization to the Trustee.

d) If the Trustee has received notice from the Master Agent of an Agent's default and Agent's failure to cure its default, then the Trustee shall not make any electronic deposits or other payments to Agent and shall make payment directly to Lender of any amount which, but for default, would be due to the corresponding Agent as recorded on the Agent Statements. Trustee shall make payments to Lender until such time as Lender provides written notification to Trustee to the contrary.

4) Distribution of Sales Commissions on Direct-Billed Policies. The Trustee shall, on or before the close of the fourth banking business day immediately following the date Master Agent delivers Agent Statements or daily summary commission reports to Trustee, distribute to Master Agent the total of Sales Commissions on Direct Billed Policies which have been credited to Agent's Account as listed on Agent Statements.

5) Distribution of Sales Commissions on Agent-Billed Policies. The Trustee shall, on or before the close of the fourth banking business day immediately following the date Master Agent delivers Agent Statements or daily summary deposit reports to Trustee, distribute to Master Agent the total of Gross Premiums on Agent Billed Policies which have been credited to Agent's Account as listed on Agent Statements. If the Net Premium portions of said Gross Premiums have been previously distributed to Master Agent, as provided in the following paragraph, then only the Sales Commissions portion of said Gross Premium shall be distributed to Master Agent.

6) Return of Other Receipts. The Trustee shall immediately return to Master Agent all Other Receipts, upon delivery by Master Agent to Trustee of a listing of all such receipts. Said listing shall include a description of each receipt and, if required by the Trustee, an affidavit from Master Agent that the listed receipts are not Sales Commissions.

7) Limitations of Trustee's Control and Responsibilities. a) Trustee shall make distributions only in accordance with the terms of this Agreement. Distributions to any other person or entity are strictly prohibited. Trustee shall be responsible for distribution of those receipts deposited to the Receipts Trust Account and shall not be responsible for distribution of any receipts that are not deposited to the Receipts Trust Account.

b) Trustee shall not assume any responsibility for the timeliness or accuracy of Agent Statements prepared by the Master Agent. Trustee shall rely solely on copies of Agent Statements prepared by Master Agent and delivered to the Trustee. However, if Trustee deems necessary for meeting its responsibilities pursuant to this agreement, the Trustee may access Master Agent's Company Billings for verification of Sales Commissions information. It is agreed that, in all instances, Company Billings shall be the only source for verifying information about Sales Commissions and that the absence of a specific reference on a corresponding Company Billing is sufficient to demonstrate that an item is not Sales Commissions.

c) Trustee shall make distributions of Sales Commissions to the Master Agent in the amounts recorded by the Master Agent on the Agent Statements, except in the case where Master Agent is in receivership or incapable of compiling Agent Statements, in which event the Trustee shall hold all Sales Commissions until such time as the Master Agent is capable of resuming its duties or until another entity assumes the Master Agent's duties to the extent provided in the Agent Agreements or the Collateral Preservation Agreements.

d) The Trustee is not authorized, and shall not, mediate or become involved in disputes between Master Agent and Agent or Master Agent and Lender. Any such disputes shall be resolved by Master Agent and Agent or Master Agent and Lender in accordance with the corresponding Agent Agreement or Collateral Preservation Agreement.

e) Trustee acknowledges and agrees that Master Agent is the sole owner of the Receipts Trust Account subject to the rights and obligations granted to Trustee herein. Therefore, Master Agent shall control investment of money deposited into any Receipts Trust Account and is entitled to all gains and responsible for all losses associated with the investment of money deposited into any Receipts Trust Account. The Trustee shall not be responsible for monitoring the activity in any Receipts Trust Account and shall not be responsible for compiling the information required to gather deposits by electronic withdrawal from the Receipts Trust Account.

8) Trustee's Accounting. As of each month end, Trustee shall provide Master Agent with an accounting of: all investments made on Master Agent's behalf; daily deposits gathered from Receipts Trust Accounts; distributions of Sales Commissions made to Master Agent; return of Other Receipts to Master Agent; and, settlement of Agent's Accounts made with Agents or Lenders.

9) Third Party Claims. In the event that Trustee receives or is served by a third party with any type of legal action, levy, attachment, writ or court order with respect to a Receipts Trust Account, Sales Commissions or Net Premiums, Trustee shall promptly deliver to Master Agent and any corresponding Lender copies of all court papers, orders, documents and other materials concerning such proceedings or claims. The Trustee shall continue to distribute Sales Commissions and return Other Receipts while any such proceeding is pending unless Trustee is explicitly prohibited by order of such court or tribunal from distributing said funds. Expenses of the Trustee, including reasonable counsel fees, incurred as a result of such proceedings shall be borne by Master Agent.

OBLIGATIONS TO BE PERFORMED BY MASTER AGENT

10) Grant of Dominion and Control. Master Agent hereby grants Trustee exclusive dominion and control over the Receipts Trust Account subject to the terms set forth herein.

11) Delivery of Agreements. Master Agent shall provide Trustee with fully legible and complete copies via the Internet of all Collateral Preservation Agreements and/or Agent Agreements to which Master Agent is a party. Master Agent shall provide necessary passwords to Trustee to permit Internet access and viewing. Further, if Trustee is unable to access any such agreement via Internet, upon Trustee's request Master Agent shall provide fully legible and complete hard copies of the agreements Trustee is unable to access via Internet.

12) Delivery of Agent Statements. Master Agent shall deliver to Trustee an Agent Statement for each Agent contracted with the Master Agent. Regardless of notice requirements set forth herein, Master Agent may deliver any such Agent Statements to Trustee via tele-fax.

13) Deposits to Receipts Trust Account. Master Agent shall promptly deposit all Sales Commissions and Other Receipts received from Companies or customers to a Receipts Trust Account.

14) Deposits to Receipts Trust Account by Agents. Master Agent will cause Agent Agreements dated after the date hereof, or any rules and procedures manual referenced by said Agent Agreement, to contain a provision requiring Agent to promptly deposit all Sales Commissions and Other Receipts received from Companies or customers to a Receipts Trust Account.

15) Restrictions on Withdrawals. Master Agent shall limit all withdrawals from Receipt Trust Accounts to electronic transfers of funds initiated by Trustee directly to Trustee for Trustee's investment on behalf of Master Agent and distribution pursuant hereto. Master Agent shall deliver to Trustee a confirmation from the institution where each such Receipt Trust Account is established confirming that Master Agent's ability to withdraw from Receipt Trust Accounts is so limited.

MISCELLANEOUS

16) Fees. Trustee shall be entitled to the fees set forth in the attached fee schedule, as same shall be amended from time to time. Such fee schedule shall also include the costs and expenses for which Trustee shall be reimbursed by Master Agent.

17) Resignation and Removal of Trustee. Trustee may resign for any reason with 30 days written notice to Master Agent with a copy to Lender. Such resignation shall not be effective until a successor trustee shall have assumed the duties of Trustee hereunder; provided however, that Master Agent shall use its best efforts to cause a successor trustee to assume Trustee's duties hereunder within 30 days of Trustee's written notice of resignation. Master Agent with cause upon two business days, and without cause, upon 30 days' prior written notice to the Trustee, may remove and discharge the Trustee (or any successor trustee thereafter appointed) from the performance of its obligations under this Agreement. The following represent sufficient cause for the immediate removal of Trustee: a material breach of this Agreement; the misconduct of Trustee; Trustee's under capitalization, insolvency or the filing of a voluntary or involuntary petition relating to Trustee's solvency; Trustee's failure to maintain required bonding or insurance; actions by Trustee which would in Master Agent's sole determination cause damage to Master Agent's or Lender's reputation; Trustee's unethical or unacceptable business practices; Trustee's gross negligence or recklessness; or Trustee's inadequate qualifications. In the event of resignation or removal, Trustee shall cooperate with the successor trustee and promptly transfer to the successor trustee, as directed in writing by Master Agent, all the files, records and documents under Trustee's control or in Trustee's possession pursuant to this Agreement.

18) Amendments. This Agreement may not be modified, revised, altered, added to, or extended in any manner, or superseded other than by an instrument in writing signed by all of the parties hereto.

19) Assignment. Trustee cannot assign, transfer or delegate all or any part of its rights, title, interest and obligations hereunder without the prior written consent of Master Agent. However, the parties agree that Master Agent may assign, transfer or delegate all or any part of its rights, title, interest and obligations hereunder upon written notice to Trustee.

20) Indemnification; Hold Harmless. Master Agent agrees to indemnify and hold harmless the Trustee and its directors, officers, agents and employees against any and all claims, damages, losses, liabilities or expenses (including, but not limited to, reasonable attorneys' fees, court costs and costs of investigation) of any kind or nature whatsoever arising out of or in connection with this Agreement; provided, however, that this shall not relieve Trustee from liability for its breach of any of its agreements under this Agreement or for its own willful misconduct, recklessness, bad faith or gross negligence, nor for the gross negligence, recklessness, bad faith or willful misconduct of its officers, directors, employees or agents. The provisions of this paragraph shall survive the resignation or removal of the Trustee or any successor trustee and the termination of this Agreement.

21) Notices. Any notices required hereunder shall be deemed effective if in writing, and delivered by hand or mailed by United States Mail, postage prepaid, or mailed by certified mail, with return receipt requested or mailed by express courier with confirmed deliver date. The effective date of notice shall be the day of delivery by hand, and if mailed by regular mail, four days following the mailing thereof, and if by certified mail or express courier, the date of receipt thereof. For purposes of notification, a business day shall be deemed any day on which the United States Postal Service shall have regular mail deliveries to the address to which the notice is mailed. Unless otherwise directed in writing, notices shall be sent to the following addresses:

Master Agent
Brooke Corporation
Attn:_____
205F Street, 2nd Floor
Phillipsburg, KS 67661

Trustee

_____
_____
_____

22) Execution in Duplicate. This Agreement may be executed in duplicate, each of which shall be deemed an original, but all of which together shall constitute one and the same instrument representing the agreement of the parties hereto.

23) Enforceability, Severability. The failure by any party to enforce any provision of this Agreement shall not be in any way construed as a waiver of any such provision nor prevent that party thereafter from enforcing each and every other provision of this Agreement. The invalidity or non-enforceability of any particular provision of this Agreement shall not affect the other provisions hereof, and this Agreement shall be construed in all respects as if such invalid or unenforceable provision were omitted.

24) Binding Effect. This Agreement shall be binding upon and inure to the benefit of the parties hereto and their heirs , administrators, successors, assigns and legal representatives, but the rights and property interests hereunder shall not be assignable by any party except as set out herein. The use of the masculine shall include the feminine, and the use of the singular shall include the plural.

25) Entire Agreement. This Agreement contains the entire agreement between the parties hereto and shall supersede and take precedence over any and all prior agreements, arrangements or understanding between the parties relating to the subject matter hereof. No oral understanding, oral statements, oral promises or oral inducements exist. No representations, warranties, covenants or conditions, express of implied, whether by statue or otherwise, other than as set forth herein, have been made by the parties hereto.

26) Governing Law. This Agreement shall be construed and governed by the laws of the State of Kansas. At the option of Master Agent, jurisdiction and venue for any dispute arising under or in relation to this Agreement will lie only in Kansas with the Phillips County District Court, Phillipsburg, Kansas, or the U.S. District Court with jurisdiction over Kansas. In the event a lawsuit or litigation is brought with respect to this Agreement, the prevailing party shall be entitled to be reimbursed for and/or have judgment for all of their costs and expenses, including reasonable attorney's fees and legal expenses.

27) Timeliness. Timeliness and punctuality are essential elements of this Agreement.

Executed on the date above written.

MASTER AGENT: **TRUSTEE:**

_____   _____
By: By:
Its: Its:

SUBAGENT AGREEMENT

THIS AGREEMENT made and entered into this _____ day of _____, _____, (which with all addenda shall be referred to herein as the "Agreement") by and between _____, having its principal place of business at _____ referred to hereafter as "Franchise Agent"; and, _____, by and through _____, its _____, whose offices and primary place of business is located at _____, _____ referred to hereafter as ("Subagent").

WITNESSETH:

WHEREAS, Subagent is in or may enter the business of selling, servicing and/or delivering Policies from the agency offices referenced above; and

WHEREAS, Franchise Agent is in the business of providing certain services and assistance to businesses selling insurance; however, Franchise Agent is in or may enter the business of selling, servicing and/or delivering other Policies and may provide certain services and assistance to businesses selling same; and

WHEREAS, Franchise Agent has entered into an agreement ("Franchise Agreement") with Brooke Corporation ("Brooke") pursuant to which Brooke provides certain services and assistance to Franchise Agent with respect to Franchise Agent's business; and

WHEREAS, Pursuant to the Franchise Agreement, Brooke provides certain services with respect to accounting for and processing of Policies associated with Customer Accounts, including without limitation, sub coding at Franchise Agent's instructions accounting entries to identify those entries related to Customer Accounts owned by Franchise Agent and Subagent;

WHEREAS, Brooke has granted the authority to Franchise Agent to enter into Subagent Agreement pursuant to which Franchise Agent provides to Subagent services similar to the services provided to Franchise Agent by Brooke with respect to accounting for and processing of Policies associated with Customer Accounts;

WHEREAS, Brooke has agreed with Franchise Agent to sub code information to the Franchise Agent Account based solely upon the instructions given to Brooke by Franchise Agent which Franchise Agent shall use in performing its duties set forth in this Agreement;

WHEREAS, Subagent and Franchise Agent desire to associate together effective _____, _____, for the purpose of Franchise providing certain services and assistance to Subagent with respect to Subagent's business.

NOW THEREFORE, in consideration of the mutual promises set forth herein and other good and valuable consideration, the receipt and sufficiency of which is hereby acknowledged, the parties agree as follows:

1. DEFINITIONS OF TERMS USED IN THIS AGREEMENT:

For purposes of this Agreement, the following terms shall have the following meanings unless the context clearly requires otherwise:

1.1 Agency-Billed Policies: Any Policies for which a Subagent is responsible for all or any part of premium or fee billing and collection.

1.2 Agent of Record: Person designated on Company's records as the agent or representative regarding a specific Policy and the owner of all Sales Commissions.

1.3 Company: A company issuing, brokering, selling or making a market for Policies and which has a contract with Brooke..

Page 1 of 13

1.4 Company Billings: Statements or billings received by Brooke from Companies for amounts due Brooke from Companies and for amounts due Companies from Brooke.

1.5 Customer Account: A Person who has a Policy purchased from, serviced, renewed or delivered through Subagent. Customer Accounts shall be owned by Subagent.

1.6 Direct-Billed Policies: Any Policies for which a Company is responsible for premium or fee billing and collection.

1.7 Franchise Agent Account: An account on Brooke's ledgers to which Brooke records amounts due Brooke from Franchise Agent and amounts due Franchise Agent from Brooke.

1.8 Gross Premiums: Total premium, fees or other amounts due from the sale, renewal, service or delivery of Policies including the corresponding Sales Commissions.

1.9 Insurance, Investment, Banking and/or Credit Services: Insurance services include but are not limited to the sale, renewal, service or delivery of insurance policies, annuities, insurance brokering services, insurance customer services, risk management services and insurance related consulting or advisory services. Investment services include, but are not limited to, the sale, renewal, service or delivery of mutual funds, stocks, bonds, notes, debentures, real estate services, investment customer services, and investment related consulting, and financial, investment, or economic advisory services. Banking services include any banking service Subagent is allowed to perform under federal and/or state laws. Credit services include, but are not limited to, origination or brokerage of loans or mortgages, credit customer services, and credit related consulting or advisory services. At any point in time, Insurance, Investment, Banking and Credit Services shall be limited to those services then offered by Franchise Agent.

1.10 Net Premium: Gross Premiums on Agency Billed Policies less the corresponding Sales Commissions.

1.11 Other Receipts: Deposits made to the Receipts Trust Account that are not Sales Commissions. Such receipts may include but are not limited to: Profit Sharing Commissions; Net Premiums, advertising reimbursements, proceeds from sale of personal money orders; Gross Premiums for Direct Billed Policies (e.g. on line payments); loan proceeds; Company refunds; supplier refunds; and vendor refunds.

1.12 Person: Any individual, sole proprietorship, partnership, joint venture, trust, unincorporated organization, association, corporation, limited liability company, institution or other entity.

1.13 Policies: Any and all insurance services, policies, coverages or products sold, renewed, serviced or delivered through Subagent to any Person. Policies include, but are not limited to, any and all Insurance, Investment, Banking or Credit Services, or policies, coverages or products associated therewith sold, renewed, serviced or delivered through Subagent to any Person.

1.14 Profit Sharing Commissions: Commissions or fees which are not associated with the sale of a specific Policy through Subagent. Profit Sharing Commissions are typically contingent upon factors such as sales volume, premium volume, profitability and other special concessions negotiated by the Brooke. Profit Sharing Commissions include, but are not limited to, payments identified by the Companies as profit sharing commissions, contingency commissions, advertising allowances, prizes, override commissions, expense reimbursements and bonus commissions.

1.15 Receipts Trust Account: An account established and owned by Brooke, but controlled by a trustee, to which premiums, fees, Sales Commissions and Other Receipts received by Subagent, Franchise Agent or Brooke from Companies or customers shall be deposited and from which Brooke, or its designee, makes regular withdrawals by Electronic Funds Transfer.

1.16 Return Commissions: Direct Bill Policy commissions that are unearned because Policy premium or fee was reduced or Policy canceled.

1.17 Sales Commissions: Commissions paid by Companies to Brooke or assigned by Subagent to Brooke for the sale, renewal, service or delivery of a specific Policy through Subagent. Sales Commissions are not normally contingent upon factors such as loss ratio, premium volume, sales volume or negotiated special concessions . For the purposes of this Agreement, Sales Commissions shall specifically exclude Profit Sharing Commissions and other similar payments. However, Sales Commissions shall specifically include amounts paid by Franchise Agent pursuant to a bonus plan, the terms of which are defined by Franchise Agent in its sole discretion and for which Franchise Agent makes no representation regarding future payments or Subagent's eligibility. Sales Commissions shall also include any consulting fees, advisory fees, placement fees, service fees, renewal fees, or any similar payments paid on or related to any Customer Account by any Person.

1.18 Subagent Account: An account on Franchise Agent's ledgers to which is recorded amounts due Franchise Agent from Subagent and amounts due Subagent from Franchise Agent. The record or statement of Subagent Account may be prepared in whole or in part by another Person for or on behalf of Franchise Agent.

2. OBLIGATIONS TO BE PERFORMED BY FRANCHISE AGENT:

2.1 (a) As of the effective date of this agreement, Franchise Agent shall provide services with respect to accounting for and processing of Policies for Subagent. Franchise Agent may provide other services as may be agreed upon by Franchise Agent and Subagent from time to time.

(b) Franchise Agent agrees to sub code all accounting entries to distinguish those entries related to Customer Accounts owned by Subagent from all other entries to Franchise Agent Account. Such sub coding information shall be used by Franchise Agent to credit and debit correct amounts to the Subagent Account. If another Person prepares reports relating to the Subagent Account on Franchise Agent's behalf or performs accounting or processing services for Franchise Agent in connection with the Subagent Account, such Person shall rely exclusively on the sub coding information and instructions provided by Franchise Agent without any duty to verify or confirm same.

2.2 Franchise Agent shall account for all Sales Commissions on Direct Bill Policies issued, renewed, endorsed, changed, serviced, delivered or canceled on behalf of Customer Accounts. Franchise Agent shall credit Subagent Account for Sales Commissions received by Franchise Agent from Brooke for Customer Accounts in the amounts indicated on the appropriate statement of Franchise Agent Account. Franchise Agent shall debit Subagent Account for Return Commissions due to Brooke by Franchise Agent for Customer Accounts in the amounts indicated on the appropriate statement of Franchise Agent Account.

2.3 (a) Franchise Agent shall account for all Net Premiums on Agency Bill Policies issued, renewed, endorsed, changed, serviced, delivered or canceled on behalf of Customer Accounts. Franchise Agent shall debit Subagent Account for Net Premiums due to Franchise Agent for Customer Accounts in the amounts indicated on the appropriate statement of Franchise Agent Account. Franchise Agent shall credit Subagent Account for Net Premiums returned to Franchise Agent from Brooke for Customer Accounts in the amounts indicated on the appropriate statement of Franchise Agent Account. Subagent has no right, title or interest in such amounts. (b) Franchise Agent shall credit Subagent Account for Agent Billed Policy premiums received from any insured or other Person for a Customer Account. At Franchise Agent's option, Franchise Agent may defer any such credit for Agent Billed Policy premiums until a corresponding charge is made to Subagent Account for Net Premiums in accordance with subparagraph 2.3 (a).

2.4 Franchise Agent shall calculate and credit Subagent Account monthly for amounts due Subagent by Franchise Agent. Amounts due Subagent shall be _____ percent (__%) of any Sales Commissions from Companies for Customer Accounts.

2.5 Subject to the prior approval of the insurance company involved, Franchise Agent shall cause Subagent to be covered by Brooke's errors and omissions insurance policy to provide errors and omissions insurance coverage for Subagent. Franchise Agent shall calculate and debit the Subagent Account for Subagent's share of the errors and omissions insurance policy premium. Franchise Agent may adjust said policy premium to maintain a Subagent deductible fund. Franchise Agent shall calculate Subagent's share of said errors and omissions insurance policy premium by dividing the estimated annual commissions received on Customer Accounts by the total estimated annual commissions received by Franchise Agent from all Companies. However, Subagent's share of Franchise

Agent's annual policy premium shall not be less than the minimum annual premium that is set from time to time by Franchise Agent. Subagent has the responsibility to provide Franchise Agent with copies of those documents which Franchise Agent deems necessary for errors & omissions documentation.

2.6 Franchise Agent will pay for 50% of advertising that is pre-approved by Franchise Agent and shall be reimbursed by Subagent for Subagent's share of payments made to advertisers on behalf of Subagent.

2.7 Franchise Agent shall account for and debit Subagent Account monthly for any other supplies or services provided by Franchise Agent to Subagent if previously agreed upon by Franchise Agent and Subagent.

2.8 Franchise Agent shall forward a record of the Subagent Account (which shall include billings or debits for Franchise Agent's share of Sales Commissions, errors and omissions premiums or other services provided by Franchise Agent) to Subagent on or about the 20th day of each month. Upon written notice to Subagent, Franchise Agent may change the date on or about which statements are forwarded.

2.9 Franchise Agent, or its designee, shall pay to Subagent the credit balance recorded on the Subagent Account on or about the 22nd day of each month. Subagent shall pay the debit balance recorded on the Subagent Account by the 22nd day of each month. Upon written notice to Subagent, Franchise Agent may change the date on or about which Subagent's account credit or debit balance is to be paid by Franchise Agent or Subagent, respectively.

2.10 Franchise Agent shall provide Subagent with a rules and procedures manual that has been adopted by Franchise Agent and shall provide Subagent with notice of any changes made by Franchise Agent to said manual from time to time.

2.11 Franchise Agent shall provide Subagent with a unique written list of Companies that have been approved for Subagent use by Franchise Agent and shall provide Subagent with notice of any changes made by Franchise Agent to said list from time to time.

2.12 Franchise Agent shall provide Subagent with a unique written list specifying Subagent authority for binding Companies to Policies or coverages and shall provide Subagent with notice of any changes made by Franchise Agent to said list from time to time.

2.13 Unless otherwise agreed in writing by Franchise Agent, Subagent shall do business under the name "Brooke Financial Services" or "Brooke Insurance and Financial Services". Therefore Subagent is permitted the use of its trade names, trademarks, service marks, logotypes, commercial symbol and promotional materials for the purpose of advertising such relationship. Franchise Agent does not represent or guarantee that Subagent will have exclusive use of such name, that such name is available for use in Subagent's market and/or that there are no competing names or uses. If such name is not available for use, Subagent shall do business under a name mutually agreed upon by the parties.

2.14 Franchise Agent shall provide Subagent full and complete access to Franchise Agent's records of Customer Accounts provided that it shall be upon reasonable advance request and during such times and upon such conditions as shall not unreasonably impair the operations of Franchise Agent.

2.15 Franchise Agent shall permit Subagent to use Brooke's proprietary Document Manager system provided that Subagent purchase, license, install and maintain all software and hardware, other than Brooke's proprietary Document Manager programs, which may be required to use the Document Manager system and provided that Subagent not sell, lease or authorize the use of the Document Manager programs to anyone else and provided that Subagent not configure, program or change any Document Manager programs. Subagent may access customer information through the Internet. Subagent acknowledges that access to customer information through the Internet is provided by Franchise Agent as a convenience to Subagent and not as a required manner of access to such information. Accordingly, Subagent, its owners, officers, directors, employees and independent contractors agree to release, indemnify and hold Franchise Agent harmless for and from any and all claims, losses, liabilities, damages or expenses (including, but not limited to reasonable attorneys' fees, court costs, and costs of investigation) of any kind or nature whatsoever incurred by Subagent, its owners, officers, directors, employees and independent contractors resulting from an interruption in Internet services or from any unauthorized use of or access to Customer

Account information through the Internet.   This release, indemnification and hold harmless shall survive the termination of this Agreement.

3. OBLIGATIONS TO BE PERFORMED BY SUBAGENT:

3.1 Upon the signing of this Agreement, Subagent shall do business under the name "Brooke Financial Services" or "Brooke Insurance and Financial Services", unless otherwise approved in writing by Franchise Agent.

3.2 Subagent shall provide competent and qualified personnel for the sale, renewal, service and delivery of Policies and to serve as liaison or contact with Customer Accounts.

3.3 On or before the effective date of this Agreement, Subagent shall, subject to prior approval of the Companies involved, change the Agent of Record for all existing Customer Accounts to Brooke.

3.4 After the effective date of this Agreement, Subagent shall process all applications for Policies exclusively through the facilities of Franchise Agent.

3.5 Subagent shall make Brooke (for the purposes of this subparagraph, "Brooke" shall include a subsidiary or affiliate of Brooke) the Agent of Record for all Policies sold, renewed, serviced or delivered by Subagent with an effective date for coverage after the effective date of this agreement, unless prior written approval is obtained from Franchise Agent. If a Company refuses to make Brooke the Agent of Record for all Policies sold, renewed, serviced or delivered by Subagent, then Subagent shall assign all Sales Commissions and Profit Sharing Commissions associated with such Policies to Brooke. Subagent agrees and acknowledges that by making Brooke the Agent of Record, all Sales Commissions and Profit Sharing Commissions are assigned to Brooke for accounting and distribution through Franchise Agent to Subagent Account pursuant to this Agreement. Subagent appoints Brooke as its attorney in fact to endorse or deposit checks made payable to Subagent by customers, Companies or master general agents. Subagent also agrees to obtain from its producers an appointment of Brooke as attorney in fact to endorse or deposit checks made payable to such producers by customers, Companies or master general agents.

3.6 Subagent shall apply for issuance of Direct Bill Policies if payment of premiums in this manner is permitted by the Company providing coverages. Subagent shall obtain specific approval of Franchise Agent prior to submitting any application for issuance of an Agency Bill Policy.

3.7 Subagent shall be solely responsible for the collection of all Agency Bill Policy premiums from Customer Accounts, which amounts shall be made payable to Brooke Corporation. Subagent shall not have authority to endorse or deposit such payments to its own account. Subagent appoints Brooke as its attorney in fact to endorse or deposit checks made payable to Subagent by customers, Companies or master general agents. Subagent also agrees to obtain from its producers an appointment of Brooke as attorney in fact to endorse or deposit checks made payable to such producers by customers, Companies or master general agents. Brooke shall establish a Receipts Trust Account to which all premiums, fees, Sales Commissions and Other Receipts from Companies or customers shall be deposited and from which Brooke, or its designee, makes regular withdrawals by Electronic Funds Transfer.

3.8 Subagent shall be responsible for payment to Franchise of all Agency Bill Policy net premiums and Direct Bill Policy return commission resulting from Customers Accounts owned by Subagent.

3.9 Subagent authorizes Franchise Agent to retain _____ percent (___%) of any Sales Commissions from Companies under contract with Brooke for Customer Accounts; Subagent shall pay its share of errors and omissions insurance policy premiums; fees for any other supplies and services provided by Franchise Agent if previously agreed upon by Subagent and Franchise Agent.

3.10 Subagent shall pay to Franchise Agent, or its designee, the debit balance recorded on the Subagent Account by the 22nd day of each month.

3.11 Subagent shall be responsible for providing to Franchise Agent any information regarding Subagent or Subagent's owners, officers, employees and independent contractors that may be required from Franchise Agent by any self regulatory organization, governmental agency, Brooke or any Company. Subagent shall be responsible for ensuring that Subagent and Subagent's owners, officers, employees and independent contractors comply with all federal, state and local requirements including but not limited to the sales practices, education and licensing requirements of all governmental agencies, Brooke and any Company. Subagent shall provide evidence satisfactory to Franchise Agent that Subagent and Subagent owners, officers, employees and independent contractors have complied with such requirements. If Subagent does not comply with the terms of this paragraph, it is cause for immediate termination of this Agreement without any liability on or against Franchise Agent.

3.12 Subagent shall abide by and conform to the rules and procedures adopted from time to time by Franchise Agent. Subagent acknowledges that said rules and procedures include, among other requirements, a requirement that Subagent provide Franchise Agent with copies of all Policy applications and all other records or documents originated, received or processed by Subagent which are related to Customer Accounts, Policies or Subagent's business. Subagent acknowledges the importance of complete and timely transmittal of all records and documents and agrees to submit in a timely manner to Franchise Agent all such records and documents.

3.13 Subagent shall apply for coverages only with the Companies that are authorized for Subagent's use from time to time by Franchise Agent. Subagent acknowledges that Franchise Agent, in its sole and absolute discretion, shall decide which Companies Subagent may use.

3.14 Subagent shall abide by and conform to the conditions and limits of authority for binding Companies to insurance and other coverages which are set forth from time to time by Franchise Agent.

3.15 Subagent shall obtain the prior written consent of Franchise Agent before using Brooke's trade names, trademarks, service marks, logotypes or commercial symbols on any advertising literature, promotional materials, signs or business forms that are not provided by Franchise Agent.

3.16 Immediately upon termination of this Agreement for whatever reason, Subagent shall cease the dissemination of any advertising material containing any of Brooke's trade names, trademarks, service marks, logotypes or commercial symbols. Franchise Agent shall have a cause of action against Subagent for failure to immediately cease using the same upon any such termination.

3.17 Subagent shall purchase a standard Business Owners Policy providing coverage for Subagent's place of business with liability limits of not less than $1,000,000 / $1,000,000 unless such requirement is waived in writing by Franchise Agent. Subagent shall also purchase a Workers Compensation insurance policy with liability limits of not less than $500,000/$500,000 unless such requirement is waived in writing by Franchise Agent.

3.18 Subagent shall be responsible for payment of all defense and other claims expenses in amounts up to $2,500 per incident for any errors and omissions related claims made as a result of Subagent's actions or lack of actions.

3.19 Subagent shall obtain Franchise Agent's prior written approval of any agreement for Subagent to purchase insurance or other agencies' assets.

3.20 Subagent shall immediately and fully report to Franchise Agent any policyholder related legal or regulatory issues such as errors and omissions claims, insurance department or other regulatory complaints, legal summons and subpoenas. Subagent shall not make any written or verbal comments or responses regarding said issues to anyone until fully discussed with Franchise Agent. Subagent acknowledges that Franchise Agent shall coordinate and control responses to any such issues.

3.21 Subagent shall provide Franchise Agent full and complete access to records of Customer Accounts and other records and documents deemed necessary by Franchise Agent to perform an audit to determine compliance with the provisions of this Agreement; provided however, that access shall be upon reasonable advance request and during such times and upon such conditions as shall not unreasonably impair the operations of Subagent.

4. PROTECTIVE AND RESTRICTIVE COVENANTS

4.1 Subagent shall not transfer to Franchise Agent any incident of ownership of the Customer Accounts. Customer lists, Policy expiration lists and other records shall remain Subagent's exclusive property, and Subagent shall be fully vested in the ownership thereof.

4.2 All Customer Accounts shall be coded on Franchise Agent's records to Subagent. Franchise Agent shall not be authorized or permitted to change the coding of Customer Accounts without the written consent of Subagent.

4.3 Franchise Agent and Subagent acknowledge that all information with respect to Customer Accounts is confidential information constituting trade secrets and shall be treated as such. Franchise Agent shall not divulge any such confidential information to anyone without the consent of Subagent unless disclosure is compelled by law. Subagent authorizes Franchise Agent to provide information with respect to Customer Accounts to Brooke, its successors or designees; a subsidiary or affiliate of Brooke, its successors or designees; or any Person pursuant to a loan document executed by Franchise Agent. Franchise Agent shall obtain the agreement of such Person to treat such confidential information as confidential.

4.4 Subagent shall not have any authority to incur any liability in the name of or on behalf of Franchise Agent. Franchise Agent and Subagent agree that the relationship of Franchise Agent to Subagent shall be that of an independent contractor.

4.5 Franchise Agent and Subagent shall not assume any liability of the other, and any such liability shall remain the exclusive individual liabilities of each. In addition, Franchise Agent and Subagent each agree to release, indemnify, and hold each other harmless from any and all losses, damages and expenses, including legal expenses, attorneys fees, discovery expenses and costs which are suffered or incurred by the other by reason of the actions, omissions or liability of any kind created, caused or allowed by each indemnifying party, individually or in conjunction with any other Person.

4.6 Subagent, its owners, officers, directors, employees and independent contractors release, indemnify and hold Franchise Agent harmless for and from any and all claims, losses, liabilities, damages or expenses (including, but not limited to reasonable attorneys' fees, court costs, and costs of investigation) of any kind or nature whatsoever incurred by Subagent, its owners, officers, directors, employees and independent contractors arising out of or in connection with interruptions of service caused by an act of God or any other event outside the direct control of Franchise Agent. This release, indemnification and hold harmless shall survive the termination of this Agreement.

4.7 Subagent, its owners, officers, directors, employees and independent contractors release, indemnify and hold Franchise Agent harmless if Franchise Agent permits Subagent its owners, officers, directors, employees and independent contractors to use an insolvent Company and Subagent, its owners, officers, directors, employees or independent contractors incur any claims, losses, liabilities, damages or expenses of any kind or nature whatsoever resulting therefrom. This release, indemnification and hold harmless shall survive the termination of this Agreement.

4.8 Subagent agrees that Franchise Agent may rely on statements, representations, requests, instructions, commitments and agreements (without verification or confirmation of same) of Subagent's owners, officers, directors, employees or independent contractors as if same had been made or delivered to Franchise Agent by Subagent unless and until written instructions limiting Franchise Agent's right to rely on such statements representations, requests, instructions, commitments and agreements have been provided by Subagent and received by Franchise Agent. Subagent agrees to release, indemnify and hold harmless Franchise Agent, its owners, officers, directors, employees, and independent contractors (for purposes of subparagraphs 4.8 and 4.9, collectively, "Franchise Agent") for and from any and all claims, losses, liabilities, or damages or expenses (including, but not limited to reasonable attorneys' fees, court costs, and costs of investigation) of any kind or nature whatsoever arising out of or in connection with Franchise Agent's reliance or which Subagent, its owners, officers, directors, employees, and independent contractors may incur as a result of Franchise Agent's reliance on same. This release, indemnification and hold harmless shall survive termination of the Agreement.

4.9   The duties and obligations of Subagent set forth herein apply to Subagent, its owners, officers, directors, employees and independent contractors. In as much as this Agreement is by and between Subagent and Franchise Agent, Subagent is responsible for the compliance of its owners, officers, directors, employees and independent contractors with the terms of this Agreement and any rules and procedures adopted from time to time by Franchise Agent. Subagent agrees that it is fully responsible for the acts and omissions of its owners, officers, directors, employees and independent contractors (for purposes of this subparagraph, collectively "Subagent").   Accordingly, Subagent agrees to release, indemnify and hold harmless Franchise Agent for and from any and all claims, losses, liabilities, or damages or expenses (including, but not limited to reasonable attorneys' fees, court costs, and costs of investigation) of any kind or nature whatsoever arising out of or in connection with Subagent's acts or omissions or which Franchise Agent or Subagent may incur as a result of Subagent's acts or omissions.   This release, indemnification and hold harmless shall survive termination of the Agreement.

5. REPRESENTATIONS AND WARRANTIES OF EACH PARTY:

5.1 If a corporation, Franchise Agent warrants and represents that it is a corporation, duly organized, existing and in good standing under the laws of the state of in which it was organized and incorporated. Subagent, if a corporation, warrants and represents that it is duly organized, existing and in good standing under the laws of the state in which it was organized and incorporated.

5.2 Subagent represents and warrants that all of Subagent's owners, officers, directors, employees or independent contractors that are required to be duly and fully licensed by any self regulatory organization, governmental agency or any Company shall be, at all times during the term of this Agreement, duly and fully licensed as insurance agents or representatives and have all other requisite licenses, registrations, and authority to sell, renew, service or deliver Policies in any state in which Subagent sells, renews, services or delivers such Policies.

5.3 Subagent shall notify Franchise Agent of any and all litigation to which Subagent or any of Subagent's owners, directors, officers, employees or independent contractors may become a party, whether as plaintiff or defendant, and represents and warrants that no such litigation is now pending.

5.4 Subagent shall notify Franchise Agent of any investigations of or hearings related to Subagent or any of Subagent's owners, directors, officers, employees or independent contractors by any self regulatory organization, governmental agency, or Company and represents and warrants that no such investigations or hearings are now pending.

5.5 If a corporation, Franchise Agent has taken all necessary corporate action, including, but not limited to, binding resolutions of its directors to enter into this Agreement and to carry out the terms and conditions thereof. Subagent, if represented in the beginning paragraph of this Agreement to be a corporation, has taken all necessary corporate action, including, but not limited to, binding resolutions/actions of all of its directors and/or shareholders to enter into this Agreement and to carry out the terms and conditions thereof.

5.6 Franchise Agent does not warrant, guarantee or make any representations regarding the accuracy and/or timeliness of any billings provided by Companies or Brooke.

6. TERMINATION OF AGREEMENT:

6.1 The term of this Agreement is for five years and is renewable at expiration.

6.2 Franchise Agent shall have the right to terminate or refuse to renew this Agreement only upon good and sufficient cause which shall be defined as:

(a) material and substantial breach of the terms of this Agreement by Subagent (unless otherwise agreed in writing, for the purposes of paragraph 6.2 and all its subparagraphs, "Subagent" shall include Subagent's owners, officers, directors, employees and independent contractors);

(b) refusal by the insurance company which provides errors and omissions insurance coverages to Brooke to endorse said insurance policy to provide errors and omissions insurance coverage for Subagent;

(c) such public actions by Subagent, which in the judgment of Franchise Agent, shall be materially injurious to the reputation of Franchise Agent or the cumulative goodwill related to Franchise Agent or the use of Brooke's name, trademarks, service marks, logotypes or commercial symbols;

(d) insurance coverage or Policy underwriting practices by Subagent, which in the opinion of a Franchise Agent, may jeopardize Franchise Agent's continued contractual agency relationship with Brooke or any Company;

(e) the commission or omission of any act by Subagent, which in the opinion of Franchise Agent, would be sufficient cause for the revocation of a license, registration, or other authority by any self regulatory organization, governmental agency or Company in any state in which Subagent sells, renews, services or delivers Policies;

(f) legal proceedings involving Subagent, which in the opinion of Franchise Agent, may impair Subagent's capacity to perform Subagent's obligations as set forth in this Agreement;

(g) business practices by Subagent, which in the opinion of Franchise Agent are unethical or unacceptable to the general business community;

(h) inadequate qualifications of Subagent, which in the opinion of Franchise Agent, may impair the ability of Subagent to provide adequate assistance and service to Customer Accounts;

(i) the partial or total sale or transfer of Subagent ownership or the partial or total sale or transfer of ownership of Customer Accounts without Franchise Agent's prior written consent;

(j) the location or relocation of Subagent's agency office to an address other than the address designated in the beginning paragraph of this Agreement without Franchise Agent's prior written consent;

(k) the establishment by Subagent of an additional agency office at an address other than the address designated in the beginning paragraph of this Agreement without Franchise Agent's prior written consent;

(l) bankruptcy of Subagent;

(m) dishonor of a draft or electronic funds transfer drawn by Franchise Agent, or its designee, on Subagent's checking account, if such draft is authorized by this Agreement;

(n) failure to provide proof of liability insurance as mandated by 3.17;

(o) the agreement (oral or written) of Subagent to enter a brokerage, commission sharing, account sharing or service center agreement with any Person not on the company list described in paragraph 2.11 or obligated by contract (either through an agreement with Brooke or a Brooke franchise agent) to process all applications for Policies exclusively through the facilities of Brooke or a Brooke franchise agent;

(p) the refusal by Subagent to provide a description of brokerage, commission sharing, account sharing or service center agreements Subagent has entered into, and copies of the agreements memorializing same, within 30 days of entering any such agreement or after receipt of Franchise Agent's written request for same, if sooner. Franchise Agent's receipt of any such agreement shall not charge Franchise Agent with actual or implied knowledge of its terms nor shall such agreement have any binding effect on Franchise Agent unless Franchise Agent is expressly a party thereto in a written document signed by Franchise Agent.

(q) the termination of (or Franchise Agent's receipt or delivery of notice to terminate) the Franchise Agreement for any reason.

6.3 In the event Franchise Agent shall terminate or refuse to renew this Agreement for cause as aforesaid, it shall give Subagent written notice of its intent to terminate or non-renew, which notice shall state all of the material facts upon which Franchise Agent relies as grounds for termination. Such notice shall fix an effective date of termination which shall be not sooner than 30 days from the date of the notice.

6.4 Subagent shall have the unilateral right to terminate this Agreement for any reason upon not less than 30 days advance notice to Franchise Agent.

6.5 Upon termination of this Agreement, Franchise Agent shall request Brooke to request that the pertinent Companies involved make the Subagent the Agent of Record for all Customer Accounts. In the event that a Company refuses to make the Subagent the Agent of Record for Customer Accounts, then Subagent shall, on or before the next Policy term expiration date following termination of this Agreement, obtain replacement coverages for said Customer Accounts with another Company. Franchise Agent shall continue to account for and process Customer Accounts until the Policy term expiration date following termination of this Agreement. Although Franchise Agent shall not be obligated to assist Subagent in obtaining replacement coverages for Customer Accounts, Franchise Agent shall provide to Subagent the Policy term expiration data and Customer Account data available through Brooke's Document Manager system. If the Subagent does not obtain replacement coverages for Customer Accounts on or before the policy term expiration date following termination of this Agreement, then Franchise Agent shall obtain coverages for said Customer Accounts and Subagent thereby relinquishes to Franchise Agent all ownership of, possession of, or other right to or interest in said Customer Accounts and any related files.

6.6 Upon termination of this Agreement and for as long as necessary thereafter, Franchise Agent shall continue to account for all Sales Commissions on Direct Bill Policies audited, endorsed, changed, or canceled on behalf of Customer Accounts processed through the facilities of Franchise Agent. Franchise Agent shall continue to record Customer Account activity on Subagent Account as set forth in paragraph 2.2 and 2.4 of this Agreement.

6.7 Upon termination of this Agreement and for as long as necessary thereafter, Franchise Agent shall continue to account for all Net Premiums on Agency Bill Policies audited, endorsed, changed, renewed, serviced, or canceled on behalf of Customer Accounts processed through the facilities of Franchise Agent. Brooke shall continue to record Customer Account activity on Subagent Account as set forth in paragraph 2.3 and 2.4 of this Agreement.

6.8 After the termination of this Agreement, Subagent shall remain responsible for payment to Franchise Agent of all Agency Bill Policy net premiums and Direct Bill Policy return commissions incurred on behalf of Customer Accounts processed through the facilities of Franchise Agent.

6.9 If entries are recorded to Subagent Account in the month of or any month after the termination of this Agreement, Franchise Agent shall forward a record of Subagent Account to Subagent on or about the 20th of said month. Subagent shall pay Franchise Agent, or its designee, on or about the 22nd of each month any amount owed by Subagent. Upon written notice to Subagent, Franchise Agent may change the date such records are forwarded to Subagent and the date Subagent shall pay Franchise Agent amounts owed Franchise Agent by Subagent.

6.10 Upon termination of this Agreement, Brooke shall cease to provide errors and omissions insurance coverage for Subagent and Subagent shall not be entitled to any refund of errors and omissions insurance policy premiums.

6.11 Upon termination of this Agreement, Franchise Agent shall be permitted to retain copies of any files and records with respect to Customer Accounts as it shall deem reasonably necessary to account for and process Customer Accounts and for any other legitimate business purposes including preparation of tax returns and audits thereof, defense of litigation, collection of Subagent Account, or otherwise.

6.12 In the event Subagent elects to sell some or all Customer Accounts owned by Subagent, Franchise Agent shall have the first right to purchase such assets at a price equal to the amount offered to or by any other bona fide purchaser Franchise Agent may assign or transfer this first right to purchase to Brooke.

7. TRUST ARRANGEMENT:

7.1 Subagent acknowledges that Brooke may enter into or has entered into a trust agreement (the "Trust Agreement") which among other terms provides for a trustee's control of all Sales Commissions. Accordingly, Subagent agrees with Franchise Agent that all premiums, fees, Sales Commissions and Other Receipts received by Subagent, Franchise Agent or Brooke from Companies or customers which are related in any way to the sale, renewal, service or delivery of Policies through Subagent shall be promptly deposited in the Receipts Trust Account.

7.2 Subagent agrees that said Receipts Trust Account shall be owned by Brooke, but controlled by the trustee. Trustee shall have sole right to withdraw funds from the Receipts Trust Account. Trustee shall distribute to Franchise Agent and/or Brooke Sales Commissions and Other Receipts in accordance with the terms of the Trust Agreement. However, unless otherwise agreed upon by the parties in writing, nothing in the Trust Agreement shall change amounts due Subagent, as shown on the statement of Subagent Account pursuant to the terms of this Agreement or amounts payable by Subagent to Franchise Agent as shown on the statement of Subagent Account pursuant to the terms of this Agreement.

7.3 Reserved for future use.

7.4 Subagent agrees to release, indemnify and hold harmless Franchise Agent, its owners, officers, directors, employees, and independent contractors (for the purposes of this subparagraph, collectively "Franchise Agent") for and from any and all claims, losses, liability, or damages or expenses (including, but not limited to reasonable attorneys' fees, court costs, and costs of investigation) of any kind or nature whatsoever arising out of or in connection with the Trust Agreement, the deposit or withdrawal of money from the Receipts Trust Account or which Subagent, its owners, officers, directors, employees, and independent contractors may incur as a result of Franchise Agent's performance of its rights, obligations or duties hereunder or in connection with the deposit or withdrawal of money from the Receipts Trust Account. Provided, however, that this shall not relieve Franchise Agent from liability for its breach of any of its agreements under this Agreement or for its own willful misconduct, recklessness, bad faith or gross negligence, nor for the gross negligence, recklessness, bad faith or willful misconduct of its owners, officers, directors, employees, or independent contractors. This release, indemnification and hold harmless shall survive termination of the Agreement.

7.5 Subagent, its owners, officers, directors, employees and independent contractors agree to release, indemnify and hold harmless the trust, its trustee, its owners, officers, directors, employees, and independent contractors (collectively, "trust") for and from any and all claims, losses, liability, or damages or expenses (including, but not limited to reasonable attorneys' fees, court costs, and costs of investigation) of any kind or nature whatsoever arising out of or in connection with the Trust Agreement or which Subagent, its owners, officers, directors, employees, and independent contractors may incur as a result of trust's performance of its rights, obligations or duties under the terms of the Trust Agreement. This release, indemnification and hold harmless shall survive termination of the Agreement. Upon Franchise Agent's request, Subagent agrees to sign a separate document (to which trustee may be a party) releasing, indemnifying and holding harmless the trust.

8. SPONSOR AGENT ARRANGEMENT:

8.1 The following Person(s) (collectively, "Sponsor Agent") endorse and sponsor Subagent in its application to Franchise Agent to become a Subagent. Franchise Agent shall pay to Sponsor Agent a percentage of Sales Commissions received on any Customer Accounts as follows:

SPONSOR AGENT	SPONSOR AGENT SUBCODE	SALES COMMISSION PERCENTAGE SHARE
1.		
2.		
3.		

If no Sponsor Agent is listed, then Franchise Agent is not obligated to pay any share of Sales Commissions on Customer Accounts to any party other than Subagent.

8.2 Sponsor Agent vouches for and represents that Subagent is of sound character and integrity and has the professional credentials and ability to perform the obligations and duties set forth in this Agreement.

8.3 Sponsor Agent has entered into a separate Subagent Agreement ("Sponsor Agent's Subagent Agreement") with the Franchise Agent. It is agreed that upon termination of a Sponsor Agent's Subagent Agreement with Franchise

Agent, such Sponsor Agent shall no longer be entitled to any share of Subagent's Sales Commissions pursuant to this Agreement. Correspondingly, upon termination of a Sponsor Agent's Subagent Agreement with Franchise Agent, such Sponsor Agent shall incur no additional liability pursuant to this Agreement for Subagent's actions or omissions that occur thereafter. However, such Sponsor Agent shall remain liable pursuant to this Agreement for any of Subagent's actions or omissions that occurred prior to termination of Sponsor Agent's Subagent Agreement with Franchise Agent.

8.4 The parties agree that Franchise Agent and Subagent shall not enter into any additional agreements, or make changes to this Agreement without the prior written consent of Sponsor Agent, unless Sponsor Agent has terminated Sponsor Agent's Subagent Agreement with Franchise Agent. The parties further agree that Sponsor Agent and Subagent may enter into additional agreements with each other for services such as commissions sharing, consulting or service.

9. MISCELLANEOUS PROVISIONS:

9.1 Franchise Agent shall not be obligated to pay Subagent any share of Profit Sharing Commissions.

9.2 Any notices required hereunder shall be deemed effective if in writing, and delivered by hand or mailed by United States Mail, postage prepaid, or mailed by certified mail, with return receipt requested or mailed by express courier with confirmed delivery date. The effective date of notice shall be the day of delivery by hand, and if mailed by regular mail, four days following the mailing thereof, and if by certified mail or express courier, the date of receipt thereof. A business day shall be deemed any day on which the United States Postal Service shall have regular mail deliveries to the address to which the notice is mailed.

9.3 This Agreement may not be modified, revised, altered, added to, or extended in any manner, or superseded other than by an instrument in writing signed by all of the parties hereto.

9.4 This Agreement may be executed in duplicate, each of which shall be deemed an original, but all of which together shall constitute one and the same instrument representing the agreement of the parties hereto.

9.5 The failure by an party to enforce any provision of this Agreement shall not be in any way construed as a waiver of any such provision nor prevent that party thereafter from enforcing each and every other provision of this Agreement.

9.6 The invalidity or non-enforceability of any particular provision of this Agreement shall not affect the other provisions hereof, and this Agreement shall be construed in all respects as if such invalid or unenforceable provisions were omitted.

9.7 This Agreement shall be binding upon and inure to the benefit of the parties hereto and their heirs and legal representatives but the rights and property interests hereunder shall not be assignable by any party except Franchise Agent may assign its rights and property interest to Brooke, a company affiliated with Brooke, or their successors and assigns and except as otherwise set out herein.

9.8 This Agreement (including all Exhibits and Addenda hereto) contains the entire agreement between the parties hereto and shall supersede and take precedence over any and all prior agreements, arrangements or understandings between the parties relating to the subject matter hereof. No oral understandings, oral statements, oral promises or oral inducements exist. No representations, warranties, covenants or conditions, express or implied, whether by statute or otherwise, other than as set forth herein, have been made by the parties hereto.

9.9 Subagent agrees to sign, acknowledge, deliver, and/or file any additional documents, certifications or statements that Franchise Agent may deem necessary to carry out the intent of this Agreement.

9.10 Subagent acknowledges receipt of the Franchise Agreement and a complete and current franchise offering circular. Further, Subagent acknowledges that the Franchise Agreement is by and between Brooke and Franchise Agent. Franchise Agent may use information, data or reports or other materials provided to Franchise Agent by Brooke pursuant to the Franchise Agreement in performing Franchise Agent's duties hereunder. Subagent acknowledges that Brooke has no duties or obligations to Subagent. Subagent is not a party to the Franchise Agreement, has no standing to enforce the terms thereof and is not a direct or indirect beneficiary of its terms.

9.11 This Agreement shall be subject to and not take effect until it is approved by Brooke. However, Franchise Agent and Subagent agree that Brooke's approval does not make Brooke a party to, a guarantor of or subject to the terms of this Agreement nor does Brooke's approval of same constitute a warranty of this Agreement's enforceability or suitability for Franchise Agent's or Subagent's purposes or any other purpose.

9.12 This Agreement shall be construed and governed by the laws of the State of _____.   At the option of Franchise Agent, jurisdiction and venue for any dispute arising under or in relation to this Agreement will lie only in the state of _____ with the _____ County District Court, _____,_____ or in the U.S. District Court having jurisdiction over _____ County_____.   In the event a lawsuit or litigation is brought with respect to this Agreement, the prevailing party shall be entitled to be reimbursed for and/or have judgment for all of their costs and expenses, including reasonable attorney's fees and legal expenses.

9.13 Timeliness and punctuality are essential elements of this Agreement.

IN WITNESS WHEREOF, Subagent and Franchise Agent have executed this Agreement as of the day and year first above written.

SUBAGENT: FRANCHISE AGENT:

By:_____   By:_____

Title:_____   Title:_____

GUARANTY AGREEMENT

If Subagent is a corporation or limited liability company, we the undersigned, as individuals, jointly and severally guarantee the faithful performance of Subagent to perform all duties and obligations set forth in the forgoing agreement including without limitation the duty to pay any sum which Subagent may become liable to pay Franchise Agent by virtue of the foregoing agreement.

IN WITNESS WHEREOF, the undersigned has executed this Guaranty Agreement as of the day and year first above written.

_____   _____

individually   individually

SPONSOR AGREEMENT

The undersigned agrees to and is bound by the terms of the Sponsor Arrangement set forth in paragraph 8 herein and specifically acknowledges that the undersigned has received consideration for same. Further if Sponsor Agent is a corporation or limited liability company, the undersigned, as individuals jointly and severally guarantee Sponsor Agent's obligations.

IN WITNESS WHEREOF, the undersigned has executed this Agreement as of the day and year first above written.

_____   _____

individually   individually

Page 13 of 13

BROKER AGREEMENT

THIS AGREEMENT made and entered into this _____ day of _____, _____, (which with all addenda shall be referred to herein as the "Agreement") by and between The American Agency, Inc., a Kansas Corporation, having its principal place of business at 10895 Grandview Drive, Suite 250, Overland Park, Kansas referred to hereafter as "American"; and, _____, by and through _____, its _____, whose offices and primary place of business is located at _____, _____.

The proprietorship, partnership, corporation or other Person referenced above is referred to hereafter as "Broker".

WITNESSETH:

WHEREAS, Broker is in or may enter the business of selling, servicing and/or delivering Policies through agents from the agency offices referenced above; and

WHEREAS, American is primarily in the business of providing certain services and assistance to businesses selling insurance; however, American is in or may enter the business of selling, servicing and/or delivering other Policies and may provide certain services and assistance to businesses selling same; and

WHEREAS, Broker and American desire to associate together effective _____, _____, for the purpose of American providing certain services and assistance to Broker with respect to Broker's business;

NOW THEREFORE, in consideration of the mutual promises set forth herein and other good and valuable consideration, the receipt and sufficiency of which are hereby acknowledged, the parties agree as follows:

1. DEFINITIONS OF TERMS USED IN THIS AGREEMENT:

For purposes of this Agreement, the following terms shall have the following meanings unless the context clearly requires otherwise:

1.1 Agency Bill Policies: Any Policies for which a Broker is responsible for all or any part of premium or fee billing and collection.

1.2 Agent of Record: Person designated on Company's records as the agent or representative regarding a specific Policy and the owner of all Sales Commissions.

1.3 Broker Account: An account on American's ledgers to which American records amounts due American from Broker and amounts due Broker from American.

1.4 Company: A company issuing, brokering, selling or making a market for Policies and which has a contract with American.

1.5 Company Billings: Statements or billings received by American from Companies for amounts due American from Companies and for amounts due Companies from American.

1.6 Customer Account: An agent who has a Policy purchased from, serviced, renewed or delivered through Broker pursuant to a brokerage producer agreement. Customer Accounts shall be owned by Broker or a Subbroker.

1.7 Direct Bill Policies: Any Policies for which a Company is responsible for premium or fee billing and collection.

1.8 Gross Premiums: Total premium, fees or other amounts due from the sale, renewal, service or delivery of Policies including the corresponding Sales Commissions.

1.9 Insurance, Investment, Banking and/or Credit Services: Insurance services include but are not limited to the sale, renewal, service or delivery of insurance policies, annuities, insurance brokering services, insurance customer services, risk management services and insurance related consulting or advisory services. Investment services include, but are not limited to, the sale, renewal, service or delivery of mutual funds, stocks, bonds, notes, debentures, real estate services, investment customer services, and investment related consulting, and financial, investment, or economic advisory services. Banking services include any banking service Broker is allowed to perform under federal and/or state laws. Credit services include, but are not limited to, origination or brokerage of loans or mortgages, credit customer services, and credit related consulting or advisory services. At any point in time, Insurance, Investment, Banking and Credit Services shall be limited to those services then offered by American and relating to _____.

1.10 Net Premium: Gross Premiums on Agency Billed Policies less the corresponding Sales Commissions.

1.11 Other Receipts: Deposits made to the Receipts Trust Account that are not Sales Commissions. Such receipts may include but are not limited to: Profit Sharing Commissions; Net Premiums, advertising reimbursements, proceeds from sale of personal money orders; Gross Premiums for Direct Billed Policies (e.g. on line payments); loan proceeds; Company refunds; supplier refunds; and vendor refunds.

1.12 Person: Any individual, sole proprietorship, partnership, joint venture, trust, unincorporated organization, association, corporation, limited liability company, institution or other entity.

1.13 Policies: Any and all insurance services, policies, coverages or products related to _____ sold, renewed, serviced or delivered through Broker to any Person. Policies include, but are not limited to, any and all Insurance, Investment, Banking or Credit Services, or policies, coverages or products associated therewith sold, renewed, serviced or delivered through Broker to any Person. Policies shall be considered related to _____ if such Policies are classified as _____ related Policies by the Companies Broker may represent in accordance with paragraph 2.11 of this Agreement.

1.14 Profit Sharing Commissions: Commissions or fees which are not associated with the sale of a specific Policy through Broker. Profit Sharing Commissions are typically contingent upon factors such as sales volume, premium volume, profitability and other special concessions negotiated by American. Profit Sharing Commissions include, but are not limited to, payments identified by the Companies as profit sharing commissions, contingency commissions, advertising allowances, prizes, override commissions, expense reimbursements and bonus commissions.

1.15 Receipts Trust Account: An account established and owned by American, but controlled by a trustee, to which premiums, fees, Sales Commissions and Other Receipts received by Broker or American from Companies or customers shall be deposited and from which American, or its designee, makes regular withdrawals by Electronic Funds Transfer.

1.16 Return Commissions: Direct Bill Policy commissions that are unearned because Policy premium or fee was reduced or Policy canceled.

1.17 Sales Commissions: Commissions paid by Companies to American or assigned by Broker to American for the sale, renewal, service or delivery of a specific Policy through Broker. Sales Commissions are not normally contingent upon factors such as American's loss ratio, premium volume, sales volume or special concessions negotiated by American. For the purposes of this Agreement, Sales Commissions shall specifically exclude Profit Sharing Commissions and other similar payments. However, Sales Commissions shall specifically include amounts paid by American pursuant to a bonus plan, the terms of which are defined by American in its sole discretion and for which American makes no representation regarding future payments or Broker's eligibility. Sales Commissions shall also include any consulting fees, advisory fees, placement fees, service fees, renewal fees, or any similar payments paid on or related to any Customer Account by any Person.

1.18 Subbroker: A Person which has entered or may enter into a Subbroker Agreement with Broker.

1.19 Subbroker Agreement. An agreement entered into by and between Broker and Subbroker and approved by American pursuant to which Subbroker is allowed vested ownership rights in Customer Accounts coded to Subbroker and Broker performs certain accounting and processing services for Subbroker.

2. OBLIGATIONS TO BE PERFORMED BY AMERICAN:

2.1 As of the effective date of this agreement, American shall provide services with respect to accounting for and processing of Policies for Broker. American may provide other services as may be agreed upon by American and Broker from time to time. Furthermore, certain duties and obligations of American set forth in this Agreement may be performed by a subsidiary or an affiliate of American.

2.2 American shall account for all Sales Commissions on Direct Bill Policies issued, renewed, endorsed, changed, serviced, delivered or canceled on behalf of Customer Accounts. American shall credit Broker Account for Sales Commissions received by American from Companies for Customer Accounts in the amounts indicated on the appropriate Company Billing. American shall debit Broker Account for Return Commissions due to Companies by American for Customer Accounts in the amounts indicated on the appropriate Company Billing.

2.3 (a) American shall account for all Net Premiums on Agency Bill Policies issued, renewed, endorsed, changed, serviced, delivered or canceled on behalf of Customer Accounts. American shall debit Broker Account for Net Premiums due to Companies by American for Customer Accounts in the amounts indicated on the appropriate Company Billing. American shall credit Broker Account for Net Premiums returned to American from Companies for Customer Accounts in the amounts indicated on the appropriate Company Billing. American has the absolute right to and is fully vested in all Net Premiums. Broker has no right, title or interest in such amounts. (b) American shall credit Broker Account for Agent Billed Policy premiums received from any insured or other Person for a Customer Account. At American's option, American may defer any such credit for Agent Billed Policy premiums until a corresponding charge is made to Broker Account for Net Premiums in accordance with subparagraph 2.3 (a).

2.4 American shall calculate and credit Broker Account monthly for amounts due Broker by American. Amounts due Broker shall be _____ percent (__%) of any Sales Commissions for Customer Accounts.

2.5 Subject to the prior approval of the insurance company involved, Brooke Corporation, American's parent company, shall endorse Brooke's errors and omissions insurance policy to provide errors and omissions insurance coverage for Broker. American shall calculate and debit Broker Account for Broker's share of the errors and omissions insurance policy premium. American may adjust said policy premium to maintain a Broker deductible fund. American shall calculate Broker's share of said errors and omissions insurance policy premium by dividing the estimated annual commissions received on Customer Accounts by the total estimated annual commissions received by American from all Companies. However, Broker's share of American's annual policy premium shall not be less than the minimum annual premium that is set from time to time by American's Board of Directors. Broker has the responsibility to provide American with copies of those documents which American deems necessary for errors & omissions documentation.

2.6 American will pay for 50% of advertising that is pre-approved by American and shall be reimbursed by Broker for Broker's share of payments made to advertisers on behalf of Broker.

2.7 American shall account for and debit Broker Account monthly for any other supplies or services provided by American to Broker if previously agreed upon by American and Broker. Broker acknowledges that, pursuant to this paragraph, American provides Broker with additional services and retains additional commissions when Policies are sold, renewed, serviced or delivered through Broker through an American subsidiary or affiliate which provides such Policies to agents.

2.8 American shall forward a record of Broker Account to Broker on or about the ___th day of each month. Upon written notice to Broker, American may change the date on or about which statements are forwarded.

2.9 American, or its designee, shall pay to Broker, by electronic funds transfer, the credit balance recorded on the Broker Account on or about the ___th day of each month. If Broker has not paid to American, or its designee, the debit balance recorded on the Broker Account by the ___th day of each month, then American, or its designee, shall withdraw the amount of any such debit balance from Broker's checking account using an electronic funds transfer. Upon written notice to Broker, American may change the date on or about which Broker's account is credited or debited.

2.10 American shall provide Broker with a rules and procedures manual that has been adopted by American and shall provide Franchise Agent with notice of any changes made by American to said manual from time to time.

2.11 American shall provide Broker with a unique written list of Companies that have been approved for Broker use by American and shall provide Broker with notice of any changes made by American to said list from time to time. Broker acknowledges that changes to the list of Companies may be made by American at its sole and absolute discretion.

2.12 American shall provide Broker with a unique written list specifying Broker authority for binding Companies to Policies or coverages and shall provide Broker with notice of any changes made by American to said list from time to time.

2.13 Unless otherwise agreed in writing by American, Broker shall do business under a variation of the name "American _____ Agency" . Therefore, American permits the use of its trade names, trademarks, service marks, logotypes, commercial symbol and promotional materials for the purpose of advertising such relationship. American does not represent or guarantee that Broker will have exclusive use of such name, that such name is available for use in Broker's market and/or that there are no competing names or uses. If such name is not available for use, Broker shall do business under a name mutually agreed upon by the parties.

2.14 American shall provide Broker full and complete access to Broker's records of Customer Accounts provided that it shall be upon reasonable advance request and during such times and upon such conditions as shall not unreasonably impair the operations of American.

2.15 American shall permit Broker to use Brooke's proprietary Document Manager system provided that Broker purchase, license, install and maintain all software and hardware, other than Brooke's proprietary Document Manager programs, which may be required to use the Document Manager system and provided that Broker not sell, lease or authorize the use of the Document Manager programs to anyone else and provided that Broker not configure, program or change any Document Manager programs. Broker may access customer information through the Internet.   Broker acknowledges that access to customer information through the Internet is provided by American as a convenience to Broker and not as a required manner of access to such information. Accordingly, Broker, its owners, officers, directors, employees and independent contractors agree to release, indemnify and hold American harmless for and from any and all claims, losses, liabilities, damages or expenses (including, but not limited to reasonable attorneys' fees, court costs, and costs of investigation) of any kind or nature whatsoever incurred by Broker, its owners, officers, directors, employees and independent contractors resulting from an interruption in Internet services or from any unauthorized use of or access to Customer Account information through the Internet.   This release, indemnification and hold harmless shall survive the termination of this Agreement.

3. OBLIGATIONS TO BE PERFORMED BY BROKER:

3.1 Upon the signing of this Agreement, Broker shall do business under a variation of the name "American _____ Agency" unless otherwise approved in writing by American.

3.2 Broker shall provide competent and qualified personnel for the sale, renewal, service and delivery of Policies through agents and to serve as liaison or contact with Customer Accounts.

3.3 On or before the effective date of this Agreement, Broker shall, subject to prior approval of the Companies involved, change the Agent of Record for all existing Customer Accounts to American.

3.4 After the effective date of this Agreement, Broker shall process all applications for Policies exclusively through the facilities of American.

3.5 Broker shall make American (for the purposes of this subparagraph, "American" shall include a subsidiary or affiliate of American) the Agent of Record for all Policies sold, renewed, serviced or delivered through Broker with an effective date for coverage after the effective date of this agreement, unless prior written approval is obtained from American. If a Company refuses to make American the Agent of Record for all Policies sold, renewed, serviced or delivered through Broker, then Broker shall assign all Sales Commissions and Profit Sharing Commissions associated with such Policies to American. Broker agrees and acknowledges that by making American the Agent of Record, all Sales Commissions and Profit Sharing Commissions are assigned to American for accounting and distribution to Broker Account pursuant to this Agreement. Broker appoints American as its attorney in fact to endorse or deposit checks made payable to Broker by customers, Companies or master general agents. Broker also agrees to obtain from its producers or Subbrokers an appointment of American as attorney in fact to endorse or deposit checks made payable to such producers or subagents by customers, Companies or master general agents.

3.6 Broker shall apply for issuance of Direct Bill Policies if payment of premiums in this manner is permitted by the Company providing coverages.

3.7 Broker shall be solely responsible for the collection of all Agency Bill Policy premiums from Customer Accounts, which amounts shall be made payable to American. Broker shall not have authority to endorse or deposit such payments to its own account. Broker appoints American as its attorney in fact to endorse or deposit checks made payable to Broker by customers, Companies or master general agents. Broker also agrees to obtain from its producers or Subbrokers an appointment of American as attorney in fact to endorse or deposit checks made payable to such producers or Subbrokers by customers, Companies or master general agents. American shall establish a Receipts Trust Account to which all premiums, fees, Sales Commissions and Other Receipts from Companies or customers shall be deposited and from which American, or its designee, makes regular withdrawals by Electronic Funds Transfer.

3.8 Broker shall be responsible for payment to American of all Agency Bill Policy net premiums and Direct Bill Policy return commission resulting from Customers Accounts.

3.9 Broker authorizes American to retain _____ percent (__%) of any Sales Commissions for Customer Accounts; Broker shall pay its share of errors and omissions insurance policy premiums; fees for any other supplies and services provided by American if previously agreed upon by Broker and American.

3.10 If Broker has not paid to American, or its designee, the debit balance recorded on the Broker Account by the ____ day of each month, then Broker authorizes American, or its designee, to withdraw the amount of such debit balance from Broker's checking account using an electronic funds transfer.

3.11 Broker shall be responsible for providing to American any information regarding Broker or Broker's owners, officers, employees and independent contractors that may be required from American by any self regulatory organization, governmental agency or any Company. Broker shall be responsible for ensuring that Broker and Broker's owners, officers, employees and independent contractors comply with all federal, state and local requirements including but not limited to the sales practices, education and licensing requirements of all governmental agencies and any Company. Broker shall provide evidence satisfactory to American that Broker and Broker's owners, officers, employees and independent contractors have complied with such requirements. If Broker does not comply with the terms of this paragraph, it is cause for immediate termination of this Agreement without any liability on or against American.

3.12 Broker shall abide by and conform to the rules and procedures adopted from time to time by American. Broker acknowledges that said rules and procedures include, among other requirements, a requirement that Broker provide American with copies of all Policy applications and all other records or documents originated, received or processed by Broker which are related to Customer Accounts, Policies or Broker's business. Franchise Agent acknowledges the importance of complete and timely transmittal of all records and documents and agrees to submit in a timely manner to American all such records and documents.

3.13 Broker shall apply for coverages only with the Companies that are authorized for Broker's use from time to time by American. Broker acknowledges that American, in its sole and absolute discretion, shall decide which Companies Broker may use.

3.14 Broker shall abide by and conform to the conditions and limits of authority for binding Companies to insurance and other coverages which are set forth from time to time by American.

3.15 Broker shall obtain the prior written consent of American before using American's trade names, trademarks, service marks, logotypes or commercial symbols on any advertising literature, promotional materials, signs or business forms that are not provided by American.

3.16 Immediately upon termination of this Agreement for whatever reason, Broker shall cease the dissemination of any advertising material containing any of American's trade names, trademarks, service marks, logotypes or commercial symbols. American shall have a cause of action against Broker for failure to immediately cease using the same upon any such termination.

3.17 Broker shall purchase a standard Business Owners Policy providing coverage for Broker's place of business with liability limits of not less than $1,000,000 / $1,000,000 unless such requirement is waived in writing by American. Broker shall also purchase a Workers Compensation insurance policy with liability limits of not less than $500,000/$500,000 unless such requirement is waived in writing by American.

3.18 Broker shall be responsible for payment of all defense and other claims expenses in amounts up to $2,500 per incident for any errors and omissions related claims made as a result of Broker's or its Subbroker's actions or lack of actions.

3.19 Broker shall obtain American's prior written approval of any agreement for Broker to purchase insurance or other agencies' assets.

3.20 Broker shall immediately and fully report to American any policyholder related legal or regulatory issues such as errors and omissions claims, insurance department or other regulatory complaints, legal summons and subpoenas. Broker shall not make any written or verbal comments or responses regarding said issues to anyone until fully discussed with American. Broker acknowledges that American shall coordinate and control responses to any such issues.

3.21 Broker shall provide American full and complete access to records of Customer Accounts and other records and documents deemed necessary by American to perform an audit to determine compliance with the provisions of this Agreement; provided however, that access shall be upon reasonable advance request and during such times and upon such conditions as shall not unreasonably impair the operations of Broker.

3.22 Broker shall be responsible for collection from Customer Accounts of _____ related taxes and other such taxes or assessments made by states and other regulatory authorities. Unless otherwise agreed in writing, Broker is responsible for gathering and reporting all such taxes, assessments and tax/assessment information. If American agrees or is required to file any information or reports regarding such taxes or assessments, Broker shall assist American with gathering such tax information for such filing.

3.23 Broker shall require all Customer Accounts to execute a Brokers Agreement approved by American which defines Broker's relationship with the Customer Account. Broker may not make any changes to the Broker Agreement without American's prior written approval.

3.24 Broker agrees to limit solicitations of Customer Accounts to the states of _____. However, Broker may accept unsolicited applications for Policies from any other state in which Broker and American have the necessary authority to conduct the business of selling, servicing, renewing or delivering Policies through agents.

4. PROTECTIVE AND RESTRICTIVE COVENANTS

4.1 Broker shall not transfer to American any incident of ownership of the Customer Accounts. Customer lists, Policy expiration lists and other records shall remain Broker's (or its Subbroker's, as applicable) exclusive property, and Broker (or Subbroker) shall be fully vested in the ownership thereof.

4.2 All Customer Accounts shall be coded on American's records to Broker. American shall not be authorized or permitted to change the coding of Customer Accounts without the written consent of Broker.

4.3 American and Broker acknowledge that all information with respect to Customer Accounts is confidential information constituting trade secrets and shall be treated as such. American shall not divulge any such confidential information to anyone without the consent of Broker unless disclosure is compelled by law.

4.4 Broker shall not have any authority to incur any liability in the name of or on behalf of American. American and Broker agree that the relationship of American to Broker shall be that of an independent contractor.

4.5 American and Broker shall not assume any liability of the other, and any such liability shall remain the exclusive individual liabilities of each. In addition, American and Broker each agree to release, indemnify and hold each other harmless from any and all losses, damages and expenses, including legal expenses, attorneys fees, discovery expenses and costs which are suffered or incurred by the other by reason of the actions, omissions or liability of any kind created, caused or allowed by each indemnifying party, individually or in conjunction with any other Person.

4.6 Broker, its owners, officers, directors, employees and independent contractors release, indemnify and hold American harmless for and from any and all claims, losses, liabilities, damages or expenses (including, but not limited to reasonable attorneys' fees, court costs, and costs of investigation) of any kind or nature whatsoever incurred by Broker, its owners, officers, directors, employees and independent contractors arising out of or in connection with interruptions of service caused by an act of God or any other event outside the direct control of American. This release, indemnification and hold harmless shall survive the termination of this Agreement.

4.7 Broker, its owners, officers, directors, employees and independent contractors release, indemnify and hold American harmless if American permits Broker its owners, officers, directors, employees and independent contractors to use an insolvent Company and Broker, its owners, officers, directors, employees or independent contractors incur any claims, losses, liabilities, damages or expenses of any kind or nature whatsoever resulting therefrom. This release, indemnification and hold harmless shall survive the termination of this Agreement.

4.8 Broker agrees that American may rely on statements, representations, requests, instructions, commitments and agreements (without verification or confirmation of same) of Broker's owners, officers, directors, employees or independent contractors as if same had been made or delivered to American by Broker unless and until written instructions limiting American's right to rely on such statements representations, requests, instructions, commitments and agreements have been provided by Broker and received by American. Broker agrees to release, indemnify and hold harmless American, its owners, officers, directors, employees, and independent contractors (for purposes of subparagraphs 4.8 and 4.9, collectively, "American") for and from any and all claims, losses, liabilities, or damages or expenses (including, but not limited to reasonable attorneys' fees, court costs, and costs of investigation) of any kind or nature whatsoever arising out of or in connection with American's reliance or which Broker, its owners, officers, directors, employees, and independent contractors may incur as a result of American's reliance on same. This release, indemnification and hold harmless shall survive termination of the Agreement.

4.9 The duties and obligations of American set forth herein apply to Broker, its owners, officers, directors, employees and independent contractors. In as much as this Agreement is by and between Broker and American, Broker is responsible for the compliance of its owners, officers, directors, employees and independent contractors with the terms of this Agreement and any rules and procedures adopted from time to time by American. Broker agrees that it is fully responsible for the acts and omissions of its owners, officers, directors, employees and independent contractors (for purposes of this subparagraph, collectively "Broker"). Accordingly, Broker agrees to release, indemnify and hold harmless American for and from any and all claims, losses, liabilities, or damages or expenses (including, but not limited to reasonable attorneys' fees, court costs, and costs of investigation) of any kind or nature whatsoever arising out of or in connection with Broker's acts or omissions or which American or Broker may incur as a result of Broker's acts or omissions. This release, indemnification and hold harmless shall survive termination of the Agreement.

5. REPRESENTATIONS AND WARRANTIES OF EACH PARTY:

5.1 American warrants and represents that it is a corporation, duly organized, existing and in good standing under the laws of the state of Kansas. Broker, if a corporation, warrants and represents that it is duly organized, existing and in good standing under the laws of the state in which it was organized and incorporated.

5.2 Broker represents and warrants that all of Broker's owners, officers, directors, employees or independent contractors that are required to be duly and fully licensed by any self regulatory organization, governmental agency or any Company contracted with American shall be, at all times during the term of this Agreement, duly and fully licensed as insurance agents or representatives under the auspices of American and have all other requisite licenses, registrations, and authority to sell, renew, service or deliver Policies in any state in which Broker sells, renews, services or delivers such Policies.

5.3 Broker shall notify American of any and all litigation to which Broker or any of Broker's owners, directors, officers, employees or independent contractors may become a party, whether as plaintiff or defendant, and represents and warrants that no such litigation is now pending.

5.4 Broker shall notify American of any investigations of or hearings related to Broker or any of Broker's owners, directors, officers, employees or independent contractors by any self regulatory organization, governmental agency, or Company and represents and warrants that no such investigations or hearings are now pending.

5.5 American has taken all necessary corporate action, including, but not limited to, binding resolutions of its directors to enter into this Agreement and to carry out the terms and conditions thereof. Broker, if represented in the beginning paragraph of this Agreement to be a corporation, has taken all necessary corporate action, including, but not limited to, binding resolutions/actions of all of its directors and/or shareholders to enter into this Agreement and to carry out the terms and conditions thereof.

5.6 American does not warrant, guarantee or make any representations regarding the accuracy and/or timeliness of any billings provided by Companies.

6. TERMINATION OF AGREEMENT:

6.1 The term of this Agreement is for five years and is renewable at expiration.

6.2 American shall have the right to terminate or refuse to renew this Agreement upon 90 days written notice and shall have the right to terminate this Agreement upon 30 days written notice upon good and sufficient cause which shall be defined as:

(a) material and substantial breach of the terms of this Agreement by Broker (unless otherwise agreed in writing, for the purposes of paragraph 6.2 and all its subparagraphs, "Broker" shall include Broker's owners, officers, directors, employees and independent contractors);

(b) refusal by the insurance company which provides errors and omissions insurance coverages to Brooke to endorse said insurance policy to provide errors and omissions insurance coverage for Broker;

(c) such public actions by Broker, which in the judgment of American, shall be materially injurious to the reputation of American or the cumulative goodwill related to the use of American's name, trademarks, service marks, logotypes or commercial symbols.

(d) insurance coverage or Policy underwriting practices by Broker, which in the opinion of American, may jeopardize American's continued contractual agency relationship with any Company;

(e) the commission or omission of any act by Broker, which in the opinion of American, would be sufficient cause for the revocation of a license, registration, or other authority by any self regulatory organization, governmental agency or Company in any state in which Broker sells, renews, services or delivers Policies;

(f) legal proceedings involving Broker, which in the opinion of American, may impair Broker's capacity to perform Broker's obligations as set forth in this Agreement;

(g) business practices by Broker, which in the opinion of American are unethical or unacceptable to the general business community;

(h) inadequate qualifications of Broker, which in the opinion of American, may impair the ability of Broker to provide adequate assistance and service to Customer Accounts;

(i) the partial or total sale or transfer of Broker ownership or the partial or total sale or transfer of ownership of Customer Accounts without American's prior written consent;

(j) the location or relocation of Broker's agency office to an address other than the address designated in the beginning paragraph of this Agreement without American's prior written consent;

(k) the establishment by Broker of an additional agency office at an address other than the address designated in the beginning paragraph of this Agreement without American's prior written consent;

(l) bankruptcy of Broker;

(m) dishonor of a draft or electronic funds transfer drawn by American, or its designee, on Broker's checking account, if such draft is authorized by this Agreement;

(n) failure to provide proof of liability insurance as mandated by 3.17;

(o) the agreement (oral or written) of Broker to enter a , Customer Account sharing or service center agreement with any Person not obligated by contract (either through an agreement with Brooke, American, a Brooke franchise agent or an American broker with a contract similar to this Agreement) to process all applications for Policies exclusively through the facilities of Brooke, American, a Brooke franchise agent or an American broker.

(p) the refusal by Broker to provide a description of brokerage, commission sharing, account sharing or service center agreements Broker has entered into, and copies of the agreements memorializing same, within 30 days of entering any such agreement or after receipt of American's written request for same, if sooner. American's receipt of any such agreement shall not charge American with actual or implied knowledge of its terms nor shall such agreement have any binding effect on American unless American is expressly a party thereto in a written document signed by American.

6.3 In the event American shall terminate or refuse to renew this Agreement for cause as aforesaid, it shall give Broker written notice of its intent to terminate or non-renew. If terminated for cause stated above, the notice shall state all of the material facts upon which American relies as grounds for termination.

6.4 Broker shall have the unilateral right to terminate this Agreement for any reason upon not less than 30 days advance notice to American.

6.5 Upon termination of this Agreement, American shall request the pertinent Companies involved to make the Broker the Agent of Record for all Customer Accounts. In the event that a Company refuses to make the Broker the Agent of Record for Customer Accounts , then Broker shall, on or before the next Policy term expiration date following termination of this Agreement, obtain replacement coverages for said Customer Accounts with another Company. American shall continue to account for and process Customer Accounts until the Policy term expiration date following termination of this Agreement. Although American shall not be obligated to assist Broker in obtaining replacement coverages for Customer Accounts, American shall provide to Broker the Policy term expiration data and Customer Account data available through Brooke's Document Manager system. If the Broker does not obtain replacement coverages for Customer Accounts on or before the policy term expiration date following termination of this Agreement, then American shall obtain coverages for said Customer Accounts and Broker thereby relinquishes to American all ownership of, possession of, or other right to or interest in said Customer Accounts and any related files.

6.6 Upon termination of this Agreement and for as long as necessary thereafter, American shall continue to account for all Sales Commissions on Direct Bill Policies audited, endorsed, changed, or canceled on behalf of Customer Accounts processed through the facilities of American.   American shall continue to record Customer Account activity on Broker Account as set forth in paragraph 2.2 and 2.4 of this Agreement.

6.7 Upon termination of this Agreement and for as long as necessary thereafter, American shall continue to account for all Net Premiums on Agency Bill Policies audited, endorsed, changed, renewed, serviced, or canceled on behalf of Customer Accounts processed through the facilities of American.   American shall continue to record Customer Account activity on Broker Account as set forth in paragraph 2.3 and 2.4 of this Agreement.

6.8 After the termination of this Agreement, Broker shall remain responsible for payment to Broker of all Agency Bill Policy net premiums and Direct Bill Policy return commissions incurred on behalf of Customer Accounts processed through the facilities of American.

6.9 If entries are recorded to Broker Account in the month of or any month after the termination of this Agreement, American shall forward a record of Broker Account to Broker on or about the ____ of said month. Broker shall pay American, or its designee, on or about the ____ of each month any amount owed by Broker. Upon written notice to Broker, American may change the date such records are forwarded to Broker and the date Broker shall pay American amounts owed American by Broker.

6.10 Upon termination of this Agreement, American shall cease to provide errors and omissions insurance coverage for Broker and Broker shall not be entitled to any refund of errors and omissions insurance policy premiums.

6.11 Upon termination of this Agreement, American shall be permitted to retain copies of any files and records with respect to Customer Accounts as it shall deem reasonably necessary to account for and process Customer Accounts and for any other legitimate business purposes including preparation of tax returns and audits thereof, defense of litigation, collection of Broker Account, or otherwise.

6.12 In the event Broker elects to sell some or all Customer Accounts owned by Broker, American shall have the first right to purchase such assets at a price equal to the amount offered to or by any other bono fide purchaser. American shall have a right to purchase Customer Accounts owned by Subbrokers second only to Broker's right to purchase same.

7. TRUST ARRANGEMENT:

7.1   Broker acknowledges that American may enter into or has entered into a trust agreement (the "Trust Agreement") which among other terms provides for a trustee's control of all Sales Commissions. Accordingly, Broker agrees that all premiums, fees, Sales Commissions and Other Receipts received by Broker or American from Companies or customers which are related in any way to the sale, renewal, service or delivery of Policies through Broker shall be promptly deposited in the Receipts Trust Account.

7.2   Broker agrees that said Receipts Trust Account shall be owned by American, but controlled by the trustee. Trustee shall have sole right to withdraw funds from the Receipts Trust Account. Trustee shall distribute to Broker and/or American Sales Commissions and Other Receipts in accordance with the terms of the Trust Agreement. However, unless otherwise agreed upon by the parties in writing, nothing in the Trust Agreement shall change amounts due Broker, as shown on the statement of Broker Account pursuant to the terms of this Agreement or amounts payable by Broker to American as shown on the statement of Broker Account pursuant to the terms of this Agreement.

7.3   Broker acknowledges and agrees that Trustee (as an authorized designee of American under paragraphs 2.9, 3.10 and 6.9 hereof) shall initiate an electronic deposit to Broker's business account of all amounts due to Broker by American as shown on the statement of Broker Account and in accordance with Broker's pre-authorization, or that Trustee shall initiate an electronic withdrawal from Broker's business account of all amounts due to American by Broker as shown on the statement of Broker Account and in accordance with Broker's pre-authorization.

7.4 Broker agrees to release, indemnify and hold harmless American, its owners, officers, directors, employees, and independent contractors (for the purposes of this subparagraph, collectively "American") for and from any and all claims, losses, liability, or damages or expenses (including, but not limited to reasonable attorneys' fees, court costs, and costs of investigation) of any kind or nature whatsoever arising out of or in connection with the Trust Agreement or the deposit or withdrawal of money from the Receipts Trust Account or which Broker, its owners, officers, directors, employees, and independent contractors may incur as a result of American's performance of its rights, obligations or duties hereunder or under the terms of the Trust Agreement or in connection with the deposit or withdrawal of money from the Receipts Trust Account or Broker's business account. Provided, however, that this shall not relieve American from liability for its breach of any of its agreements under this Agreement or for its own willful misconduct, recklessness, bad faith or gross negligence, nor for the gross negligence, recklessness, bad faith or willful misconduct of its owners, officers, directors, employees, or independent contractors. This release, indemnification and hold harmless shall survive termination of the Agreement.

7.5 Broker, its owners, officers, directors, employees and independent contractors agree to release, indemnify and hold harmless the trust, its trustee, its owners, officers, directors, employees, and independent contractors (collectively, "trust") for and from any and all claims, losses, liability, or damages or expenses (including, but not limited to reasonable attorneys' fees, court costs, and costs of investigation) of any kind or nature whatsoever arising out of or in connection with the Trust Agreement or which Broker, its owners, officers, directors, employees, and independent contractors may incur as a result of trust's performance of its rights, obligations or duties under the terms of the Trust Agreement.   This release, indemnification and hold harmless shall survive termination of the Agreement. Upon American's request, Broker agrees to sign a separate document (to which trustee may be a party) releasing, indemnifying and holding harmless the trust.

8. SUBBROKER ARRANGEMENTS:

8.1 Transfer of Customer Accounts may result in termination of this Agreement in accordance with paragraph 6.2(i). However, American authorizes Broker to enter into agreements ("Subbroker Agreements") with qualified Subbrokers which provide for the vesting of ownership in Customer Account to Subbrokers. Said authorization is contingent upon the following:

(a) Broker agrees to provide a copy of this Agreement and a complete and current offering circular to all prospective Subbrokers. Broker acknowledges that said franchise offering circular has been prepared for disclosure to prospective brokers and is provided to Subbroker to disclose Broker's direct relationship with American.

(b) Broker agrees not to make any oral agreements, modifications or representations with or to any Subbroker or prospective Subbroker with regard to the subject matter of this Agreement or any Subbroker Agreement. All such agreements and representations must be in writing, true and complete, and without a tendency to mislead. Further, Broker agrees not to furnish any oral or written representations, information or projections concerning the actual or potential sales, costs, income profits or performance of any Subbroker's or prospective Subbroker's agency. Any modifications to a Subbroker Agreement must be in writing and are subject to the prior approval of American. Such approval shall be at American's sole discretion.

(c) Broker acknowledges that American shall not be a party to any agreements between Broker and Subbroker. Broker agrees to enforce for the benefit of American all provisions in Subbroker Agreements executed by Broker that pertain to or benefit American and Broker agrees not to waive any provisions which pertain to or benefit American.

(d) Broker agrees to submit to American a Subbroker Application, in a form approved by American, at least five (5) business days prior to the proposed effective date of any Subbroker Agreement. A fully completed, but not executed, Subbroker Agreement must be attached to the Subbroker Application. Broker shall not enter into a Subbroker Agreement until Broker receives written approval from American. Such approval shall be at American's sole discretion. American's approval of same shall not be deemed American's warranty of such agreement's compliance with any laws, enforceability or suitability for Broker's purposes or any other purpose.

(e) Broker agrees to provide a fully completed, but not executed, Subbroker Agreement to the Subbroker at least five (5) business days prior to the proposed effective date of the Subbroker Agreement.

(f) Subbroker Agreements shall be executed in triplicate prior to the effective date of the Subbroker Agreement and Broker shall deliver one fully executed original to American.

(g) Broker agrees to identify Subbroker ownership by assigning a specific Subbroker sub code to all Customer Accounts owned by Subbroker. Broker agrees to ensure that this Subbroker sub code is recorded on all applications and to otherwise ensure that American receives the information necessary to sub code those Customer Accounts for which ownership has been vested in a Subbroker.

(h) Broker acknowledges that American's accounting responsibilities to the Broker with regard to Subbrokers is limited to the recording of the Subbroker sub coding information provided by the Broker and that the accuracy of said sub code information is the exclusive obligation of Broker. American agrees to record said sub code information in a manner which permits the separation of all entries to the Broker Account so that Broker can provide statements of Subbroker's account with Broker. Broker acknowledges and agrees that American may rely exclusively on sub coding instructions, statements and information provided to American by Broker and American is not required to verify or confirm same. Broker agrees to release , indemnify and hold harmless American, its owners, officers, directors, employees and independent contractors for and from any and all claims, losses, liabilities, damages or expenses (including, but not limited to reasonable attorneys' fees, court costs, and costs of investigation) of any kind or nature whatsoever arising out of or in connection with American's reliance on Broker's sub coding instructions, statements or information.

(i) Broker acknowledges that it is responsible for collection of all amounts due from Subbroker and payment of all amounts due to Subbroker pursuant to the Subbroker Agreement. The Broker further acknowledges that the entire Broker Account balance shall be paid to American when due, irrespective of whether the Broker has collected amounts due Broker from Subbroker.

(j) Broker acknowledges that its Company list may be modified or restricted as a result of entering into a Subbroker Agreement.

8.2 Subject to the approval of the insurance company involved, Brooke Corporation, American's parent company, shall endorse Brooke's errors and omissions insurance policy to provide errors and omissions insurance coverage for Subbroker. Upon termination of the Subbroker Agreement, errors and omissions insurance coverage for Subbroker shall no longer be provided to Subbroker under Brooke's errors and omissions insurance policy.

8.3. American shall provide Customer Account and document information to Broker pursuant to this Agreement. Such information may subsequently be made available by Broker to Subbroker at Broker's discretion. At Broker's discretion, Broker may authorize Subbrokers to use Brooke's proprietary software under Broker's license; provided however, such authorization is subject to the same restrictions applied to Broker pursuant hereto.

8.4 Broker shall immediately notify American when any Subbroker Agreement is terminated and, upon Broker's written request, Brooke shall request the pertinent Companies involved to make Subbroker the Agent of Record for all Customer Accounts identified by the sub code information provided by Broker.

9. MISCELLANEOUS PROVISIONS:

9.1 American shall not be obligated to pay Broker any share of Profit Sharing Commissions.

9.2 Any notices required hereunder shall be deemed effective if in writing, and delivered by hand or mailed by United States Mail, postage prepaid, or mailed by certified mail, with return receipt requested or mailed by express courier with confirmed delivery date. The effective date of notice shall be the day of delivery by hand, and if mailed by regular mail, four days following the mailing thereof, and if by certified mail or express courier, the date of receipt thereof. A business day shall be deemed any day on which the United States Postal Service shall have regular mail deliveries to the address to which the notice is mailed.

9.3 This Agreement may not be modified, revised, altered, added to, or extended in any manner, or superseded other than by an instrument in writing signed by all of the parties hereto.

9.4 This Agreement may be executed in duplicate, each of which shall be deemed an original, but all of which together shall constitute one and the same instrument representing the agreement of the parties hereto.

9.5 The failure by an party to enforce any provision of this Agreement shall not be in any way construed as a waiver of any such provision nor prevent that party thereafter from enforcing each and every other provision of this Agreement.

9.6 The invalidity or non-enforceability of any particular provision of this Agreement shall not affect the other provisions hereof, and this Agreement shall be construed in all respects as if such invalid or unenforceable provisions were omitted.

9.7 This Agreement shall be binding upon and inure to the benefit of the parties hereto and their heirs and legal representatives but the rights and property interests hereunder shall not be assignable by any party except as set out herein.

9.8 This Agreement (including all Exhibits and Addenda hereto) contains the entire agreement between the parties hereto and shall supersede and take precedence over any and all prior agreements, arrangements or understandings between the parties relating to the subject matter hereof. No oral understandings, oral statements, oral promises or oral inducements exist. No representations, warranties, covenants or conditions, express or implied, whether by statute or otherwise, other than as set forth herein, have been made by the parties hereto.

9.9 Broker agrees to sign, acknowledge, deliver, and/or file any additional documents, certifications or statements that American may deem necessary to carry out the intent of this Agreement.

9.10 This Agreement shall be construed and governed by the laws of the State of Kansas. At the option of American, jurisdiction and venue for any dispute arising under or in relation to this Agreement will lie only in Kansas with the Johnson County District Court or in the U.S. District Court having jurisdiction over Johnson County Kansas. In the event a lawsuit or litigation is brought with respect to this Agreement, the prevailing party shall be entitled to be reimbursed for and/or have judgment for all of their costs and expenses, including reasonable attorney's fees and legal expenses.

9.11 Timeliness and punctuality are essential elements of this Agreement.

IN WITNESS WHEREOF, American and Broker have executed this Agreement as of the day and year first above written.

AMERICAN: BROKER:

By:_____   By:_____

Title:_____   Title:_____

GUARANTY AGREEMENT

If Broker is a corporation or limited liability company, we the undersigned, as individuals, jointly and severally guarantee the faithful performance of Broker to perform all duties and obligations set forth in the forgoing agreement including without limitation the duty to pay any sum which Broker may become liable to pay American by virtue of the foregoing agreement.

IN WITNESS WHEREOF, the undersigned has executed this Guaranty Agreement as of the day and year first above written.

_____   _____

_____,individually   _____, individually

PRODUCER AGREEMENT

THIS AGREEMENT ("Agreement") made and entered into this ____ day of _____, _____, by and between _____ ("Agent") and _____ ("Producer") as follows:

In consideration of the mutual promises set forth herein and other good and valuable consideration, the receipt and sufficiency of which is hereby acknowledged, the parties agree as follows:

1. DEFINITIONS

For purposes of this Agreement, the following terms shall have the following meanings unless the context clearly requires otherwise:

1.1. Company. A company issuing, brokering, selling or making a market for Policies and which has a contract with Brooke.

1.2. Insurance, Investment, Banking and/or Credit Services. Insurance services include but are not limited to the sale, renewal, service or delivery of insurance policies, annuities, insurance brokering services, insurance customer services, risk management services and insurance related consulting or advisory services. Investment services include, but are not limited to, the sale, renewal, service or delivery of mutual funds, stocks, bonds, notes, debentures, real estate services, investment customer services, investment related consulting, and financial, investment, or economic advisory services. Banking services include any banking service Agent and Producer are allowed to perform under federal and/or state laws. Credit services include, but are not limited to, origination or brokerage of loans or mortgages, credit customer services, and credit related consulting or advisory services. At any point in time, Insurance, Investment, Banking and Credit Services shall be limited to those services then offered by Agent.

1.3. Brooke. Brooke Corporation, its successors, assigns or designees. Brooke is the "agent of record" for all of Policies sold, renewed, serviced or delivered by Agent, its employees or independent contractors. Agent, its employees and independent contractors are required to sell, service, renew and deliver Policies exclusively through Brooke.

1.4 Person. Any individual, sole proprietorship, partnership, joint venture, trust, unincorporated organization, association, corporation, limited liability company, institution or other entity.

1.5 Policies. Any and all insurance services, policies, coverages or products sold, renewed, serviced or delivered by Producer to any Person. Policies include, but are not limited to, any and all Insurance, Investment, Banking or Credit Service, or policy, coverage or product associated therewith sold, renewed, serviced or delivered by Producer to any Person.

1.6 Sales Commissions. Amounts paid by Companies for sale, renewal, service or delivery of a specific Policy. Sales Commissions are not normally contingent upon factors such as Brooke's loss ratio, premium volume, sales volume or special concessions negotiated by Brooke. For the purposes of this Agreement, Sales Commissions shall specifically exclude amounts received for advertising allowances, prizes, override commissions, profit sharing commissions, supplier bonus commissions and other similar payments. Sales Commissions shall also include any consulting fees, advisory fees, placement fees, service fees, renewal fees, or any similar payments paid on or related to any Customer Account by any Person.

2. SUBJECT MATTER OF AGREEMENT

2.1 Agent has and does, hereby, contract with Producer for Producer to sell Policies to Persons.

3. INDEPENDENT CONTRACTOR

3.1 The Producer's relationship with Agent is that of an independent contractor. As such, the Producer will exercise independent judgment as to time and place of performing services under this Agreement.

Page 1 of 4

4. SALES COMMISSIONS

4.1 Agent agrees to pay to Producer an amount equal to 60% of the Sales Commissions received by Agent upon the original issuance of a Policy, the sale of which was the result of Producer's exclusive efforts and the sale of which occurred after date of this Agreement. Producer agrees to repay Agent an amount equal to any Sales Commission reduction resulting from policy premium audits, policy cancellations or commissions adjustments to said Policy. Producer's obligation to repay such amounts shall survive the termination of this Agreement. Any amounts Producer owes Agent shall represent a debt of Producer which Agent shall at its discretion be entitled to collect directly or offset against current or future Sales Commissions.

4.2 Agent agrees to pay to Producer an amount equal to 40% of the Sales Commissions received by Agent upon the renewal of a Policy, the original sale of which was the result of Producer's exclusive efforts and the original sale of which occurred after the date of this Agreement. Producer agrees to repay Agent an amount equal to any Sales Commission reduction resulting from policy premium audits, policy cancellations or commission adjustments to said Policy. Producer's obligation to repay such amounts shall survive the termination of this Agreement. Any amounts Producer owes Agent shall represent a debt of Producer which Agent shall at its discretion be entitled to collect directly or offset against current or future Sales Commissions.

4.3 Payment of Sales Commissions by Agent to Producer shall be made on or about the_____ day of the month following the month in which Sales Commissions are received by Agent. The amount of Sales Commissions shall be derived from periodic statements provided to Agent by Brooke.

4.4 Unless otherwise agreed, Producer shall not be entitled to any other payment or commission such as advertising allowances, prizes, awards, override commissions, profit sharing commissions, supplier bonus commissions and other similar payments.

5. ERRORS AND OMISSIONS INSURANCE

5.1 During the term of this agreement, Agent shall provide errors and omissions insurance coverage for Producer. However, Producer shall be responsible for payment of all defense and other claims expenses in amounts up to $2500 per incident for any errors and omissions insurance related claim resulting from Producer's actions or omissions.

6. OFFICE FACILITIES AND SUPPLIES

6.1 Agent will provide office facilities for Producer's use, which includes phone, desk, fax machine, copy machine, camera, and personal computer.

6.2 Producer shall be responsible for payment of expenses such as supplies, transportation, education, training and long distance phone call expenses.

7. ADDITIONAL OBLIGATIONS OF PRODUCER

7.1 Producer shall abide by and conform to the rules and procedures adopted from time to time by Agent. Producer acknowledges that said rules and procedures include, among other requirements, a requirement that Producer provide Agent with copies of all Policy applications and all other records or documents originated, received or processed by Producer which are related to Policies. Producer acknowledges the importance of complete and timely transmittal of all records and documents and agrees to submit in a timely manner to Agent all such records and documents.

7.2 Producer shall apply for coverages only with the Companies that are authorized for Producer's use from time to time by Agent. Producer shall abide by and conform to the conditions and limits of authority for binding Companies to insurance and other coverages which are set forth from time to time by Agent.

7.3 During the term of this Agreement, Producer shall do business under the name "_____," unless otherwise approved in writing by Agent. Upon termination of this Agreement, Producer shall immediately cease using such name and any other materials pertaining or referring to Brooke or Agent.

7.4 After the date of this Agreement, Producer shall sell, service, renew and deliver Policies exclusively for Agent. Producer shall process all applications for Policies exclusively through the facilities of Agent with Companies that are authorized for Producer's use. Producer shall make Brooke "Agent of Record" for all policies sold renewed services or delivered by Producer after the date of this Agreement. If a company refuses to make Brooke the Agent of Record for such Policies, then Producer shall assign all Sales Commissions and bonuses, profit sharing commissions, advertising allowances, prizes, awards and other similar payments associated with such Policies to Brooke.

7.5 Producer shall provide to Agent any information regarding Producer that may be required from Agent, Brooke, any self regulatory organization, government agency or any Company. Producer shall comply with all federal, state and local requirements including but not limited to the sales practices, education and licensing requirements of all government agencies and any Company.

7.6 Producer shall immediately report to Agent any legal or regulatory issues, investigations or hearings such as errors and omissions claims, insurance department or other regulatory complaints, legal summons and subpoenas related to Producer or Policies. Producer shall not make any written or verbal comments or responses regarding said issues, investigations or hearings to anyone until authorized to do so. Agent will coordinate and control responses to same.

7.7 Producer shall provide Agent with full and complete access to Producer's records and documents deemed necessary by Agent to perform an audit to determine compliance with the provisions of this Agreement or for other legitimate business purposes.

7.8 Producer shall not have authority to incur any liability in the name of or on behalf of Agent. Neither party shall assume any liability of the other. Such liability shall remain the exclusive individual liabilities of each.

7.9 Producer shall respect the confidentiality of client files, client lists, policy expiration information, business plans, operations plans, marketing plans, business documents, customer and other information ("confidential information") owned by, developed by or in the possession of Agent, its owners, employees, officers or independent contractors (for the purposes of this paragraph collectively referred to as "Agent"). Producer shall not remove any confidential information from premises owned or rented by Agent without the express written consent of Agent. Producer shall not sell, trade or gift any confidential information. Producer agrees that all confidential information remains the exclusive property of Agent.

8. TERMINATION OF THIS AGREEMENT

8.1 Without cause, either Agent or Producer may terminate this Agreement upon ____ days written notice to the other party. In the event of conduct by Producer adverse to the interests of Agent, this Agreement may be terminated immediately upon discovery of such an occurrence or event, without the necessity of further notice.

8.2 Any errors and omissions coverage provided by or through Agent shall cease upon termination of this Agreement.

8.3. Upon termination of this Agreement, Agent shall not be obligated to pay Sales Commissions, new or renewal, to Producer for any Policy issued before or after the date of termination.

9. COVENANT NOT TO SOLICIT

9.1 Producer agrees that, for a period of three (3) years following the effective date of the termination of this Agreement, Producer will not directly or indirectly solicit or write for any customers that are a part of the book of business of Agent and will not directly or indirectly attempt to divert any customer that is a part of the book of business of Agent from continuing to do business with Agent.

9.2 Producer agrees that the covenants set forth herein are reasonable and necessary and that Producer's association with Agent and the opportunities afforded Producer pursuant to this Agreement are ample consideration for same.

9.3 Producer understands that Producer is not prohibited from working for any other company or in any particular line of work, but that this post termination covenant not to solicit only restricts the Producer from directly or indirectly writing Policies for or contacting in person, by telephone, by mail, or by any other means those current or prior customers or potential customers of Agent.

10. LENDER PROTECTION PROVISION

10.1 Producer acknowledges that Agent or a principal thereof has been or may be extended credit by a lending institution or other Person ("Lender"). In such instances, Lender shall be granted a security interest in the assets of Agent (including assets that are Sales Commission based) to secure Lender's loan. Producer acknowledges and agrees that if Agent or a principal thereof has been extended credit, Lender's interest in the assets of Agent is prior and superior to Producer's interest in any such assets.

11. MISCELLANEOUS

11.1 This Agreement shall supersede and take precedence over any and all prior agreements, arrangements or understandings between Agent and the Producer relating to the subject matter hereof.

11.2 No oral understanding, oral statement, or oral promises or oral inducements on the subject of this Agreement exists.

11.3 The waiver by Agent of any breach of any provision of this Agreement by Producer shall not operate or be construed as a waiver of any subsequent breach by the Producer.

11.4 Any notice required or permitted to be given under this Agreement shall be sufficient in writing, and if hand delivered or sent by registered mail to Producer's residence or to Agent's principal office.

11.5 The rights and obligations of Agent under this Agreement shall inure to the benefit of and shall be binding upon the successors and assigns of Agent.

11.6 This Agreement may not be modified, revised, altered, added to, or extended in any manner, superseded other than by an instrument in writing signed by all the parties hereto.

IT IS SO AGREED.

AGENT

witness

By:
Its:

PRODUCER

witness

COMMISSION SHARING AGREEMENT

THIS AGREEMENT (the "Agreement) is made and entered into by and between _____ ("Franchise Agent") and _____ ("Agent").

WHEREAS, Franchise Agent and Agent are in the business of selling, servicing and/or delivering Policies;

WHEREAS, Franchise Agent and Agent desire to associate together for the purpose of sharing Sales Commissions for the joint sale, service, delivery or renewal of Policies.

NOW THEREFORE, in consideration of the mutual promises set forth herein and other good and valuable consideration, the receipt and sufficiency of which are hereby acknowledged, the Franchise Agent and Agent agree as follows:

1. DEFINITIONS

For purposes of this Agreement, the following terms shall have the following meanings unless the context clearly requires otherwise:

Brooke. Brooke Corporation, its successors, assigns or designees. Brooke is the "agent of record" for all of Policies sold, renewed, serviced or delivered through Franchise Agent and Agent. Franchise Agent and Agent are required to sell, service, renew and deliver Policies exclusively through Brooke.

Company. A company issuing, brokering, selling or making a market for Policies and which has a contract with Brooke.

Customer Account. A Person who has a Policy purchased from, serviced, renewed or delivered through Franchise Agent. Customer Accounts shall be owned by Franchise Agent.

Insurance, Investment, Banking and/or Credit Services. Insurance services include but are not limited to the sale, renewal, service or delivery of insurance policies, annuities, insurance brokering services, insurance customer services, risk management services and insurance related consulting or advisory services. Investment services include, but are not limited to, the sale, renewal, service or delivery of mutual funds, stocks, bonds, notes, debentures, real estate services, investment customer services, investment related consulting, and financial, investment, or economic advisory services. Banking services include any banking service Franchise Agent and Agent are allowed to perform under federal and/or state laws. Credit services include, but are not limited to, origination or brokerage of loans or mortgages, credit customer services, and credit related consulting or advisory services. At any point in time, Insurance, Investment, Banking and Credit Services shall be limited to those services then offered by Franchise Agent .

Franchise Agent Account: An account on Brooke's ledgers to which Brooke records amounts due Brooke from Franchise Agent and amounts due Franchise Agent from Brooke.

Person. Any individual, sole proprietorship, partnership, joint venture, trust, unincorporated organization, association, corporation, limited liability company, institution or other entity.

Policies. Any and all insurance services, policies, coverages or products sold, renewed, serviced or delivered to any Person. Policies include, but are not limited to, any and all Insurance, Investment, Banking or Credit Service, or policy, coverage or product associated therewith sold, renewed, serviced or delivered to any Person.

Sales Commissions. Commissions paid by Companies to Brooke or assigned by Franchise Agent to Brooke for the sale, renewal, service or delivery of a specific Policy. Sales Commissions are not normally contingent upon factors such as Brooke's loss ratio, premium volume, sales volume or special concessions negotiated by Brooke. For the purposes of this Agreement, Sales Commissions shall specifically exclude Profit Sharing Commissions and other similar payments. Sales Commissions shall specifically exclude amounts paid by Brooke pursuant to a bonus plan, the terms of which are defined by Brooke in its sole discretion and for which Brooke makes no representation regarding future payments or Franchise Agent's eligibility. Sales Commissions shall also include any consulting fees, advisory fees, placement fees, service fees, renewal fees, or any similar payments paid on or related to any Customer Account by any Person.

2. SALES COMMISSIONS

Franchise Agent agrees to share Sales Commissions with Agent on the Policies sold to the Customer Accounts identified on the attached list through the joint efforts of Franchise Agent and Agent.

Franchise Agent agrees to pay to Agent an amount equal to _____% of the Sales Commissions credited to Franchise Agent Account upon the original issuance of a Policy, the sale of which was the result of Franchise Agent's and Agent's joint effort and the sale of which occurred after date of this Agreement. Agent agrees to repay Franchise Agent an amount equal to any Sales Commission reduction resulting from policy premium audits, policy cancellations or commissions adjustments to said Policy. Agent's obligation to repay such amounts shall survive the termination of this Agreement. Any amounts Agent owes Franchise Agent shall represent a debt of Agent which Franchise Agent shall at its discretion be entitled to collect directly or offset against current or future Sales Commissions.

Franchise Agent agrees to pay to Agent an amount equal to ___% of the Sales Commissions received by Franchise Agent upon the renewal of a Policy, the original sale of which was the result of Franchise Agent's and Agent's joint efforts and the original sale of which occurred after the date of this Agreement. Agent agrees to repay Franchise Agent an amount equal to any Sales Commission reduction resulting from policy premium audits, policy cancellations or commission adjustments to said Policy. Agent's obligation to repay such amounts shall survive the termination of this Agreement. Any amounts Agent owes Franchise Agent shall represent a debt of Agent which Franchise Agent shall at its discretion be entitled to collect directly or offset against current or future Sales Commissions.

Payment of Sales Commissions by Franchise Agent to Agent shall be made on or about the_____ day of the month following the month in which Sales Commissions are received by Franchise Agent. The amount of Sales Commissions shall be derived from periodic statements provided to Franchise Agent by Brooke.

Unless otherwise agreed, Agent shall not be entitled to any other payment or commission such as advertising allowances, prizes, awards, override commissions, profit sharing commissions, supplier bonus commissions and other similar payments.

3. SERVICING RESPONSIBILITY

Unless otherwise agreed in writing, Franchise Agent shall be solely responsible for the servicing of such Policies including, but not limited to, the collection of any agency bill premiums.

4. OWNERSHIP OF CUSTOMER ACCOUNTS

Franchise Agent's agreement to pay a percent of Sales Commissions associated with certain Customer Accounts does not convey any ownership in any Customer Accounts to Agent. Agent acknowledges and agrees that Customer Accounts shall be exclusively Franchise Agent's and that the Franchise Agent's client and prospective client lists, policy expiration lists and other such records or information shall remain Franchise Agent's exclusive property and Franchise Agent shall be fully vested in the ownership thereof.

5. COMPLIANCE

Franchise Agent and Agent each represent and warrant to the other that each has all necessary licenses and registrations to sell, service, renew and deliver Policies. Franchise Agent and Agent shall comply with all federal, state and local requirements including but not limited to the sales practices, education and licensing requirements of all government agencies and any Company. Further, for the purposes of this Agreement, Agent shall abide by and conform to the rules and procedures adopted from time to time by Franchise Agent.

During the term of this Agreement, Agent shall immediately report to Franchise Agent any legal or regulatory issues, investigations or hearings such as errors and omissions claims, insurance department or other regulatory complaints, legal summons and subpoenas related to the Policies sold through the joint efforts of Agent and Franchise Agent.

6. LIABILITIES

Neither party shall have the authority to incur any liability in the name of or on behalf of the other. Neither party shall assume any liability of the other. Such liability shall remain the exclusive individual liabilities of each.

7. ERRORS AND OMISSIONS INSURANCE

During the term of this Agreement, Franchise Agent and Agent shall each have errors and omissions insurance coverage. However, Agent shall reimburse Franchise Agent for payment of all defense and other claims expenses in amounts up to $2500 per incident for any errors and omissions insurance related claim which is the result of Agent's actions or omissions.

8. ACCESS TO RECORDS

Agent shall provide Franchise Agent with full and complete access to Agent's records and documents pertaining to the Policies sold pursuant to this Agreement deemed necessary by Franchise Agent for a legitimate business purpose; provided however, that access shall be upon reasonable advance request and during such times and upon such conditions as shall not unreasonably impair the operations of Agent.

9. CONFIDENTIALITY

Agent shall respect the confidentiality of client files, client lists, policy expiration information, business plans, operations plans, marketing plans, business documents, customer and other information ("confidential information") owned by or in the possession of Franchise Agent, its owners, employees, officers or independent contractors (for the purposes of this paragraph collectively referred to as "Franchise Agent"). Agent shall not convert or use any such confidential information to directly or indirectly solicit or write Policies for Customer Accounts other than pursuant to this Agreement and shall not disseminate in any way such confidential information. Agent shall not remove any confidential information from premises owned or rented by Franchise Agent without the express written consent of Franchise Agent. Agent shall not sell, trade or gift any confidential information. Agent agrees that all confidential information remains the exclusive property of Franchise Agent.

10. TERMINATION OF THIS AGREEMENT

Without cause, either Franchise Agent or Agent may terminate this Agreement at any time upon ____ days written notice to the other party. In the event of conduct by Agent adverse to the interests of Franchise Agent, this Agreement may be terminated with cause immediately upon discovery of such an occurrence or event, without the necessity of further notice.

Upon termination of this Agreement without cause, Franchise Agent shall continue to pay Sales Commissions, first year and renewal, to Agent for any Policy sold (as evidenced by a signed application) before the date of termination as a result of Franchise Agent's and Agent's joint efforts. If this Agreement is terminated for cause, Franchise Agent shall discontinue payment of any Sales Commissions to Agent.

11. COVENANT NOT TO SOLICIT

Agent agrees that during the term of this Agreement and for a period of 3 years after the termination of this Agreement, Agent will not directly or indirectly solicit or write Policies for any Customer Account on the attached list or which purchased a Policy sold through the joint efforts of Franchise Agent and Agent pursuant to this Agreement and will not directly or indirectly attempt to divert to Agent any Customer Account on the attached list or which purchased a Policy sold through the joint efforts of Franchise Agent and Agent. Agent acknowledges that such solicitation will cause substantial harm to Franchise Agent and Agent agrees to liquidated damages of $10,000 per incident (sale or solicitation) or actual damages, whichever is greater. Further, Franchise Agent is entitled to seek injunctive relief or any other remedy available to Franchise Agent at law or in equity.

Agent agrees that the covenants set forth herein are reasonable and necessary and that Agent's association with Franchise Agent and the opportunities afforded Agent pursuant to this Agreement are ample consideration for same.

Agent understands that Agent is not prohibited from working for any other company or in any particular line of work, but that this covenant not to solicit only restricts the Agent from directly or indirectly writing Policies for or contacting in person, by telephone, by mail, or by any other means those Customer Accounts on the attached list or which purchased a Policy sold through the joint efforts of Franchise Agent and Agent.

12. LENDER PROTECTION PROVISION

Agent acknowledges that Franchise Agent or a principal thereof has been or may be extended credit by a lending institution or other Person ("Lender"). In such instances, Lender shall be granted a security interest in the assets of Franchise Agent (including assets that are Sales Commission based) to secure Lender's loan. Agent acknowledges and agrees that if Franchise Agent or a principal thereof has been extended credit, Lender's interest in the assets of Franchise Agent is prior and superior to Agent's interest in any such assets.

13. MISCELLANEOUS

This Agreement shall supersede and take precedence over any and all prior agreements, arrangements or understandings between Franchise Agent and Agent relating to the subject matter hereof.

No oral understanding, oral statement, or oral promises or oral inducements on the subject of this Agreement exists.

The waiver by Franchise Agent of any breach of any provision of this Agreement by Agent shall not operate or be construed as a waiver of any subsequent breach by the Agent.

Any notice required or permitted to be given under this Agreement shall be sufficient in writing, and if hand delivered or sent by registered mail to the other party's principal office.

The rights and obligations of Franchise Agent under this Agreement shall inure to the benefit of and shall be binding upon the successors and assigns of Franchise Agent.

This Agreement may not be modified, revised, altered, added to, or extended in any manner, superseded other than by an instrument in writing signed by all the parties hereto.

IT IS SO AGREED.

FRANCHISE AGENT

_____   _____
Witness   By:
                                                                          Its:

                                                                     AGENT

_____   _____
Witness

BROKERAGE PRODUCER AGREEMENT

The undersigned, a duly licensed property/casualty agency or brokerage firm in the State of _____, ("Producer"), desiring to submit to American Insurance Agency ("AIA") applications for insurance agrees as follows:

Authority. Producer is acting as agent and/or broker for the applicant and in the applicant's behalf, not as an agent of AIA, and that no binding authority is granted or delegated by this agreement.

Cancellations. Without exception, if coverage is bound by AIA, a charge is made in accordance with the policy terms. Flat cancellations are not allowed. If Producer does not make timely payment of any sums due AIA, then AIA may, in addition to other remedies available to it, cancel the policy for non payment of premium. Upon cancellation, Producer shall pay AIA return commissions at the same rate as originally credited.

Premium Collection. Producer accepts full and entire responsibility to AIA for the collection and payment of all premiums due on those accounts whereby the Producer has requested AIA to bind coverage and AIA has agreed to provide coverage. Such premiums are due to AIA whether or not Producer has collected the premiums. AIA may add 1.5% per month to any past due balance owed, and in the event of default, be paid reasonable collection charges and/or attorneys fees.

Uncollectable adjustable premiums. Premiums which have been determined by audits, retrospective rating adjustments and/or interim reports are fully earned at time of invoicing by AIA. Producer may be relieved of the responsibility of such premiums if AIA is notified in writing within 30 days after invoice date, stating that such premiums are uncollectable and that a diligent effort has been made. Commission on premiums deemed not collectable in this manner will be forfeited and Producer shall pay AIA return commission at the same rate as originally credited. Failure to give AIA timely notice shall constitute acceptance of the responsibility to pay such premiums.

Venue. In the event of any dispute under this agreement, the proper venue for any legal action will be Johnson County in the State of Kansas.

Ownership of business. AIA agrees to pay or allow the Producer commissions as may be negotiated; and provided that all premiums or unearned commissions are fully paid as herein agreed, the Producer shall retain full ownership and control of all expirations.

Licensing. In order to comply with certain state resident agent countersignature laws, AIA may request Producer to obtain a license with the carrier(s) for which AIA places Producer's accounts. Producer agrees that such license, when procured, shall be used by Producer for countersigning purposes only and that no binding authority is extended to the Producer as a result of such license.

E & O. Producer warrants and represents that he/she has errors and omissions insurance in effect throughout the term of this agreement.

        E & O Carrier_____ **Limit of Liability**_____

Cancellation of Agreement. This agreement may be canceled at any time by written notice to the other, but such cancellation shall not alter in any way the continued application of this agreement to insurance policies in effect prior to the date of cancellation.

Other provisions. Producer understands that AIA assumes no responsibility toward any policy holder or subproducer with regard to the adequacy, amount or form of coverage and agrees to hold AIA harmless from any claim asserted against AIA in following instructions of Producer.

**Producer's
business name:** _____

Address: _____

It is agreed:

PRODUCER   AMERICAN INSURANCE AGENCY

By:_____   By:_____

Title:_____   Title:_____

Please attach a copy of current Agent and/or Broker license

SERVICE CENTER AGREEMENT

THIS AGREEMENT ("Agreement") is made and entered into this _____ day of _____, ____, by and between _____ ("Servicer") having its principal place of business at _____and _____("Agent").

NOW THEREFORE, in consideration of the mutual promises set forth herein and other good and valuable consideration, the receipt and sufficiency of which are hereby acknowledged, the parties agree as follows:

DEFINITIONS

For purposes of this Agreement, the following terms shall have the following meanings unless the context clearly requires otherwise:

Brooke. Brooke Corporation, its successors, assigns or designees. Brooke is the "agent of record" for all of Policies sold, renewed, serviced or delivered by Agent.

Insurance, Investment, Banking and/or Credit Services. Insurance services include but are not limited to the sale, renewal, service or delivery of insurance policies, annuities, insurance brokering services, insurance customer services, risk management services and insurance related consulting or advisory services. Investment services include, but are not limited to, the sale, renewal, service or delivery of mutual funds, stocks, bonds, notes, debentures, real estate services, investment customer services, investment related consulting, and financial, investment, or economic advisory services. Banking services include any banking service Agent and Servicer are allowed to perform under federal and/or state laws. Credit services include, but are not limited to, origination or brokerage of loans, or mortgages, credit customer services, and credit related consulting or advisory services. At any point in time, Insurance, Investment, Banking and Credit Services shall be limited to those services then offered through Servicer.

Person. Any individual, sole proprietorship, partnership, joint venture, trust, unincorporated organization, association, corporation, limited liability company, institution or other entity.

Policies. Any and all insurance services, policies, coverages or products sold, renewed, serviced or delivered to any Person. Policies include, but are not limited to, any and all Insurance, Investment, Banking or Credit Service, or policy, coverage or product associated therewith sold, renewed, services or delivered to any Person.

Sales Commissions. Amounts paid for sales, renewal, service or delivery of a specific Policy. Sales Commissions shall include any commissions, consulting fees, advisory fees, placement fees, service fees, renewal fees, or any similar payments paid on or related to any customer account by any Person.

TERMS AND CONDITIONS

Agent shall pay Servicer twenty-five percent (25%) of any Sales Commissions resulting from the sale, service, renewal or delivery of Policies to Agent's customer accounts by Servicer or Agent. The amount of Sales Commissions shall be derived without further adjustment from monthly agent statements prepared by Brooke. Agent authorizes Servicer to deduct any such amounts from any balances due Agent from Servicer. In the event that the balances due Agent from Servicer are not sufficient to pay Servicer in full, then Agent shall pay any remaining amounts to Servicer within five (5) business days of billing.

During the term of this Agreement, Servicer agrees to provide the following services to Agent at Servicer's offices located at the address stated above:

1. use of office space, desks, chairs, computers, fax machine, copy machine, receptionist, and local phone facilities which is sufficient for a typical Agent to operate its agency business.
2. use of licensed service representatives which is sufficient for a typical Agent to operate its agency business.
3. customer and policy accounting using Brooke's Document Manager system and Brooke's Internet site.

Agent agrees to reimburse Servicer for postage, long distance telephone charges, travel and transportation expenses, entertainment expenses, supply expenses, and education expenses incurred by Servicer on behalf of Agent. Agent agrees not to use Servicer's office space for any purposes other than selling, renewing, servicing or delivering Policies.

Agent and its owners, officers, directors, employees, independent contractors, and guests shall not:

1. use of permit the use of abusive or discourteous language, threats, or fighting in or near Servicer's office space;
2. use or permit the use of alcohol or illegal drugs in or near Servicer's office space;
3. gamble or possess weapons in or near Servicer's office space;
4. create an offensive environment in or near Servicer's office space including but not limited to unwanted sexual advances, the use of sexually explicit or vulgar language, the presence of sexually explicit photographs or other materials, the use of racist language or rhetoric, the presence of racial materials, or the telling of sexual or racist stories;
5. obstruct hallways, clutter common areas, or otherwise inconvenience others working in or near Servicer's office space;
6. store files on, load programs on, or re-configure in any way Servicer's office server computer or programs or sell, lease or authorize the use of same without Servicer's prior written consent;
7. conduct themselves and their business in an unprofessional or inappropriate manner or in a manner that would harm the reputation of the Servicer or the service center; or
8. violate the policies or procedures prescribed by Servicer or violate any other agreement Agent has with Servicer as such policies, procedures or agreements may be amended from time to time.

Agent agrees to respect the confidentiality of customer information owned or controlled by Servicer or by other agents or subagents that have entered into a service center agreement or other agreement with Servicer or to which Agent may inadvertently or in any manner obtain access to through Brooke, Servicer, or other agent or subagent under contract with or otherwise associated or affiliated with Brooke, the service center or Servicer. Agent shall not use any such confidential information to directly or indirectly solicit or write Policies and shall not disseminate in any way such confidential information. Agent acknowledges that Servicer and Brooke do not have the authority to restrict other agents or subagents that have entered into service center agreements, franchise agent agreements, or subagent agreements with Servicer or Brooke from soliciting or writing Policies from customer accounts owned by Agent. Correspondingly, Servicer acknowledges that Agent is not restricted from soliciting Policies from customer accounts owned by other agents that have entered into service center agreements, franchise agreements or subagent agreements provided that confidential information is not used as set forth in the above.   The provisions set forth herein shall survive termination of this Agreement.

During the term of this Agreement, for a period of two (2) years from and after the termination of this Agreement, Agent will not directly or indirectly solicit employees or independent contractors of Servicer to become employees or independent contractors of Agent, and will not directly or indirectly attempt to divert any employee or independent contractor of Servicer from continuing to be an employee or independent contractor Servicer.

Agent authorizes Brooke to release to Servicer any confidential information regarding Agent's customer accounts and Agent agrees to release, indemnify and hold Brooke harmless for the release of any such information to Servicer.

The term of this Agreement shall be for a period of not less than one month beginning on _____, ____, after which this Agreement may be terminated by either party upon 30 days written notice. This Agreement may be terminated immediately upon Agent or Agent's owners, directors, officers, employees, independent contractors or guests violation of one or more of the terms hereof.

This Agreement shall supersede and take precedence over any and all prior agreements, arrangements or understandings between Servicer and Agent relating to the subject matter hereof. No oral understanding, oral statement, or oral promises or oral inducements on the subject of this agreement exists.

The waiver by Servicer of any breach of any provision of this Agreement by Agent shall not operate or be construed as a waiver of any subsequent breach by the Agent.

Any notice required or permitted to be given under this Agreement shall be sufficient in writing, and if hand delivered or sent by first class mail to Servicer's or Agent's principal business address.

The rights and obligations of Agent shall not be assignable unless otherwise agreed to in writing.

This Agreement may not be modified, revised, altered, added to, or extended in any manner, superseded other than by an instrument in writing signed by all the parties hereto.

IN WITNESS WHEREOF, Agent and Servicer have executed this Agreement as of the day and year first above written.

SERVICER: AGENT:

By:_____   By:_____

Title:_____   Title:_____

CONSULTING AGREEMENT

THIS AGREEMENT made and entered into this ____ day of _____, ____ by and between _____ ("Client") and _____, ("Consultant").

WHEREAS, Client is desirous of purchasing property and casualty insurance coverages or products ("Coverage") to cover the following types of risks (specifically describe type of risk) and/or to cover the following property (specifically describe property, its location, uses and type of risk):

_____

_____

WHEREAS, Client is desirous of engaging Consultant to assist Client in evaluating risks and exposures, and identifying, negotiating, and procuring Coverage.

WHEREAS, Consultant wishes to help Client evaluate risks and exposures and identify, negotiate, and procure Coverage.

NOW THEREFORE, for and in consideration of the mutual promises and in consideration of the remuneration herein set forth, the parties agree as follows:

1. TERM. Client hereby engages Consultant and grants to Consultant, subject to the terms hereof, the authority to help Client evaluate risks and exposures and identify, negotiate and procure Coverage during the term of this Agreement which shall begin on _____ and expire on _____. This Agreement may be terminated without cause for any reason by either party upon ten (10) days written notice to the other. In the event of conduct by Consultant adverse to the interests of Client, this Agreement may be terminated immediately upon discovery of such an occurrence or event, without the necessity of further notice.

2. CLIENT'S RIGHT TO PROFESSIONAL COUNSEL. Client acknowledges and agrees that the procurement of Coverage encompasses many professional disciplines, and while Consultant possesses considerable general knowledge, Consultant is not expert in matters of law, tax, finance, structural conditions, hazardous materials, engineering, etc. Client acknowledges that Client has been advised by Consultant to seek professional expert assistance and advice in those and other areas of professional expertise. In the event that Consultant provides to Client names or sources for such advice and assistance, Client acknowledges and agrees that Consultant does not warrant or guarantee such advice, assistance, services and/or products.

3. CLIENT'S ROLE. Client agrees to work and cooperate with Consultant and assist Consultant in the process of evaluating risks and exposures and identifying, negotiating and procuring Coverage. Client agrees to provide to Consultant the complete and correct information Consultant needs to perform Consultant's services hereunder. Consultant acknowledges that such information may be confidential and agrees to only disseminate such information to prospective suppliers of Coverage and other persons who need to know or have access to such information for Consultant to provide services hereunder.

4. CLIENT'S RESPONSIBILITY. The duties of Consultant contained herein do not relieve Client from the responsibility of protecting Client's own interests. Client should read carefully all agreements and policies to assure that they adequately express Client's understanding of the Coverage. Client shall sign all authorizations, applications or other agreements associated with procuring Coverage; Consultant is not authorized to do so.

5. CONSULTANT'S AUTHORITY AND ROLE. Consultant is hereby authorized to evaluate risks and exposures, identify and present Coverage options to Client, to present prices and terms of Coverage to Client, and to negotiate prices and terms of Coverage on Client's behalf. Consultant agrees to: (a) meet with Client to discuss risks and exposures, Coverage objectives, Coverage requirements, time schedules, Client's financial capability, Coverage options, Coverage acquisition strategies and other procurement factors; (b) assist Client in identifying and examining available Coverages suitable for Client's purposes; (c) assist Client in presenting underwriting and other data to prospective Coverage suppliers; and (d) assist Client in negotiating, applying for, and acquiring a contract for Coverage.

6. COVERAGE DATE. Client desires that Coverage be procured by _____, ____.

7. PREMIUM CONSIDERATIONS. Client desires to expend a maximum premium of _____ per _____ (month, quarter, year, etc.) for Coverage. Client is responsible for and agrees to pay for Coverage procured and accepted by Client. Unless otherwise agreed, Consultant shall not be authorized to pay premiums on Client's behalf. However, if Client gives Consultant such authority, Client shall reimburse Consultant for such premiums.

8. COMPENSATION. Client agrees to pay as compensation to Consultant a fee of $_____ ("Consulting Fee"). **Unless otherwise agreed in writing, the Consulting Fee shall be above and in addition to the commissions or compensation received by Consultant from the supplier of Coverage.** Client agrees to pay out-of-pocket expenses reasonably incurred by Consultant which are directly attributed to services performed pursuant hereto and on behalf of Client not to exceed $_____.

The Consulting Fee will be paid by Client within ___ days after Coverage is procured. Expenses will be paid to Consultant within ___ days of billing.

Client agrees to pay the Consulting Fee and expenses set forth above if Client procures Coverage identified and presented to Client by Consultant from Consultant or any other person during the term of this Agreement or within _____ days of the termination of this Agreement. If Coverage is not procured due to Client's failure to cooperate or perform its duties hereunder and through no fault of Consultant, Consultant shall be entitled to reasonable expenses as set forth above and a consulting fee of $_____ for consultation time.

9. TRANSFER OR ASSIGNMENT. This Agreement shall not be transferred or assigned without the prior written consent of all parties. Any assignee shall fulfill all the terms and conditions of this Agreement. This Agreement shall inure to the benefit of, and be binding upon, the parties hereto, their heirs, successors, administrators, executors and assigns.

10. INDEMNIFICATION OF CONSULTANT. Although Consultant will use best efforts to identify and negotiate Coverage acceptable to Client, Consultant's failure to identify and negotiate Coverage acceptable to Client is not a breach of this Agreement. Further, Client agrees to indemnify Consultant and to hold Consultant harmless on account of any and all loss or damage arising out of this Agreement, provided Consultant is not at fault, including, but not limited to, attorney's fees reasonably incurred by Consultant.

11. ADDITIONAL PROVISIONS. _____
_____
_____
_____

EXECUTED on the date above written.

CLIENT   **CONSULTANT**

By: _____   By: _____
Its: _____   Its: _____

(Note: Depending on the jurisdiction, this agreement may be subject to Insurance Department review and approval.)

AGREEMENT FOR PURCHASE OF AGENCY ASSETS

THIS AGREEMENT MADE this ___ day of _____, _____ (the "Agreement") by and between
_____, a/an_____ of _____, _____, hereinafter referred to as
"Seller", and _____, a/an_____ of _____, _____,
hereinafter referred to as "Purchaser".

DEFINITIONS

For purposes of this Agreement, the following terms shall have the following meanings unless the context clearly
requires otherwise:

Company. A company issuing, brokering, selling or making a market for Policies .

Insurance, Investment, Banking and/or Credit Services. Insurance services include but are not limited to the
sale, renewal, service or delivery of insurance policies, annuities, insurance brokering services, insurance customer
services, risk management services and insurance related consulting or advisory services. Investment services
include, but are not limited to, the sale, renewal, service or delivery of mutual funds, stocks, bonds, notes,
debentures, real estate services, investment customer services, and investment related consulting and financial,
investment, or economic advisory services. Banking services include any banking service Seller is allowed to
perform under federal and/or state laws.   Credit services include, but are not limited to, origination or brokerage of
loans or mortgages, credit customer services, and credit related consulting or advisory services.

Person.   Any individual, sole proprietorship, partnership, joint venture, trust, unincorporated organization,
association, corporation, limited liability company, institution or other entity.

Policies. Any and all insurance services, policies, coverages or products sold, renewed, serviced or delivered
through Seller to any Person. Policies include, but are not limited to, any and all Insurance, Investment, Banking or
Credit Services, or policies, coverages or products associated therewith sold, renewed, serviced or delivered
through Seller to any Person.

Now, therefore, in consideration of the mutual promises, covenants, and agreements set forth hereinafter, the Seller
does hereby agree to sell and the Purchaser does hereby agree to purchase the agency assets hereinafter described on
the terms and conditions set forth as follows:

TERMS AND CONDITIONS

1. **Subject Matter of the Agreement**. Seller hereby agrees to sell, transfer, assign and convey unto the Purchaser
all of the Seller's right, title and interest in and to the general agency assets owned by Seller. Such sale shall
include: the "book of business"; customer accounts associated with all Policies; goodwill; customer lists; customer
files; customer renewals; customer records; and all other intangible assets associated with Seller's general agency
business which does business as _____ or which may have done business from any other
location under any other trade name. Such sale shall also include the office equipment and other personal property
specifically identified on the listing attached hereto as Exhibit C. All assets shall be conveyed unto Purchaser, free
and clear of any claims, liens and encumbrances whatever.   The assets described in this paragraph shall be
collectively referred to as "agency assets."

2. **Purchase Price**. In consideration of the sale of the above described agency assets, the Purchaser agrees to pay
the total sum of _____ Dollars ($_____) in the following manner:

(A) The sum of _____Dollars ($_____) as earnest money, the receipt of which is hereby
acknowledged.

(B) The sum of _____Dollars ($_____) shall be paid to Seller at the date of closing.

(C) The balance of the purchase price in the amount of _____ Dollars ($_____) shall be paid in _____ annual installments of _____ Dollars ($_____) which shall be due on the anniversary date of the closing of this Agreement.

3. Conveyance of Title and Delivery of Property.

(A) Seller shall convey title to the above described agency assets by a Bill of Sale which shall be executed, acknowledged, and delivered to the Purchaser on the closing date of this Agreement, free of all liens and encumbrances whatever. The bill of sale shall be in the form attached hereto as Exhibit A and made a part hereof by reference.

(B) Seller shall transfer to Purchaser the Policies that are a part of the book of business sold pursuant to this Agreement by delivering Transfer Letters to the Purchaser on the closing date of this agreement. The transfer letter shall be in the form attached hereto as Exhibit B and printed on Seller's letterhead and with Seller's original signatures. Seller furthermore agrees to sign any additional forms or letters which may be required to transfer said Policies.

(C) Seller shall deliver to Purchaser's primary office on the closing date of this Agreement the entire contents of all paper and electronic files for all of Seller's past, current and prospective customers.   Electronic files may be delivered in electronic text format using comma separated values or in paper format by printing customer lists, customer data, customer notes, customer accounting, customer history, Policy expiration lists, Policy notes, Policy accounting, Policy history, claims notes and other records which are stored in Seller's electronic files.

(D) Seller shall deliver to Purchaser's primary office on the closing date of this Agreement all office equipment and other personal property specifically identified on the listing attached hereto as Exhibit C.

4. Closing.
Closing of this sale shall occur on _____ (the "closing date"), unless (i) Purchaser, upon 5 days written notice to Seller, exercises its unilateral right to postpone the closing date ___ days, or (ii) another date is agreed upon in writing by the parties.

5. Effective Date of Transfer of Business and Obligations.

(A) All of the agency assets conveyed under the terms of this Agreement shall be transferred as of the closing date. For the purpose of this Agreement, the Policy inception date will determine on which day the Policy was written. If premiums are paid by a Policyholder to a Company in installments, it is agreed that the due date of each installment shall be considered a new Policy inception date. The Purchaser shall be entitled to all commissions for Policies written by Seller, or Seller's, owners, directors, officers, employees and independent contractors on or subsequent to the closing date.

(B) Seller shall be liable for all debts, premiums, claims and obligations incurred prior to the closing date. All accounts receivables for Policies written prior to the closing date shall remain the separate property of the Seller, provided that Seller pays all debts, premiums, claims and obligations on Policies written prior to closing date. Seller acknowledges that the value of the assets sold pursuant to this Agreement is diminished if Seller does not promptly pay its obligations to Customers, Companies and managing general agents for the net policy premiums on Policies written prior to the closing date. As such, if Purchaser becomes aware that any such net policy premiums are not paid when due, then Purchaser may elect, but is not obligated, to pay any such amounts on behalf of Seller, in which event Seller agrees to fully and promptly reimburse Purchaser.

(C) Purchaser will attempt to collect all funds owed to Seller for Policies written prior to the closing date. Seller appoints Purchaser as its attorney in fact to endorse checks made payable to Seller by Policy owners, Companies, managing general agents or other Persons. Any funds collected by Purchaser for the Seller will be remitted to Seller on a monthly basis. For a period of sixty (60) days after closing, Purchaser shall provide Seller with access to monthly agent statements for the specific purpose of verifying the amount of agency billed premiums or direct billed commissions which may be due Seller for Policies written prior to the closing date and attributable to Policies that are part of the book of business sold pursuant to this Agreement. Such access shall be upon reasonable advance written request and during such times and upon such conditions as shall not unreasonably impair the operations of Purchaser. Seller agrees to respect the confidential nature of such information.

(D) After the closing date, Seller shall not be responsible for payment to Purchaser of commissions on any reduction of premiums which result from policy cancellations, policy endorsements or policy audits for Policies and which are reflected on any Company statement dated after the closing date. After the closing date, Seller shall be responsible for any additional amounts due Customer, Companies or Managing General Agents which result from policy cancellations, policy endorsements, or policy audits for Policies and which are reflected on any Company statement dated prior the closing date. Correspondingly, after the closing date, Purchaser shall not be responsible for payment to Seller of commissions on any additional premiums which result from Policy endorsements or Policy audits for Policies and which are reflected on any Company statement dated after the closing date. After the closing date, Purchaser shall be responsible for any additional amounts due Customer, Companies or Managing General Agents which result from policy cancellations, policy endorsements, or policy audits for Policies and which are reflected on any Company statement dated after the closing date.

(E) Seller shall remit to Purchaser on the closing date any funds received by Seller for Policies written on or subsequent to the closing date.

(F) Purchaser shall be entitled to all profit sharing commissions, bonus commissions, prizes, advertising allowances or override commissions received on or after the closing date.

6. Hold Harmless Guaranty.

(A) Seller hereby agrees and promises to hold Purchaser harmless for any and all liability that may arise by reason of Seller's or Seller's owner's, directors, officers, employees and independent contractors negligence or failure to renew, issue or otherwise service any Policy prior to the date of closing, it being agreed that any liability for such errors and omissions in the transaction of business shall vest solely with Seller.

(B) Purchaser hereby agrees and promises to hold Seller harmless for any and all liability that may arise by reason of Purchaser's or Purchaser's owner's, directors, officers, employees and independent contractors negligence or failure to renew, issue or otherwise service any Policy after the date of closing, it being agreed that any liability for such errors and omissions in the transaction of business shall vest solely with Purchaser.

7. Contingencies. This agreement is further subject to Purchaser being approved for agency contracts with all Companies currently represented by the Seller. In the event of non-approval of one or more contracts, this Agreement may, at option of the Purchaser, become null and void and Purchaser shall be entitled to the return of all earnest money payments and all parties shall thereupon be released from any further liability under this Agreement. Further, this Agreement is subject to Purchaser's verification of Seller's information set forth in the Seller's Survey attached hereto as Exhibit I. In the event that a due diligence audit should disclose that Seller's information is not as stated in Exhibit I, this Agreement may be declared null and void and Purchaser shall be entitled to the return of all sum theretofore advanced, and all parties shall thereupon be released from any further liability under this Agreement.

8. Covenants of Seller.

(A) Seller does, hereby, covenant and agree that its owners, directors, officers and employees will, at all times, assist and cooperate with Purchaser in transferring to Purchaser all Policies previously written, serviced or sold by Seller or Seller's owners, directors, officers, employees or independent contractors.

(B) Seller and _____, individually, further agree that they will not engage directly or indirectly in the business of selling Policies in or within a _____ mile radius of _____, _____ for a period of five (5) years from and after the closing date. Seller and _____,individually, further agree that for a period of five (5) years from and after the closing date, they will not directly or indirectly solicit or write Policies for any customers that are a part of the book of business sold pursuant to this Agreement and will not directly or indirectly attempt to divert any customer that is a part of the book of business sold pursuant to this Agreement from continuing to do business with Purchaser. The parties acknowledge that the covenants set forth in this paragraph 8(B) are material to this agreement and that unless otherwise specifically stated herein, one-fourth (1/4) of the purchase price set forth in paragraph 2 shall be allocated to this covenant not to solicit and not to compete. Seller agrees that the covenants contained in this paragraph are reasonable and necessary and that Purchaser has paid ample consideration for same.

(C) Seller does hereby covenant and agree to deliver to buyer all evidence of ownership and origin of all agency assets.

(D) Seller does, hereby, covenant and agree to enforce, for the continued benefit of Purchaser, all non solicitation agreements or non compete agreements currently in force between Seller and its owners, producers, directors, officers, independent contractors and employees.

9. **Warranties and Representations of the Purchaser**. The Purchaser warrants and represents that it is a corporation, duly organized, existing and in good standing under the laws of the State of Kansas. Purchaser warrants and represents that it has taken all necessary corporate action, including, but not limited to, binding resolutions of all of its directors to enter into this agreement and to carry out the terms and conditions thereof.

10. **Warranties and Representations of the Sellers**.

(A) If Seller is a corporation, then Seller warrants that it is duly organized, existing and in good standing under the laws of the State of _____ and Seller warrants and represents that it has taken all necessary corporate action, including, but not limited to, binding resolutions/actions of all of its directors and shareholders to enter into this Agreement and to carry out the terms and conditions thereof.

(B) The Seller warrants and represents that it has received sales commissions, excluding profit sharing commissions and brokered policies commissions, of at least _____ Dollars ($_____), for the twelve (12) month period ending _____, _____. The Seller warrants and represents that it has provided accurate and complete third party documents containing commissions information and that an affidavit, a copy of which is attached hereto as Exhibit D, has been executed and attached to said documents.

(C) The Seller warrants and represents that it is the sole and legitimate owner of the agency assets to be purchased and sold pursuant to this Agreement.

(D) The Seller warrants and represents that it currently has an errors and omissions insurance policy in force and that a "tail" policy will be or has been purchased which provides for continuing errors and omissions insurance coverages, and will provide Purchaser with proof of such coverage upon request.

(E) The Seller warrants and represents that it has fully and accurately disclosed to Purchaser in writing in the form attached hereto as Exhibit E all of the written and verbal agreements that it currently has, or has had during the past twelve (12) months, with licensed producers, representatives, agents or other Persons related to Seller's agency assets.

(F) The Seller warrants and represents that it has fully and accurately disclosed to Purchaser in writing in the form attached hereto as Exhibit F : all trade names Seller currently uses or has used; all locations at or from which Seller conducts or has conducted agency business; Seller's chief executive office if Seller conducts business at more than one location; place of individual Seller's current and past places of residence (past five years) and the period during which Seller resided at such place; names of prior owners of any of the agency assets; and, the location of agency assets for preceding five (5) years.

(G) The Seller warrants and represents that it has fully and accurately disclosed to Purchaser all information elicited by the Seller's Survey attached hereto as Exhibit I.

11. **Use of Name and PO Box and Telephone Number**. As a result of the sale contemplated herein, the Purchaser shall on and after the date of closing be entitled to the use of the trade name described in paragraph 1 hereof. Furthermore, the Seller shall not use or authorize anyone else to use said trade name. The Purchaser shall acquire all rights to the telephone listings, telephone numbers and post office boxes listed under said trade name.

12. **Security Interest.**

(A) To secure the payment of the sums described in paragraph 2(C) hereof, Purchaser hereby grants to Seller a security interest in and to the agency assets which are purchased from Seller pursuant to this Agreement.

(B) The Purchaser agrees to execute and deliver to the Sellers a UCC-1 financing statement evidencing said security interest in form suitable for filing.

13. Default.

(A) Time is of the essence of this Agreement. In the event that the Purchaser shall fail to pay the amount due on the date of closing as described in paragraph 2(B) hereof, then this agreement shall immediately become null and void and the Seller shall be entitled to retain the earnest money described in paragraph 2(A) hereof as liquidated damages. In said event, this Agreement shall thereafter be null and void.

(B) In the event that the Purchaser shall fail to make any of the installment payments described in paragraph 2(C) hereof within fifteen (15) days of the payment due date, then the Seller, or their authorized agents, shall give written notice of such default to the Purchaser at the address shown hereinafter. In the event that such default is not cured within thirty (30) days of the mailing of such notice, then the Seller shall be entitled to take possession and control of all of the agency assets secured hereunder, subject to any other security interests, and in said event the Purchaser agrees to transfer, convey, and deliver all of said assets peacefully to the Seller.

14. Assignment of Purchaser's Interest. It is agreed that Purchaser has the unconditional right to assign or transfer all of Purchaser's rights and obligations obtained or incurred pursuant to this agreement to a qualified assignee or purchaser capable and having financial resources to honor all commitments contained herein, as may be determined by Purchaser. In the event of any such assignment or transfer, Purchaser hereby guaranties all payments due Seller under the terms of this Agreement.

15. Miscellaneous Agreements of the Parties. Unless specifically identified on the listing attached hereto as Exhibit G, the Purchaser shall not assume any of Seller's obligations with regards to employees, producers, independent contractors, lessors (real or personal property), vendors, suppliers, advertisers or utility companies.

16. Entire Agreement

(A) This Agreement contains all of the terms and conditions of agreement between the parties hereto relative to the subject matter hereof, and no other agreement relative thereto between them, whether past, present or future, shall be valid unless the same is reduced to writing and signed by each of the parties.

(B) Upon execution of this agreement, the confidentiality agreement previously signed by Purchaser, a copy of which is attached hereto as Exhibit H, is no longer valid and no longer enforceable.

(C) The parties agree that the following listed exhibits are an integral part of this agreement. The parties acknowledge that Exhibit C, Exhibit E, Exhibit F and Exhibit G are fully executed original documents. The parties further acknowledge that Exhibit D, Exhibit H and Exhibit I are copies of fully executed original documents.

Exhibit A- Bill of Sale
Exhibit B-Transfer Letter
Exhibit C-Listing of Office Equipment and Other Personal Property
Exhibit D-Affidavit
Exhibit E-List of Agreements
Exhibit F-Disclosure of Trade Names, etc.
Exhibit G- Listing of Obligations Assumed by Purchaser
Exhibit H- Confidentiality Agreement
Exhibit I - Seller's Survey

17. **Amendments.** This Agreement may not be modified, revised, altered, added to, or extended in any manner, or supersded other than by an instrument in writing signed by all the parties hereto. No waiver of any provision hereof shall be effective unless agreed to in writing by all parties hereto. Any modification or waiver shall only be effective for the specific instance and for the specific purpose for which given.

18. **Failure to Enforce, Not Waiver.** The failure by either party to enforce any provision of this Agreement shall not be in any way construed as a waiver of any such provision nor prevent such party thereafter from enforcing each and every other provision of this Agreement.

19. **Invalidity or Non-enforceability.** The invalidity or non-enforceability of any particular provision of this Agreement shall not affect the other provisions hereof, and this Agreement shall be construed in all respects as if such invalid or unenforceable provisions were omitted.

20. **Governing Law.** This Agreement shall be construed and governed by the laws of the State of Kansas. At the option of Purchaser, jurisdiction and venue for any dispute arising under or in relation to this Agreement will lie only in the State of Kansas with the Phillips County District Court, or the U.S. District Court having jurisdiction over Phillips County in the State of Kansas. In the event that a lawsuit, administrative proceeding or litigation is brought with respect to this Agreement, the prevailing party shall be entitled to be reimbursed for, and/or have judgment entered with respect to, all of its costs and expenses, including reasonable attorney's fees' and legal expenses.

21. **Notices.** Notices which may be required to be sent by Seller or Purchaser in accordance with this Agreement shall be sent to the address set forth below or such other address as may be designated by such party provided notice of such change in address has been given to the other party. Notices shall be deemed effective if in writing, and delivered by hand or mailed by United States Mail, postage prepaid, mailed by certified mail, with return receipt requested, or mailed by express courier with date of receipt confirmed. The effective date of notice shall be the day of delivery by hand; if mailed by regular mail, four business days following the mailing thereof; and, if by certified mail or express courier, the date of receipt thereof :

Seller Address   **Purchaser Address**

_____   _____
_____   _____
_____   _____

18. **Binding Effect.** This agreement executed in triplicate shall be binding upon each of the parties hereto, their heirs, administrators, successors and assigns. The use of the masculine shall include the feminine, and the use of the singular shall include the plural.

19. **Timeliness.** Timeliness and punctuality are essential elements of this Agreement.

SELLER: PURCHASER:

By:_____   By:_____

Title:_____   Title:_____

AGREEMENT NOT TO SOLICIT OR COMPETE

The undersigned agree(s) to and is (are) bound by the covenants not to solicit and not to compete set forth in paragraph 8(B) herein and specifically acknowledge that the covenants contained in said paragraph are reasonable and necessary and that the undersigned has received ample consideration for same.

_____   _____
_____,individually   _____, individually

AGREEMENT FOR ADVANCEMENT OF LOAN

THIS AGREEMENT FOR ADVANCEMENT OF LOAN (the "Agreement") is made and entered into as of the _____ day of _____,____, by and between _____ ("Lender") and _____ ("Borrower").

RECITALS

WHEREAS, Lender has agreed to loan to Borrower the amount of $_____ for the purpose of _____; and

WHEREAS, this Agreement and the Loan Documents, as defined herein shall apply to all existing and future loans or advances made by Lender to Borrower.

NOW, THEREFORE, in consideration of the terms and conditions set forth herein and of any loans or advances now or hereafter made to or for the benefit of Borrower by Lender, and for other good and valuable consideration, the receipt and sufficiency of which are hereby acknowledged, Lender and Borrower agree as follows:

DEFINITIONS

For purposes of this Agreement, the following terms shall have the following meanings unless the context clearly requires otherwise:

Agency's Assets. All of Borrower's personal property, whether tangible or intangible, and all of Borrower's interest in property and fixtures, now owned or existing or hereafter acquired and wherever located, including without limitation, the following: (a) all inventory, machinery, equipment, goods and supplies; (b) all accounts, including without limitation, the Agent's Account and Customer Accounts; (c) all instruments, documents (including, without limitation, the Customer Files) policies and certificates of insurance, money, chattel paper, investment property, deposits, warehouse receipts and things in action; (d) all general intangibles and rights to payment or proceeds of any kind, including without limitation, rights to insurance proceeds and letter of credit proceeds; (e) all contract rights and interests of any kind, including without limitation, the rights and interests set forth in the Agent Agreement and any Subagent Agreement; and (f) any and all additions, attachments, parts, repairs, accessories, accessions, replacements and substitutions to or for any of the forgoing. The above description of property shall also include, but not be limited to, any and all telephone numbers, rights to the lease of office space, post office boxes or other mailing addresses, rights to trademarks and use of trade names, rights to software licenses, and rents received by Borrower for the lease of office space. Proceeds and products of the above property are also covered.

Agent Account. An account on Master Agent's ledgers to which the Master Agent records amounts due Master Agent from Borrower and amounts due Borrower from Master Agent.

Agent Agreement. Agreement which has been or will be executed by and between Borrower and Master Agent providing for Borrower to sell, renew, service or deliver Policies exclusively through Master Agent which has been or will be signed by Borrower and Master Agent.

Agent of Record. Person designated on Company's records as the agent or representative regarding a specific Policy and the owner of all Sales Commissions.

Closing Date. The date upon which the Lender extends credit to Borrower.

Collateral Preservation Agreement. Agreement, as amended from time to time, between the Master Agent and Lender which requires the Master Agent to help protect and preserve Lender's collateral interest in certain Agency Assets including, without limitation, Agent's Account and Customer Files.

Company. A company issuing, brokering, selling or making a market for Policies and which has a contract with Master Agent.

Customer Accounts. A Person who has a Policy purchased from, serviced, renewed or delivered through Borrower. Customer Accounts may be owned by Borrower or a Subagent of Borrower.

Customer Files. Documents, data and correspondence to or from Customer Accounts, Borrower, Master Agent, Companies, or others regarding Policies.

Insurance, Investment, Banking and/or Credit Services. Insurance services include but are not limited to the sale, renewal, service or delivery of insurance policies, annuities, insurance brokering services, insurance customer services, risk management services and insurance related consulting or advisory services. Investment services include, but are not limited to, the sale, renewal, service or delivery of mutual funds, stocks, bonds, notes, debentures, real estate services, investment customer services, investment related consulting, and financial, investment, or economic advisory services. Banking services include any banking service Borrower is allowed to perform under federal and/or state laws. Credit services include, but are not limited to, origination or brokerage of loans or mortgages, credit customer services, and credit related consulting or advisory services. At any point in time, Insurance, Investment, Banking and Credit Services shall be limited to those services then offered by Master Agent.

Lender. The Lender named above , its successors, assigns or designees.

Loan Documents. This Agreement and all other agreements, instruments and documents, including without limitation, any guaranties, mortgages, deeds of trust, notes, pledges, powers of attorney, consents, assignments, contracts, notices, security agreements, leases, subordination agreements, financing statements and all other written documents heretofore, now and/or from time to time hereafter executed by and/or on behalf of Borrower and delivered to Lender in connection therewith, including, without limitation, the documents referenced in paragraphs 1 through 11 herein.

Master Agent. The party with whom Borrower enters an Agent Agreement. Pursuant to the Agent Agreement, Master Agent is made the "agent of record" for all Policies sold, renewed, serviced or delivered throughBorrower. Master Agent is Borrower's primary contact with Companies and other suppliers.

Person. Any individual, sole proprietorship, partnership, joint venture, trust, unincorporated organization, association, corporation, limited liability company, institution or other entity.

Policies. Any and all insurance services, policies, coverages or products sold, renewed, serviced or delivered through Borrower to any Person. Policies include, but are not limited to, any and all Insurance, Investment, Banking or Credit Service, or policy, coverage or product associated therewith sold, renewed, serviced or delivered through Borrower to any Person.

Sales Commissions. Commissions paid by Companies to Master Agent or assigned by Borrower to Master Agent for the sale, renewal, service or delivery of a specific Policy through Borrower. Sales Commissions are not normally contingent upon factors such as Master Agent's loss ratio, premium volume, sales volume or special concessions negotiated by the Master Agent. For the purposes of this Agreement, Sales Commissions shall specifically exclude amounts received by the Master Agent for advertising allowances, prizes, override commissions, profit sharing commissions, supplier bonus commissions and other similar payments. However, Sales Commissions shall specifically include amounts paid to Borrower by the Master Agent pursuant to a bonus plan, the terms of which are defined by the Master Agent in its sole discretion and for which the Master Agent makes no representation regarding future payments or Borrower eligibility. Sales Commissions shall also include any consulting fees, advisory fees, placement fees, service fees, renewal fees or any similar payments paid on or related to any Customer Account by any Person.

Subagent. A Person who has entered or may enter into a Subagent Agreement with Borrower.

Page 2 of 11 (Form BCC-M Revised 03/27/00)

Subagent Agreement. An agreement entered into by and between Borrower and Subagent and approved by Master Agent pursuant to which Subagent is allowed vested ownership rights in Customer Accounts coded to Subagent and Borrower performs certain accounting and processing services for Subagent.

Trust Agreement. Trust Agreement dated _____, as such may be amended from time to time, executed by Master Agent and a trustee pursuant to which Master Agent, among other things, transfers control of Sales Commissions to a trustee for such trustee's distribution pursuant to the terms thereof.

<h2 style="text-align:center">TERMS AND CONDITIONS</h2>

This Agreement is subject to the following terms and conditions.

1. Promissory Note. Borrower shall execute a promissory note (substantially in the form attached hereto as Exhibit ___) in the amount of $_____ (the "Note"). The Note shall provide for monthly payments , payable on the first day of every month, and shall mature _____ months after the date of said Note. The Note shall also provide for an interest rate that begins at _____% and varies annually on December 31st of each year to a rate that is the New York Prime Rate, as published in the Wall Street Journal on December 31 of each year or on the next banking business day nearest to that date, plus _____percent (____%).

2. Security Agreement. Borrower shall execute a security agreement (substantially in the form attached hereto as Exhibit B) and security agreement addendum (substantially in the form attached hereto as Exhibit C) which provides for, among other terms, a purchase money security interest in the acquired Agency Assets.

3. Financing Statement. Borrower shall execute a UCC-1 financing statement form (substantially in the form attached hereto as Exhibit D) which shall be filed to perfect Lender's security interest in the Agency Assets and such other assets Lender may require.

4. Guaranty. Upon Lender's request, Borrower shall provide to Lender a duly executed continuing and unlimited guaranty agreement of Borrower's principals, officers, directors, spouse, or other Person Lender may require or Borrower may offer, substantially in the form attached hereto as Exhibit E (the "Guaranty").   The Guaranty shall unconditionally guaranty the payment and performance of each and every existing and future debt, liability and obligation of Borrower to Lender.

5. Opinions of Counsel. a) Borrower shall provide to Lender, upon Lender's request and substantially in the form attached hereto as Exhibit F, the opinion(s) of Borrower's counsel.

b) Borrower shall also provide to Lender, upon Lender's request, the opinion of Borrower's counsel as to these same or substantially similar points with regard to Borrower's purchase of Agency Assets.

6. Affidavit Regarding Financial Status and other Material Facts. Borrower shall execute on the Closing Date an affidavit substantially in the form attached hereto as Exhibit G (the Affidavit") which Affidavit shall certify, under penalty of perjury that there have been no material adverse changes in Borrower's financial status or any other circumstances which Lender deems material to its decision to extend credit.

7. Authorization to Release Information. Borrower hereby authorizes any Person that may have agency, loan, financial, credit, valuation or other confidential or non-confidential information to release to Lender such information as Lender, in its sole discretion, deems necessary to respond to regulatory inquires; for the performance of audits, quality control or other reviews or to market the Loan Documents; or for any other legitimate purpose. Furthermore, upon Lender's request, Borrower shall sign a release substantially in the form attached hereto as Exhibit H authorizing the release to Lender of any financial, credit, valuation or other confidential or non-confidential information which Lender, in its sole discretion, deems necessary to respond to regulatory inquires; to perform audits, quality control or other reviews, or to market the Loan Documents; or for any other legitimate purpose.

8. Lender's Protection Addendum. Borrower and Master Agent shall execute a Lender's Protection Addendum substantially in the form attached hereto as Exhibit I, which shall be made a part of and attached to the Agent

Agreement. The Lender's Protection Addendum sets forth terms and conditions applicable to Borrower and Master Agent and their rights and obligations pertaining to Lender, Lender's security interest and the loan. By executing the Lender's Protection Addendum, among other things, Borrower agrees to and acknowledges the existence of the Collateral Preservation Agreement and certain obligations and duties of Master Agent to Lender set forth therein which may have a material effect on Borrower.

9. Settlement or Closing Statement. Upon Lender's request, Borrower shall sign a settlement or closing statement substantially in the form attached hereto as Exhibit J, which pertains to and authorizes the distribution of loan proceeds and delineates, among other items, certain transaction fees and costs.

10. Financial Reports and Additional Documents. a) Borrower will provide to Lender annually and, as soon as is practicable at any other time following Lender's request, any financial statement or financial, credit, valuation, organizational or other such confidential or non-confidential information Lender may deem necessary in its discretion. Upon Lender's request, Borrower shall certify such statements, valuations or other information. Upon Lender's request, Borrower shall provide statements, valuations or other information audited by a qualified third party and/or prepared in accordance with generally accepted accounting practices or GAAP standards. In addition, upon Lender's request, Borrower agrees to obtain and provide to Lender any statements, valuations or other information (confidential or non-confidential) Lender may deem necessary in its discretion pertaining to any or all guarantors, and which shall, at Lender's discretion, be certified, audited, and/or prepared in accordance with generally accepted accounting practices or GAAP standards. Borrower authorizes Lender to provide any such information to trustees a party of the Trust Agreement, auditors, regulators, attorneys, consultants, rating agencies, analysts, prospective purchasers of Borrower's loan or other Person needing such information for legitimate purposes. Borrower holds Lender, its owners, officers, directors, partners, independent contractors and employees harmless from any and all claims, damages or liability resulting from any further and improper disclosure of such information by such third parties.

b) Borrower agrees to sign, acknowledge, deliver, and file any additional documents, statements or certifications that Lender may consider necessary to carry out the intent of this Agreement; to perfect, continue and preserve Borrower's obligations under any Loan Document; to perfect, continue or preserve Lender's lienholder status; to replace or correct lost, misplaced, incorrectly filed, misstated or incorrect Loan Documents; to correct or adjust for clerical errors; to complete incomplete or deficient Loan Documents; to assure that the executed Loan Documents will conform to and be acceptable in the market place in the instance of transfer, sale or conveyance by Lender of its interest in and to said Loan Documents; to assure that the Loan Documents are in compliance with all laws, rules, regulations or the requirements of any prospective purchaser to whom Lender seeks to market the Loan Documents; to enable Lender to sell, convey, seek guaranty, insure or market the Loan Document to any Person. Upon Lender's request, Borrower shall execute a limited power of attorney which grants to Lender the power and authority to sign, acknowledge, deliver and file as Borrower's attorney in fact any such additional documents, statements, or certifications. Any written request for additional documentation made by Lender shall be prima facie evidence of the necessity for same.

11. Acknowledgment. Upon Lender's request, Borrower shall deliver to Lender on or before the Closing Date, an acknowledgment of a third party in substantially the form attached hereto as Exhibit K. Pursuant to such acknowledgment, said third party shall swear and attest under penalty of perjury that he/she witnessed Borrower or Borrower's authorized representative sign the Loan Documents described in paragraphs 1 through 10 herein, and that Borrower or Borrower's authorized representative is the signatory whom he/she represents to be.

12. Assignment of Agency Assets. (a) Borrower grants, conveys and assigns to Lender as additional security all the right, title and interest in and to Borrower's Agency Assets, including without limitation, Borrower's rights, title and interest in and to the Agent Agreement, Subagent Agreements, Agent's Account and Customer Accounts. Borrower shall defend the rights of Lender in and to Agency Assets against all claims and demands of all Persons at any time claiming the same or any interest therein adverse to Lender and shall keep the Agency Assets free from liens, assignments, and other security interests except for the assignment of security interest granted pursuant to the Loans Documents.

(b) Borrower may collect, receive, enjoy and use the Agency Assets so long as Borrower is not in default under the terms of any of the Loan Documents. Borrower agrees that the assignment of Agency Assets shall be immediately effective between the parties to this Agreement and that it shall be effective as to third parties when Lender or its agent notifies Borrower of default, Borrower fails to cure such default within the time allowed hereunder, and Lender demands that the Agency Assets be transferred and paid directly to Lender.

(c) Borrower agrees that Lender, without liability to Borrower, may take actual possession of the Agency Assets without the necessity of commencing legal action and that actual possession is deemed to occur when Lender or its agent notifies Borrower of default, Borrower fails to cure such default within the time allowed hereunder, and demands that the Agency Assets be transferred and paid directly to Lender. Borrower agrees that, upon Borrower's default and failure to cure default within the time allowed hereunder, Lender may, without liability to Borrower, transfer any of the Agency Assets or evidence thereof into its own name or that of its designee and/or demand, collect, convert, redeem, receipt for, settle, compromise, adjust, sue for, foreclose or realize upon its collateral in its own name, its designee's name or in the name of Borrower.

(d) On payment in full of the obligations and all other charges owed by Borrower to Lender under the Loan Documents, Lender shall execute and deliver to Borrower a release of this assignment.

13. Default. (a) Lender may upon written notice to Borrower, declare Borrower to be in default if: Borrower fails to fulfill or perform any term, condition or obligation set forth in any Loan Document, including without limitations Borrower's failure to make payments when due in accordance with the terms of the Note; or, if any representation or warranty set forth in any Loan Document is not as represented or warranted by Borrower.

(b) In addition, Lender may upon written notice to Borrower, declare Borrower to be in default upon the occurrence of any of the following events:

i. Borrower's failure to fulfill, perform or enforce any term, condition or obligation set forth in any agreement by Borrower to purchase Agency Assets that are related to or the subject of the Loan Documents;

ii. Borrower's failure to fulfill, perform or enforce any term, condition or obligation set forth in the Agent Agreement;

iii. any representation or warranty set forth in the Agent Agreement is not as represented or warranted by Borrower;

iv. the Agent Agreement is terminated by Borrower or Master Agent;

v. the total annual Sales Commissions for the most recent calendar year (or the immediately preceding twelve month period if selected by Lender) decrease to _____ percent or less of the principal balance of the Note;

vi. a significant impairment of Lender's prospect of any payment, performance, or ability to realize upon assets in which it has a security interest arises;

vii. an individual Borrower's insolvency, death or legal incapacitation; a guarantor's insolvency, death or legal incapacitation; or, the insolvency, death or legal incapacitation of a principal, officer or owner of Borrower;

viii. the refusal by any guarantor to guaranty the payment and performance of any future debt, liability and obligation of Borrower to Lender;

ix. if at any time the total of all outstanding obligations of Borrower (and/or any guarantor of Borrower's obligations, at Lender's sole discretion) to Lender and/or any other Person exceeds _____ (Note: Lender may select market value net worth requirement or in other manner limit increases in Borrower's or a Guarantor's debt load; no such limitations indicated by "N/A");

x. if, without Lender's prior written consent, _____'s ownership interest in _____ is transferred, diluted or further encumbered in any manner, including but not limited to, the issuance of new shares, assignment or gift of shares, the substitution of shares, the hypothecation or pledge of shares (Note:

Applies at Lender's discretion, if Borrower is a corporation, or if individual Borrower pledges shares of a corporation as collateral; inapplicability indicated by "N/A");

xi. if, without Lender's prior written consent, _____ distributes in any successive 12 month period by cash, assets, salary, consulting fees, dividends, loans, payment in kind, or other such distribution directly or indirectly to Borrower; Borrower's owners, partners, principals, directors, officers, spouse; or guarantors, any amount in excess of the greater of (i) or (ii): (i)_____ ; or (ii) annual earnings of _____ before interest, taxes, depreciation and amortization, less any applicable debt payments of _____ (Note: At Lender's discretion; inapplicability indicated by "N/A") ;

x. if, Borrower does not pay obligations associated with the Agency Assets or the operation of Borrower's agency in a timely manner and Lender, in its sole discretion, determines Borrower's delinquency will materially impair Lender's security interest.

(c) A default by Borrower in performing under the terms of one Loan Document shall constitute a default under the terms of all other Loan Documents.

(d) A default by Borrower in performing the obligations and duties of any contract relating to Borrower's business shall constitute a default under the terms of this Agreement.

14. Remedies Upon and Effect of Default. In addition to any remedy or right Lender has under any Loan Document, the Uniform Commercial Code or other law, and in addition to any effect of default set forth in any other Loan Document, the Uniform Commercial Code or other law, in the event Borrower fails to cure any monetary default within five (5) calendar days or any non monetary default within fifteen (15) calendar days:

(a) Borrower shall cooperate fully with Lender or a receiver and promptly endorse, set over, transfer and deliver to Lender or a receiver any Agency Assets in Borrower's possession or held by a third party. Borrower expressly agrees and acknowledges Lender's or a receiver's right to Agency Assets, right to possession of Agency Assets and right to operate Borrower's business without the necessity of commencing legal action and without Borrower's further action or authorization.

(b) Borrower shall deposit any receipts received by Borrower in the Receipts Trust Account described in the Lender's Protection Addendum or in such other deposit account designated by Lender.

(c) For a period of three (3) years after Borrower's default, Borrower and _____, individually, shall not directly or indirectly solicit or write Policies for any of Borrower's customers and shall not directly or indirectly attempt to divert any of Borrower's customers from continuing to do business with Master Agent, its successors, assigns or designees. Borrower and _____, individually, agree that this prohibition is reasonable and necessary and that the credit extended to Borrower is ample consideration for this restriction. Borrower and _____, individually, understand that Borrower and _____, individually, are not prohibited from working for any other company or in any particular line of work, but that this covenant not to compete only restricts the Borrower and _____, individually, from writing insurance for or contacting in person, by telephone, by mail, or by any other means, those customers or potential customers he/she worked with while an agent of Master Agent.

(d) Borrower shall enforce, for the continued benefit of Lender, all non solicitation agreements or non compete agreements currently in force between Borrower and its owners, officers, directors, partners, independent contractors and employees.

(e) Borrower shall cause, Borrower's owners, officers, directors, partners, independent contractors and employees to cooperate with Lender in transferring ownership of all property to Lender.

(f) Lender, without appointing a receiver, shall be entitled, but is not required, to take possession and control of the Agency Assets and collect the rents, issues, and profits thereof. However, Lender shall be entitled, but is not required, to have a receiver appointed by a court of competent jurisdiction to take possession and control of the Agency Assets and collect the rents, issues, and profits thereof. In the event a receiver is appointed, the amount so collected by the receiver shall be applied under the direction of the court to the payment of any judgment rendered or amount found due under the Loan Documents. However, under no circumstances whatsoever shall the appointment of the receiver be considered to create a control of Borrower's business by Lender and at all times the receiver shall be an agent apart from Lender and responsible only to the appointing court.

(g) All rights and remedies of Lender under this Agreement and the Loan Documents shall be cumulative, and the exercise of one or more rights or remedies shall not preclude the exercise of any other right or remedy available under this Agreement or applicable law.

15. Contingencies; Closing Date. Lender's extension of credit to Borrower shall be contingent upon: (i) Lender's receipt of all duly executed, original (and recorded as required by Lender) Loan Documents; (ii) Lender's receipt of the duly executed, original Agent Agreement satisfactory to Lender with duly executed, original Lender's Protection Addendum attached thereto; (iii) Lender's satisfaction with the due diligence inspection conducted with respect to _____; (iv) Lender's satisfaction with Borrower's interview; (v) Borrower's purchase of Agency Assets and evidence satisfactory to Lender that Borrower has exclusive, good and marketable title to such assets; (vi) if requested by Lender, Lender's receipt of copies of the agreements described in paragraphs 17 and 28 herein;   and, (vii) Lender's receipt of duly executed, original Trust Agreement and Collateral Preservation Agreement;   (viii) Borrower's compliance with all other terms and conditions set forth in the Loan Documents, Agent Agreement and Lender's Protection Addendum. The Closing Date shall be no later than 60 days from the date hereof, unless otherwise agreed to in writing by the parties.   In the event the Closing Date does not occur within 60 days from the date hereof and the parties do not agree upon an extension of the Closing Date, Lender shall have no further duties under any Loan Document and Borrower shall reimburse Lender for any out-of-pocket expenses incurred by Lender in connection with the loan or in preparation for the extension of credit under the Loan Documents.

16. Payment of Costs and Fees; Set-off. Borrower shall pay at closing all costs, expenses (including without limitation attorney's fees and other professional fees), and taxes incurred by Lender in connection with the negotiation, preparation, execution, delivery and recording of the Loan Documents.   In addition, **Borrower shall pay immediately upon demand by Lender all costs and expenses (including without limitation attorney's fees and other professional fees) incurred by Lender in connection with the administration or enforcement of the Loan Documents relating to a breach by Borrower of any Loan Documents or otherwise.** Any such amount may be added to the principal balance of the loan or offset by Lender from any funds held by Lender or held in trust or by a third party, for Borrower's benefit or otherwise, before or after loan payoff.

17. Agreements with Employees, Independent Contractors, Owners, Directors, Officers and Producers. (a) Without Lender's prior written consent, Borrower shall not enter into any employment, producer or other agreement which purports to vest or transfer ownership of Agency Assets. Unless otherwise agreed by Lender in writing, Borrower further agrees that all owners, directors, officers, as well as all employees, independent contractors, producers or other such persons having insurance or other financial services licenses or authority, shall enter into written agreements with Borrower containing an acknowledgment of Lender's priority position in Agency Assets, and containing a covenant that such person, for a period of at least three (3) years following termination of such agreement, will not directly or indirectly solicit or write Policies for any of Borrower's customers and will not directly or indirectly attempt to divert any of Borrower's customers from continuing to do business with Borrower, its successors, assigns or designees. Borrower agrees that it shall enforce such provisions for its benefit and for the benefit of Lender. Borrower agrees to provide to Lender upon Lender's written request: copies of employment, producer or other such agreements pertaining to Borrower's business or operations; and, any employees', independent contractors', owners', directors', officers' and producers' acknowledgment of Lender's priority position in the Agency Assets and other property which are the subject of the Loan Documents or which secure the loan.

(b) Notwithstanding the restrictions set forth in paragraph 17(a), Lender authorizes Borrower to enter into Subagent Agreements so long as same are in compliance with the terms and conditions of the Agent Agreement. Lender acknowledges that pursuant to the Subagent Agreement a Subagent shall have vested ownership rights in Customer Accounts coded to Subagent as indicated on the Agent Account and that Lender's security interest in Customer Accounts owned by Subagent shall be subject to Subagent's vested interest. Lender acknowledges that Borrower does not purport to grant a security interest in the ownership rights Subagent has in Customer Accounts coded to Subagent. Instead, Borrower security interest is limited to Borrower's interest in and relating to Customer Accounts owned by Subagents. Such rights include, without limitation, contract rights and interests of any kind set forth in the Subagent Agreement, rights to payment pursuant to the Subagent Agreement, and rights to any accounts created or described in such Subagent Agreement.

18. Right to Assign or Delegate.   (a) Lender may assign or delegate all or any part of its rights, title, interest or obligations in and to this Agreement or under any Loan Document to one or more Persons without the consent of Borrower. Lender may also assign or delegate all or any part of its rights, interest or obligations to service the loan which is the subject of the Loan Documents to one or more Persons without the consent of Borrower.   Any such assignment by Lender shall be without further recourse to Lender.

(b) Borrower shall not assign or delegate all or any part of its rights, title, interest or obligations under any Loan Document, Agent Agreement or agreement to purchase agency assets without the prior written consent of Lender.

19. Indemnification and Hold Harmless. Borrower hereby agrees to and acknowledges the existence of the Trust Agreement.   Borrower agrees to hold Lender, the trust, trustees under the Trust Agreement, and their owners, officers, directors, partners, employees, and independent contractors thereof (collectively the "indemnified parties") harmless from any and all liability for the distribution of amounts in accordance with the terms and priorities of the Trust Agreement and for incorrect or improper distribution of such amounts except to the extent such incorrect or improper distribution was caused by such indemnified party's willful or gross misconduct.

20. Change in Status. Borrower agrees to notify Lender immediately upon any change in Borrower's status which may result in the material impairment of Borrower's ability to perform any or all terms of any Loan Documents or which may materially impair Lender's security interest. Such material change in status includes but is not limited to: (i) a significant loss of business, or a loss of a large Customer Account; (ii) a significant change in Borrower's health, financial circumstances, or family status; or (iii) an adverse claim, proceeding, demand or action against Borrower, or Borrower's business. In the event of such change in Borrower's status, Borrower agrees to cooperate fully with Lender to protect Lender's security interest.

21. Insurance. Borrower agrees to obtain insurance which insures Borrower's person or business, and which is of the type and in the amount which Lender deems necessary to protect its interest. Borrower agrees to obtain insurance coverage on Borrower's owners, key employees, producers, independent contractors, officers or directors of the types and in the amounts which Lender deems necessary to protect its interest. Any such insurance policies shall, at Lender's discretion, name Lender as irrevocable beneficiary or as an additional insured. In addition, Lender may, in its sole discretion, require that it be assigned the cash value of any insurance policy as additional security.

22. Agreement to Purchase Agency Assets. Borrower shall not amend or waive any material term of any agreement to purchase agency assets without the prior written consent of Lender. Further, Borrower shall enforce all material terms of such agreement, including but not limited to any agreement or covenant not to solicit or compete, for its benefit and for the benefit of Lender.

23. Protection of Property. Borrower will use its best efforts to preserve the value of Borrower's Agency Assets and the property in which Lender has a security interest. Borrower shall not directly or indirectly commit or allow any impairment, deterioration, diversion, or transfer of such property not in the ordinary course of business without Lender's prior written consent.   Borrower will not permit any substantial change in the operation of its business without Lender's prior written consent.   Borrower will pay before or as they become due all taxes, assessments, liens, encumbrances, lease payments, and other obligations relating to its business.

24. Authority to Perform. If Borrower fails to perform any duty or any of the covenants contained in any Loan Document, Agent Agreement, a Subagent Agreement or other agreement related to Borrower's business, Lender may without notice perform or cause such duty or covenant to be performed. Borrower appoints Lender as attorney in fact to sign Borrower's name or pay any amount necessary for performance. Lender's right to perform for Borrower shall not create an obligation to perform, and Lender's failure to perform will not preclude Lender from exercising any of Lender's other rights under the law or any Loan Document. Any amount paid by or incurred by Lender may be added to the principal balance of the loan or offset by Lender from any funds held by Lender or held in trust or by a third party, for Borrower's benefit or otherwise, before or after loan payoff.

25. Prior Security Interest. With regard to any other security agreement or other lien document purporting to create a prior or subordinate security interest or encumbrance on any Agency Asset, Borrower hereby agrees: (i) to make all payments when due and to perform or comply with all covenants contained therein; (ii) to promptly deliver to Lender any notices that Borrower receives from the holder of such security interest; and (iii) not to allow any modification or extension of nor to request any future advances under any note or agreement secured by the lien document without Lender's prior written consent. Borrower warrants that it has disclosed in writing any such prior or subordinate security interest to Lender and that nothing in this paragraph is to be interpreted to allow Borrower to grant a prior or subordinate security interest in the Agency Assets without Lender's prior written consent.

26. Purchase Money Security Interest. The security interest granted in the Loan Documents secures this loan (including all extensions, renewals, refinancings and modifications thereof) and any other debt Borrower has with Lender now or in the future and, if used to purchase Agency Assets, grants Lender a purchase money security interest. Borrower and Lender agree that the security interest of any future loan or advances by Lender not to purchase additional Agency Assets shall be subordinate to the security on any amounts loaned to Borrower by Lender for the purchase of Agency Assets, now or in the future.

27. Allocation of Loan Payments, Prepayments, and Payments on Default to Reduce Debt. Borrower hereby agrees that Lender may allocate the payments it receives in any manner which Lender deems necessary. This allocation may include but is not limited to current loan amounts, any prepayments, and any past due payments which may otherwise place Borrower in default. This discretion also allows Lender to determine whether to apply the loan payment proceeds to interest or principal. **Borrower hereby further agrees that the allocation of the loan payment proceeds is absolutely within the discretion of Lender and therefore waives any objections that Borrower might otherwise express with the allocation amounts.**

REPRESENTATIONS AND WARRANTIES

28. Agreement to Purchase Agency Assets. Borrower represents and warrants that it has provided a true and accurate copy of the agreement to purchase Agency Assets which are related to or the subject of the Loan Documents. Borrower also warrants that such agreement contains a covenant that the seller, for a period of at least three (3) years following closing of such agreement, will not directly or indirectly solicit or write Policies for any of Borrower's customers and will not directly or indirectly attempt to divert any of Borrower's customers from continuing to do business with Borrower, its successors, assigns or designees.

29. Other Representations and Warranties. Borrower warrants and represents to and covenants with Lender that: (a) Borrower has the right, power and capacity and is duly authorized and empowered to enter into, execute, deliver and perform this Agreement and the Loan Documents; (b) the execution, delivery and/or performance by Borrower of this Agreement and the Loan Documents shall not, by the lapse of time, the giving of notice or otherwise, constitute a violation of any applicable law or a breach of any provision contained in Borrower's Articles of Incorporation, Bylaws or similar document, or contained in any agreement, instrument or document to which Borrower is now or hereafter a party or by which it is or may be bound; (c) Borrower is now, and at all times hereafter shall be solvent, and generally paying its debts as they mature and Borrower now owns (or has an interest acceptable to Lender in) and shall at all time hereafter own (or have an interest acceptable to Lender in) property which, at a fair valuation, is greater than the sum of its debts; (d) Borrower is not and will not be, during the term hereof, in violation of any applicable federal, state or local statute, regulation or ordinance that in any respect materially and adversely affects its business, property, assets, operations or condition, financial or otherwise; (e) Borrower is not in default with respect to any indenture, loan agreement, mortgage, deed or other similar agreement relating to the borrowing of monies to which it is a party or by which it is bound; (f) since _____, there has been no material adverse change in the financial condition or other circumstances of Borrower and no change to the financial or other information provided to Lender pursuant to this Agreement; and, (g) Borrower has obtained all federal, state and local licenses necessary to conduct its business as contemplated by the Loan Documents.

MISCELLANEOUS TERMS AND CONDITIONS

30. Amendments. This agreement may not be modified, revised, altered, added to, or extended in any manner, or superseded other than by an instrument in writing signed by all the parties hereto.   No waiver of any provision hereof shall be effective unless agreed to in writing by all parties hereto. Any modification or waiver shall only be effective for the specific instance and for the specific purpose for which given. Borrower agrees and acknowledges that Lender may also be required to obtain the approval of other persons or entities before entering into an amendment or granting a waiver.

31. Failure to Enforce, Not Waiver. The failure by Lender to enforce any provision of this Agreement shall not be in any way construed as a waiver of any such provision nor prevent Lender thereafter from enforcing each and every other provision of this Agreement.

32. Execution in Duplicate. The Agreement may be executed in duplicate, each of which shall be deemed an original, but all of which together shall constitute one and the same instrument which shall represent the agreement of the parties hereto.

33. Invalidity or Non-enforceability. The invalidity or non-enforceability of any particular provision of this Agreement shall not affect the other provisions hereof, and this Agreement shall be construed in all respects as if such invalid or unenforceable provisions were omitted.

34. Binding Effect. This Agreement shall be binding upon and inure to the benefit of the parties hereto and their heirs, administrators, successors, assigns and legal representatives but the rights and property interest hereunder shall not be assignable by any party except as set forth herein. The use of the masculine shall include the feminine, and the use of the singular shall include the plural.

35. Survival. This Agreement shall create and constitute the continuing obligation of the parties hereto in accordance with its terms, and shall remain in full force and effect until the loan is paid in full. The indemnification and hold harmless provisions and the provisions of paragraph 7 hereof shall be continuing and shall survive any termination of this Agreement.

36. Integration. **This Agreement (including all exhibits and addenda hereto) together with the other Loan Documents contains the entire agreement between the parties hereto and shall supersede and take precedence over any and all prior agreements, arrangements or understandings between the parties relating to the subject matter hereof.   No oral understandings, oral statements, oral promises or oral inducements exist.   No representations, warranties, covenants or conditions, express or implied, whether by statute or otherwise, other than as set forth herein, have been made by the parties hereto. By signing below, Borrower and Lender affirm that no oral agreement between them exists.**

37. Interpretation. Provisions in the Loan Documents are intended to be cumulative. To the extent that the provisions of this Agreement conflict with those of any other Loan Document, the provision which provides Lender most protection and grants Lender the greatest rights shall control.   Likewise, if the provisions of any Loan Document conflict with those of any other Loan Document, the provision which provides Lender most protection and grants Lender the greatest rights shall control.

38. Governing Law. This Agreement shall be construed and governed by the laws of the State of Kansas except to the extent that the perfection of the interests in the Agency Assets is governed by the laws of a jurisdiction other than the State of Kansas. At the option of Lender, jurisdiction and venue for any dispute arising under or in relation to this Agreement will lie only in Kansas with the Phillips County District Court, Phillipsburg, Kansas, or the U.S. District Court having jurisdiction over Phillips County Kansas. In the event that a lawsuit, administrative proceeding or litigation is brought with respect to this Agreement, the prevailing party shall be entitled to be reimbursed for, and/or have judgment entered with respect to, all of its costs and expenses, including reasonable attorney's fees' and legal expenses.

39. Waiver of Jury Trial. <u>Borrower hereby expressly waives any right to a trial by jury in any action or proceeding to enforce or defend any rights under this Agreement, any other Loan Document, instrument or document delivered or which may in the future be delivered in connection herewith. Borrower agrees that any such action or proceeding shall be tried before a court and not a jury.</u>

40. Waiver of Marshaling of Assets. Borrower waives any and all rights to require any marshaling of Borrower's assets.

41. Commercial Loan. Borrower and Lender agree that the credit extended hereunder represents a commercial loan and is not a consumer loan subject to the UCCC.

42. Notices. Notices which may be required to be sent by Lender or Borrower in accordance with this Agreement shall be sent to the address set forth below or such other address as may be designated by such party provided notice of such change in address has been given to the other party. Notices shall be deemed effective if in writing, and delivered by hand or mailed by United States Mail, postage prepaid, mailed by certified mail, with return receipt requested, or mailed by express courier with date of receipt confirmed. The effective date of notice shall be the day of delivery by hand; if mailed by regular mail, four business days following the mailing thereof; and, if by certified mail or express courier, the date of receipt thereof :

Lender's Address: Borrower's Address:

_____   _____

_____   _____

_____   _____

43. Timeliness. Timeliness and punctuality are essential elements of this Agreement.

The undersigned agree to the foregoing and acknowledge receipt of a copy of this Agreement on this the _____day of _____, _____ .

Lender: **Borrower:**

by:_____   by:_____
title:_____   title:_____

OPINION OF BORROWER'S COUNSEL

(to be typed on firm letterhead)

Date

Brooke Credit Corporation
10895 Grandview Drive, Suite 250
Overland Park, KS 66210

RE:

Ladies and Gentlemen:

We have acted as counsel for _____ (the "Borrower") and ____ in connection with _____, and in that connection we have examined the executed originals or copies, certified or otherwise, identified to our satisfaction of:

1.   Articles of Incorporation of the Borrower and Bylaws of the Borrower, all as amended to date; (Note: If partnership, limited liability company or other entity, please reference applicable organizational documents.)

2.   A certificate of recent date of the Secretary of the State of _____ relating to the legal existence and good standing of the Borrower in _____;

3.   A   Promissory   Note   dated   as   of   _____   (the   "Note")   between _____, as Lender, and _____, as Borrower;

4.   A   Security   Agreement   dated   _____   (the   "Agreement")   between _____, as Lender, and _____, as Borrower;

5.   A Financial Statement dated as of _____ (the "Statement") of Borrower and any Guarantors;

6.   The UCC Forms dated as of _____ (the "UCC Forms") of Borrower and any Guarantors;

7.   An   Agent   Agreement   dated   _____   (the   "Agent   Agreement")   between _____, as Master Agent and _____, as Agent;

8.   An Agreement for Sale/Purchase of Insurance Agency Assets dated _____ (the   "Sale/Purchase   Agreement")   between   _____,   as   Seller,   and _____, as Buyer;

9.   An Agreement for Advancement of Loan dated _____ (the "Loan Agreement") between _____, as Lender, and _____, as Borrower;

10.   The   Personal   Guaranties   dated   _____   (the   "Guaranties")   executed   by _____, as Guarantors;

11.   The proceedings of the Board of Directors of the Borrower, authorizing, among other things, the execution and delivery by the Borrower of the Sale/Purchase Agreement and Loan Documents;

12.   The proceedings of the shareholders of the Borrower, authorizing, among other things, the execution and delivery by the Borrower of the Sale/Purchase Agreement and Loan Documents;

13.   Such other documents, instruments, certificates and corporate records as we have considered necessary for purposes of this opinion.

For purposes of this opinion, we have assumed that the Lender has all requisite power and authority and has taken all necessary corporate action to execute and deliver the instruments to which it is a party and to effect the transactions contemplated thereby. For the purposes of this opinion, the capitalized terms shall have the meaning attached to said terms in the Loan Agreement.

Based on the foregoing, we are of the opinion that:

1.   The Borrower is a corporation duly organized, validly existing and in good standing under the laws of the State of _____, with corporate powers adequate for carrying on the business now conducted by it.

2.   The Borrower has full power and authority to execute and deliver the Loan Documents and to perform its/his/her/their obligations thereunder; the Loan Documents have been duly authorized, executed and delivered by Borrower, and, subject to the qualification stated in the last paragraph of this opinion, each is a valid, legally binding obligation of the Borrower enforceable against the Borrower in accordance with its terms.

3.   The execution and delivery of the Loan Documents, and the performance by the Borrower of its/his/her/their obligations thereunder, do not and will not constitute a material default under, (or conflict with or violate any material provisions of the Borrower's Articles of Incorporation or Bylaws, both as amended to date, or applicable corporate law,) and do not and will not materially conflict with or violate or result in a material adverse effect on the Borrower under any indenture, mortgage, deed of trust, contract, agreement or other instrument to which it/he/she/they is/are a party, or any administrative regulation or court decree. (Note: If borrower is a partnership, limited liability company or other entity, reference applicable organizational documents.)

4.   There is no litigation, proceeding, investigation or notice of violation by or before any court, public board or body, pending or threatened, against or affecting the Borrower, its officers or property, challenging the validity of the Loan Documents or other documents described above, challenging Borrower's organization or authorization, challenging the solvency of Borrower, or seeking to enjoin any of the transactions contemplated by such instruments or the performance by the Borrower of its/his/her/their obligations thereunder, or challenging the acquisition or operation of the Agency. Further, there is no litigation, proceeding or investigation pending or threatened against the Borrower, its officers or property except (i) that arising in the normal course of the Borrower's business operations, and being defended by or on behalf of the Borrower, in which the probable ultimate recovery and estimated defense costs and expenses, in the opinion of the Borrower's counsel, will be entirely within applicable insurance policy limits (subject to applicable self-insurance, retentions and deductibles), or (ii) that which, if determined adversely to the Borrower, would not, in the opinion of Borrower's counsel, materially adversely affect the Borrower's operations or condition, financial or otherwise. (Note: If borrower is a partnership, limited liability company or other entity, reference to "officer" should be changed to partner or other designation as applicable.)

5.   There are no usury claims available to Borrower against Lender.

6.   There are no additional filing, recording and transfer charges, fees and taxes other than the fees associated with the recording of the Loan Documents.

7.   To the best of our knowledge, information and belief, and after review of the Loan Documents, nothing has come to our attention which would lead us to conclude that any documents executed or completed by Borrower contains any untrue statement of a material fact or omits to state any material fact required to be stated therein or necessary in order to make the statement therein, in the light of the circumstances under which they were made, not misleading.

Our opinion that the Loan Documents are enforceable in accordance with their terms is qualified to the extent that enforcement of the rights and remedies created by them is subject to bankruptcy, insolvency, reorganization and similar laws of general application affecting the rights and remedies of creditors and secured parties, and that the availability of the remedy of specific enforcement or of injunctive relief is subject to the discretion of the court before which any proceedings therefor may be brought.

Very truly yours,

(Borrower's Counsel)

AGENT AGREEMENT ADDENDUM REGARDING LENDER PROTECTION

THIS ADDENDUM ("Addendum") is made to and a part of the _____ Agreement (which with other addenda shall be the "Agreement") dated _____, by and between _____ ("Franchise Agent") and _____ ("Master Agent").

WHEREAS, the Master Agent may enter into or has entered into a Collateral Preservation Agreement with _____ ("Lender") to assist Lender in the preservation of its collateral interest in Agency Assets in the event of Franchise Agent's default on its obligations to Lender by Master Agent: 1) gathering and transferring Franchise Agent's Customer File information to Lender; 2) assisting in the immediate transfer of Franchise Agent Account to Lender; 3) allowing Lender to assume Franchise Agent's rights and obligations set forth in Franchise Agent's agreements with Master Agent; 4) and, otherwise assisting Lender in the operation of Franchise Agent's business.

NOW, THEREFORE, in consideration of the terms and conditions set forth herein, and for other good and valuable consideration, the receipt and sufficiency of which are hereby acknowledged, Master Agent and Franchise Agent agree as follows:

DEFINITIONS

For purposes of this Addendum, the following terms shall have the following meanings unless the context clearly requires otherwise:

Agency's Assets. All of Franchise Agent's personal property, whether tangible or intangible, and all of Franchise Agent's interest in property and fixtures, now owned or existing or hereafter acquired and wherever located, including without limitation, the following: (a) all inventory, machinery, equipment, goods and supplies; (b) all accounts, including without limitation, the Franchise Agent's Account and Customer Accounts; (c) all instruments, documents (including, without limitation, the Customer Files) policies and certificates of insurance, money, chattel paper, investment property, deposits, warehouse receipts and things in action; (d) all general intangibles and rights to payment or proceeds of any kind, including without limitation, rights to insurance proceeds and letter of credit proceeds; (e) all contract rights and interests of any kind, including without limitation, the rights and interests set forth in the Franchise Agent Agreement and any Subagent Agreement; and (f) any and all additions, attachments, parts, repairs, accessories, accessions, replacements and substitutions to or for any of the forgoing. The above description of property shall also include, but not be limited to, any and all telephone numbers, rights to the lease of office space, post office boxes or other mailing addresses, rights to trademarks and use of trade names, rights to software licenses, and rents received by Franchise Agent for the lease of office space. Proceeds and products of the above property are also covered.

Agency Bill Policies. Any Policies for which Franchise Agent is responsible for all or any part of premium or fee billing and collection.

Franchise Agent's Affiliates. Any Person affiliated with Franchise Agent, related to Franchise Agent, employed by Franchise Agent, contracted with Franchise Agent, business associate of Franchise Agent, shares office space with Franchise Agent or rents office space from Franchise Agent.

Agent of Record. Person designated on Company's records as the Franchise Agent or representative regarding a specific Policy and the owner of all Sales Commissions.

Franchise Agent Account. An account on Master Agent's ledgers to which the Master Agent records amounts due Master Agent from Franchise Agent and amounts due Franchise Agent from Master Agent.

Franchise Agent Statements. A record of Franchise Agent Account prepared by Master Agent listing all credit and debit entries made to Franchise Agent Account by Master Agent for a specified period of time.

Such debit and credit entries may include, but are not limited to, Sales Commissions, Net Premiums and Master Agent advances to Franchise Agent.

Company. A company issuing, brokering, selling or making a market for Policies and which has a contract with Master Agent.

Customer Accounts. A Person who has a Policy purchased from, serviced, renewed or delivered through Franchise Agent. Customer Accounts shall be owned by Franchise Agent or a Subagent.

Customer Files. Documents, data and correspondence to or from Customer Accounts, Franchise Agent, Master Agent, Companies or others regarding Policies.

Direct Bill Policies. Any Policy for which a Company is responsible for premium or fee billing and collection.

Insurance, Investment, Banking and/or Credit Services. Insurance services include but are not limited to the sale, renewal, service or delivery of insurance policies, annuities, insurance brokering services, insurance customer services, risk management services and insurance related consulting or advisory services. Investment services include, but are not limited to, the sale, renewal, service or delivery of mutual funds, stocks, bonds, notes, debentures, real estate services, investment customer services, investment related consulting, and financial, investment or economic advisory services. Banking services include any banking service Franchise Agent is allowed to perform under federal and/or state laws. Credit services include, but are not limited to, origination or brokerage of loans or mortgages, credit customer services, and credit related consulting or advisory services. At any point in time, Insurance, Investment, Banking and Credit Services shall be limited to those services then offered by Master Agent.

Lender. The Lender named above , its successors, assigns or designees.

Loan. Any and all extensions of credit and interest thereon to Franchise Agent by Lender pursuant to the Loan Agreement or any other agreement between Lender and Borrower.

Loan Agreement. Agreement for Advancement of Loan by and between Franchise Agent and Lender.

Net Premium. Agency Bill Policy gross premium or fee less Sales Commissions.

Person. Any individual, sole proprietorship, partnership, joint venture, trust, unincorporated organization, association, corporation, limited liability company, institution or other entity.

Policy. Any and all insurance services, policies, coverages or products sold, renewed, serviced or delivered through Franchise Agent to any Person. Policies include, but are not limited to, any and all Insurance, Investment, Banking or Credit Service, or policy, coverage or product associated therewith sold, renewed, serviced or delivered through Franchise Agent to any Person.

Profit Sharing Commissions. Commissions or fees which are not associated with the sale of a specific Policy through Franchise Agent. Profit Sharing Commissions are typically contingent upon factors such as sales volume, premium volume, profitability and other special concessions negotiated by the Master Agent. Profit Sharing Commissions include, but are not limited to, payments identified by the Companies as profit sharing commissions, contingency commissions, advertising allowances, prizes, override commissions, expense reimbursements and bonus commissions.

Receipts Trust Account: An account established and owned by Master Agent, but controlled by a trustee, to which premiums, fees, Sales Commissions and Other Receipts received by Franchise Agent or Master Agent from Companies or customers shall be deposited and from which Master Agent, or its designee, makes regular withdrawals by Electronic Funds Transfer.

Return Commissions. Direct Bill Policy commissions that are unearned because Policy premium or fee was reduced or Policy canceled.

Sales Commissions. Commissions paid by Companies to Master Agent or assigned by Franchise Agent to Master Agent for the sale, renewal, service or delivery of a specific Policy through Franchise Agent. Sales Commissions are not normally contingent upon factors such as Master Agent's loss ratio, premium volume, sales volume or special concessions negotiated by the Master Agent. For the purposes of this Addendum, Sales Commissions shall specifically exclude Profit Sharing Commissions and other similar payments. However, Sales Commissions shall specifically include amounts paid by the Master Agent pursuant to a bonus plan, the terms of which are defined by the Master Agent in its sole discretion and for which the Master Agent makes no representation regarding future payments or Franchise Agent eligibility. Sales Commissions shall also include any consulting fees, advisory fees, placement fees, service fees, renewal fees, or any similar payments paid on or related to any Customer Account by any Person.

Subagent. A Person which has entered or may enter into a Subagent Agreement with Franchise Agent.

TERMS AND CONDITIONS

1) Franchise Agent's Termination of Agreement. Franchise Agent agrees that it shall not terminate the Agreement prior to the Agreement's expiration date or prior to the date upon which Franchise Agent pays its Loan(s) in full, whichever date is later. Franchise Agent further agrees to renew the Agreement at the end of its expiration date until such time as Franchise Agent pays its Loan(s) in full.

2) Franchise Agent's Assignment of Agreement. Franchise Agent and Master Agent acknowledge Lender's interest, including without limitation its security interest, in the Agency Assets. Franchise Agent and Master Agent agree that, pursuant to the Loan Agreement, Lender may among other remedies assume all of the Franchise Agent's rights and obligations set forth in this Agreement upon written notice to the Franchise Agent and Master Agent by Lender that Franchise Agent is in default and has not cured the default on its obligations to Lender. Franchise Agent and Master Agent acknowledge Lender's right to assume such rights and obligations without necessity of commencing legal action and without Franchise Agent's or Master Agent's further action or authorization. Franchise Agent and Master Agent acknowledge that Lender's right to assume Franchise Agent's rights and obligations set forth in this Agreement is in addition to all of Lender's other rights and remedies.

3) Master Agent's Assignment of Agreement. Franchise Agent agrees that Master Agent may assign Master Agent's rights and obligations set forth in this Agreement to another party at its sole discretion and without further notice to Franchise Agent.

4) Sales Commissions and Profit Sharing Commissions. Franchise Agent agrees that all Sales Commissions and Profit Sharing Commissions shall be owned by the Master Agent (for the purposes of this subparagraph, "Master Agent" shall include a subsidiary or affiliate of Master Agent). Franchise Agent shall make Master Agent the Franchise Agent of Record for all Policies sold, renewed, serviced or delivered through Franchise Agent unless prior approval is obtained from Master Agent. If a Company refuses to make Master Agent the Agent of Record for all Policies, then Franchise Agent shall assign its rights in any and all Sales Commissions and Profit Sharing Commissions associated with such Policies to Master Agent. Franchise Agent appoints Master Agent as its attorney in fact to endorse or deposit checks made payable to Franchise Agent by customers, Companies or master general agents. Franchise Agent also agrees to obtain from its producers or Subagents an appointment of Master Agent as attorney in fact to endorse or deposit checks made payable to such producers or Subagents by customers, Companies or master general agents.

5) Franchise Agent Account and Customer Files. (a) Master Agent shall code or designate Franchise Agent Account, Customer Account and Customer Files in a manner which readily identifies Franchise Agent's interest in such accounts and files.

(b) Franchise Agent agrees to not request, authorize or permit Master Agent to change or transfer the designation of Franchise Agent's interest or coding for Franchise Agent Account, Customer Accounts or Customer Files unless Lender provides prior written consent.

(c) Franchise Agent and Master Agent acknowledge that, pursuant to the Loan Agreement, Franchise Agent has agreed to relinquish possession, use and enjoyment of its Franchise Agent Account, Customer Accounts and other Agency Assets to the Lender upon notice to the Franchise Agent and Master Agent that Franchise Agent is in default and has not cured the default on its obligations to Lender. Franchise Agent authorizes Master Agent, upon Master Agent's receipt of notice from Lender that Franchise Agent is in default and has not cured the default on its obligations to Lender, to make payment or instruct the trustee of the Trust Agreement described in paragraph 12 to make payment directly to Lender of any amount which, but for default, would be due to Franchise Agent as recorded on the Franchise Agent Statement.

(d) Franchise Agent agrees to provide Customer File information to Master Agent on a timely basis and Master Agent agrees to store any such Customer File information.

(e) Franchise Agent authorizes Master Agent to cooperate with Lender to endorse, set over, transfer and deliver to Lender the Franchise Agent Account, Customer Accounts, Customer Files or any other of Franchise Agent's assets associated with Franchise Agent's business which are in Master Agent's possession without any further release or authorization from Franchise Agent.

6) Agency Agreements with Companies.   (a) The parties agree that Master Agent, or a subsidiary or affiliate thereof, shall be the entity which enters into all agency agreements with Companies for the sale, renewal, service or delivery of Policies through Franchise Agent. Franchise Agent agrees that it shall not enter into any agency agreements with Companies for the sale, renewal, service or delivery of Policies without Master Agent's prior written consent.

(b)   Franchise Agent agrees that it shall not sell, renew, service or deliver Policies under any agency agreement with Companies for the sale, renewal, service or delivery of Policies except under those agency agreements entered into or pre-approved in writing by the Master Agent. Franchise Agent agrees that it shall not provide leads, contacts or referrals to Franchise Agent's Affiliates which result in the sale, renewal, service or delivery of Policies under agency agreements other than those entered into by the Master Agent and thereby circumvent the requirements of this paragraph.

7) Direct Bill Policies; Agency Bill Policies. Franchise Agent shall only apply for issuance of Direct Bill Policies if payment of premiums in this manner is permitted by the Company providing coverages. Franchise Agent shall obtain specific approval of Master Agent prior to submitting any application for issuance of an Agency Bill Policy. Franchise Agent shall be solely responsible for the collection of all Agency Bill Policy premiums or fees, which amounts shall be made payable to Master Agent. Franchise Agent shall not have authority to endorse or deposit such payments to its own account. Franchise Agent shall be responsible for payment to Master Agent of all Net Premiums and Direct Bill Policy Return Commissions. Franchise Agent appoints Master Agent as its attorney in fact to endorse or deposit checks made payable to Franchise Agent by customers, Companies or master general agents. Franchise Agent also agrees to obtain from its producers or Subagents an appointment of Master Agent as attorney in fact to endorse or deposit checks made payable to such producers or Subagents by customers, Companies or master general agents.

8) Errors and Omissions Insurance. Master Agent agrees to maintain a professional errors and omissions insurance policy and, subject to approval of the issuing insurance company, to name Franchise Agent as an additional insured on said policy. Master Agent's inability to obtain or maintain such coverage shall be grounds for termination of the Agreement. Master Agent shall calculate and debit Franchise Agent Account for Franchise Agent's share of the errors and omissions insurance policy premium. Master Agent may adjust said policy premium to maintain an Agent deductible fund. Master Agent shall calculate Franchise Agent's share of said errors and omissions insurance policy premium by dividing the estimated annual commissions received on Customer Accounts by the total estimated annual commissions received by Master Agent from all Companies. However, Franchise Agent's share of Master Agent's annual policy premium shall not be less than the minimum annual premium that is set from time to time by Master Agent. Franchise Agent has the responsibility to provide Master Agent with copies of those documents which Master Agent deems necessary for errors & omissions documentation.

9) **Amendments and Waivers**. Franchise Agent and Master Agent agree that they shall not amend or waive any term, condition or provision of this Agreement or addenda thereto which may have a materially adverse effect on Lender or Lender's security interest without Lender's prior written approval.

10) **Release of Information.** a) Franchise Agent authorizes Master Agent to release to Lender any Franchise Agent, Customer File, Sales Commissions, loan, financial, credit, valuation or other confidential or non confidential documents or information Master Agent has or may have in its possession from any source, deemed necessary by Lender to protect Lender's interest, to perform audits, quality control or other reviews, to market Franchise Agent's Loan, or for any other legitimate purpose.

b) Franchise Agent authorizes Master Agent to release to a prospective successor, assignee or designee of Master Agent or Lender any Franchise Agent, Customer File, Sales Commissions, loan, financial, credit, valuation or other confidential or non confidential documents or information Master Agent has or may have in its possession from any source, deemed necessary by Lender to protect Lender's interest, to perform audits, quality control or other reviews, to market Franchise Agent's Loan or for any other legitimate purpose.

c) Franchise Agent authorizes Master Agent to obtain from Lender, or other person or entity, such Franchise Agent, Customer File, Sales Commissions, loan, financial, credit, valuation or other confidential or non confidential information such source has or may have in its possession deemed necessary by Master Agent to perform audits, quality control or other review, or for analysis by a potential successor, assign or designee of Master Agent.

11) **Collateral Preservation Agreement**. Franchise Agent acknowledges that Master Agent may enter into or has entered into a Collateral Preservation Agreement with Lender which governs the relationship between Master Agent and Lender as such pertains to Franchise Agent's obligations to Lender. Franchise Agent agrees that the Collateral Preservation Agreement contains provisions that may require the Master Agent to act in the interests of Lender and against the interests of Franchise Agent and may also require that Master Agent's obligations to Franchise Agent be subordinate to Master Agent's obligations to Lender.

12) **Trust Agreement.** a) Franchise Agent acknowledges that Master Agent has entered into a Trust Agreement which among other terms provides for a trustee's control of all Sales Commissions. Accordingly, the Master Agent and Franchise Agent agree that all premiums, fees, Sales Commissions and other receipts received by Master Agent or Franchise Agent from Companies or customers that are related in any way to the sale, renewal, service or delivery of Policies through Franchise Agent shall be promptly deposited in the Receipts Trust Account.

b) Franchise Agent agrees that said Receipts Trust Account shall be owned by Master Agent, but controlled by the trustee. Trustee shall have sole right to withdrawal funds from the Rectipts Trust Account. Trustee shall distribute to Franchise Agent and/or Master Agent Sales Commissions and other receipts in accordance with the terms of the trust agreement. Franchise Agent acknowledges and agrees that Trustee shall initiate an electronic deposit to Franchise Agent's business account of all amounts due to Franchise Agent by Master Agent as recorded on the Franchise Agent Statements and in accordance with Franchise Agent's pre-authorization or that Trustee shall initiate an electronic withdrawal from Franchise Agent's business account of all amounts due to Master Agent by Franchise Agent as recorded on the Franchise Agent Statements and in accordance with Franchise Agent's pre-authorization.

c) Franchise Agent acknowledges and agrees that if the Trustee has received notice from the Master Agent of Franchise Agent's default and Franchise Agent's failure to cure its default, then the Trustee shall not make any electronic deposits or other payments to Franchise Agent and shall make payment directly to Lender of any amount which, but for default, would may be due to the corresponding Franchise Agent as recorded on the Franchise Agent Statements. Trustee shall make payments to Lender until such time as Lender provides written notification to notifies Trustee to the contrary.

13) Reliance on Lender's Representations. Franchise Agent agrees that Master Agent shall rely on the Lender's representations regarding default on Franchise Agent's obligations to Lender and Franchise Agent's failure to cure same, and Master Agent shall not be obligated to verify the accuracy, authenticity or enforceability of representations, information or instructions contained in any notices, instructions or requests by Lender to Master Agent regarding Franchise Agent, Franchise Agent's default or Franchise Agent's failure to cure its default.

14) Authority to Perform. Franchise Agent agrees that if Franchise Agent fails to perform any duty or any of the covenants contained in the Agreement, Master Agent may without notice perform or cause them to be performed. Franchise Agent appoints Master Agent as attorney in fact to sign Franchise Agent's name or pay any amount necessary for performance. Master Agent's right to perform for Franchise Agent shall not create an obligation to perform, and Master Agent's failure to perform will not preclude Master Agent from exercising any of Master Agent's other rights under the Agreement, at law or in equity. In addition, Master Agent may be designated or appointed as a receiver for Franchise Agent's business. Any amounts paid or incurred by Master Agent in performing such duty or covenant may be offset by Master Agent from any funds held by Master Agent or held in trust or by a third party, for Franchise Agent's benefit or otherwise.

15) Additional Documents. Franchise Agent agrees to sign, acknowledge, deliver, and/or file any additional documents, statements or certifications that Master Agent may deem necessary to carry out the intent of this Addendum.

16) Release, Indemnification and Hold Harmless. a) Franchise Agent agrees to release, indemnify and hold harmless Master Agent, its owners, officers, directors, employees, and independent contractors (collectively, "Master Agent") for and from any and all claims, losses, liability, damages or expenses (including, but not limited to reasonable attorneys' fees, court costs, and costs of investigation) of any kind or nature whatsoever arising out of or in connection with the Agreement or this Addendum or which Franchise Agent or Master Agent may incur as a result of Master Agent's performance of its rights, obligations or duties hereunder or under the terms of the Trust Agreement, Collateral Preservation Agreement, in connection with the deposit or withdrawal of monoey from the Receipts Trust Account or Franchise Agent's business account or as a result of Master Agent's compliance with Lender's instructions contained in any notice, instruction or request delivered to Master Agent by Lender. This release, indemnification and hold harmless shall survive termination of the Agreement and this Addendum.

b) Franchise Agent, its owners, officers, directors, employees and independent contractors agree to release, indemnify and hold harmless the Trust (established pursuant to the Trust Agreement described in paragraph 12 herein), its trustee(s) and its owners, officers, directors, employees, and independent contractors (collectively, "Trust") for and from any and all claims, losses, liability, damages or expenses (including, but not limited to reasonable attorneys' fees, court costs, and costs of investigation) of any kind or nature whatsoever arising out of or in connection with this Addendum or Trust Agreement or which Franchise Agent, its owners, officers, directors, employees, and independent contractors may incur as a result of Trust's performance of its rights, obligations or duties hereunder or under the terms of the Trust Agreement. This release, indemnification and hold harmless shall survive termination of the Agreement and this Addendum. Upon Master Agent's request, Franchise Agent agrees to sign a separate document (to which Trustee may be a party) releasing, indemnifying and holding harmless Trust Parties.

17) Modification of Franchise Agent Agreement. Franchise Agent and Master Agent acknowledge that this Addendum is intended to modify the Master Agent's standard agent agreement to accommodate Lender's collateral preservation conditions for the extension of credit, and therefore, the provisions in this Addendum are intended to be cumulative. Unless specifically amended hereby, all provisions, terms and conditions shall remain as set forth in the Agreement. To the extent that the provisions of this Addnedum conflict with those of the Agreement, the provisioin which provides Master Agent and Lender most protection and grants Master Agent and Lender the greatest rights shall control.

18) Termination and Survival. Franchise Agent and Master Agent agree to the provisions of this Addendum shall remain in force until Franchise Agent's Loan from Lender has been paid in full, at which time it shall terminate.   Provisions of this Addendum shall survive termination of this Addendum and/or the Agreement if specifically stated herein.

THIS ADDENDUM is executed on the _____ day of _____, _____.

FRANCHISE AGENT: **MASTER AGENT:**

_____   _____

By: By:
Its: Its:

COLLATERAL PRESERVATION AGREEMENT

This Collateral Preservation Agreement entered into this ____ day of _____ by and between _____ ("Master Agent") and _____ ("Lender").

RECITALS

WHEREAS, the Lender has entered into an Agreement for Advancement of Loan with _____ ("Agent") pursuant to which Agent has granted to Lender certain rights, title and interest in and to Agency Assets, including, without limitation, Agent's Account and Customer Files.

WHEREAS, the Master Agent has entered or shall enter into an Agent Agreement and Lender Protection Addendum with Agent. A copy of the Agent Agreement, including a Lender Protection Addendum, is attached hereto as Exhibit A.

WHEREAS, the Master Agent has entered into a Trust Agreement ("Trust Agreement") to establish a trust arrangement to help ensure that Agent's Account balances are paid to Lender in the event of Agent's default and failure to cure such default. A fully executed copy of the Trust Agreement is attached hereto as Exhibit B.

WHEREAS, the Lender requests assistance from the Master Agent in the preservation of its collateral interest in Agency Assets in the event of Agent's default on its obligations to Lender by Master Agent: 1) gathering and transferring Customer File information to Lender; 2) assisting in the immediate transfer of Agent's Account to Lender; 3) allowing Lender to assume Agent's rights and obligations set forth in Agent's agreement with Master Agent; 4) and, otherwise assisting Lender in the operation of Agent's business.

WHEREAS, Master Agent may be benefited by an increase in Sales Commissions and/or Profit Sharing Commissions as a result of Lender's extension of credit to Agent.

NOW THEREFORE, in consideration of the terms and conditions set forth herein and for other good and valuable consideration the receipt and sufficiency of which are hereby acknowledged, Lender and Master Agent agree as follows:

DEFINITIONS OF TERMS USED IN THIS AGREEMENT

For purposes of this Agreement, the following terms shall have the following meanings unless the context clearly requires otherwise:

Agent of Record. Person designated on Company's records as the agent or representative regarding a specific Policy and the owner of all Sales Commissions.

Agent Agreement. Agreement, which has been or will be executed, by and between Agent and Master Agent providing for Agent to sell, renew, service or deliver Policies exclusively through Master Agent.

Agency's Assets. All of Agent's personal property, whether tangible or intangible, and all of Agent's interest in property and fixtures, now owned or existing or hereafter acquired and wherever located, including without limitation, the following: (a) all inventory, machinery, equipment, goods and supplies; (b) all accounts, including without limitation, the Agent's Account and Customer Accounts; (c) all instruments, documents (including, without limitation, the Customer Files) policies and certificates of insurance, money, chattel paper, investment property, deposits, warehouse receipts and things in action; (d) all general intangibles and rights to payment or proceeds of any kind, including, without limitation, rights to insurance proceeds and letter of credit proceeds; (e) all contract rights and interests of any kind, including without limitation, the rights and interests set forth in the Agent Agreement and any subagent agreement; and (f) any and all additions, attachments, parts, repairs, accessories, accessions, replacements and substitutions to or for any of the forgoing. The above description of property shall also include, but not be limited to, any and all telephone numbers, rights to the lease of office space, post office boxes or other mailing addresses, rights to trademarks and use of trade names, rights to software licenses, and rents received by Agent for the lease of office space. Proceeds and products of the above property are also covered.

Page 1 of 7

Agent's Account. An account on Master Agent's ledgers to which the Master Agent records amounts due Master Agent from Agent and amounts due Agent from Master Agent.

Agent Statements. A record of Agent's Account prepared by Master Agent listing all credit and debit entries made to Agent's Account by Master Agent for a specified period of time. Such debit and credit entries may include, but are not limited to, Sales Commissions, net premiums and Master Agent advances to Agent.

Company. A company issuing, brokering, selling or making a market for Policies and which has a contract with Master Agent.

Customer Account. A Person who has a Policy purchased from, serviced, renewed or delivered through Agent.

Customer Files. Documents, data and correspondence to or from customers, Agent, Master Agent, Companies or others regarding Policies.

Insurance, Investment, Banking and/or Credit Services. Insurance services include but are not limited to the sale, renewal, service or delivery of insurance policies, annuities, insurance brokering services, insurance customer services, risk management services and insurance related consulting or advisory services. Investment services include, but are not limited to, the sale, renewal, service or delivery of mutual funds, stocks, bonds, notes, debentures, real estate services, investment customer services, investment related consulting, and financial, investment or economic advisory services. Banking services include any banking service Agent is allowed to perform under federal and/or state laws. Credit services include, but are not limited to, origination or brokerage of loans or mortgages, credit customer services, and credit related consulting or advisory services. At any point in time, Insurance, Investment, Banking and Credit Services shall be limited to those services then offered by Master Agent.

Lender. The Lender named above, its successors, assigns or designees.

Lender Protection Addendum. An addendum to the Agent Agreement which sets forth terms and conditions applicable to Agent and Master Agent and certain of their rights and obligations pertaining to Lender and Lender's security interest.

Person. Any individual, sole proprietorship, partnership, joint venture, trust, unincorporated organization, association, corporation, limited liability company, institution or other entity.

Policies. Any and all insurance services, policies, coverages or products sold, renewed, serviced or delivered through Agent to any Person. Policies include, but are not limited to, any and all Insurance, Investment, Banking or Credit Service, or policy, coverage or product associated therewith sold, renewed, serviced or delivered through Agent to any Person.

Profit Sharing Commissions. Commissions or fees which are not associated with the sale of a specific Policy through Agent. Profit Sharing Commissions are typically contingent upon factors such as sales volume, premium volume, profitability and other special concessions negotiated by the Master Agent. Profit Sharing Commissions include, but are not limited to, payments identified by the Companies as profit sharing commissions, contingency commissions, advertising allowances, prizes, override commissions, expense reimbursements and bonus commissions.

Sales Commissions. Commissions paid by Companies to Master Agent as Agent of Record or assigned by Agent to Master Agent for the sale, renewal, service or delivery of a specific Policy through Agent. Sales Commissions are not normally contingent upon factors such as Master Agent's loss ratio, premium volume, sales volume or special concessions negotiated by the Master Agent. For the purposes of this Agreement, Sales Commissions shall specifically exclude Profit Sharing Commissions and other similar payments. However, Sales Commissions shall specifically include amounts paid to Agent by the Master Agent pursuant to a bonus plan, the terms of which are defined by the Master Agent in its sole discretion and for which the Master Agent makes no representation regarding future payments or Agent eligibility. Sales Commissions shall also include any consulting fees, advisory fees, placement fees, service fees, renewal fees, or any similar payments paid on or related to any Customer Account by any Person.

TERMS AND CONDITIONS

1) Recognition of Lender's Interest in Agent Agreement. Upon Lender's notice to the Agent and Master Agent that Agent is in default and has not cured the default on its obligations to Lender, the Lender may at its option, among other remedies, immediately take possession of Agency Assets, operate Agent's business, and/or assume Agent's rights and obligations set forth in the Agent Agreement and addenda thereto. Upon Lender's written request, Master Agent agrees to recognize Lender as the successor of all of Agent's rights and obligations set forth in the Agent Agreement and addenda thereto. Upon Master Agent's request, Lender shall give Master Agent assurances or confirmation as to Lender's lawful possession and/or operation of Agent's business and Lender's lawful assumption of Agent's rights and obligations, and shall also provide to Master Agent assurances or confirmation that Lender, or its designee, has all necessary insurance licenses and other regulatory approvals required to assume Agent's rights and obligations set forth in the Agent Agreement and addenda thereto.

2) Assignment of Master Agent's Interest in Agent Agreement. a) To preserve the Lender's collateral interest from inappropriate conduct by the Master Agent, the Lender may require that the Master Agent assign its rights and obligations set forth in the Agent Agreement to the Lender but only under the following conditions:

    i) Lender demonstrates one of the following events has occurred:

        a)   Master Agent or one of its principal officers has been convicted of fraud;

        b)   Master Agent business practices which clearly demonstrate a pattern of intentionally avoiding the requirements of the Trust Agreement in a manner which shall interfere with the preservation of Lender's collateral interest;

        c)   Master Agent petitions for bankruptcy; and

    (ii) Lender promptly notifies the Master Agent in writing of the specific event and circumstances and allows the Master Agent thirty (30) days thereafter to cure the specific event; and,

    (iii) Lender provides further written notice to Master Agent that it has not cured the specific event within the 30 day time period.

(b) In the event of such assignment, then the parties acknowledge that Lender must change the Agent of Record from Master Agent to Lender for the corresponding Policies sold through Agent. Accordingly, the parties acknowledge that Lender must enter into agency agreements with those Companies through which Policies have been sold through Agent, before the Agent of Record may be changed. The parties further acknowledge that Lender may need to be a duly licensed insurance agent or obtain other regulatory approvals prior to entering into such agency agreements.

(c) In the event of such assignment, Master Agent will cooperate with Lender to effect the assignment, and will execute those documents required by Lender to change the Agent of Record for the corresponding Policies sold through Agent. Upon Lender's request, Master Agent shall execute a limited power of attorney which grants to Lender the power and authority to sign, acknowledge, deliver and file as Master Agent's attorney in fact any such additional documents.

3) Sales Commissions and Profit Sharing Commissions. Subject to the provisions of paragraph 2 herein, Lender acknowledges that all Sales Commissions and Profit Sharing Commissions are owned by the Master Agent pursuant to the Agent Agreement and that Lender does not have a collateral or other interest in Master Agent's Sales Commissions and Profit Sharing Commissions. However, nothing in this paragraph shall be interpreted to diminish Lender's collateral or other interest in Agency Assets, including, without limitation, Lender's interest in the Agent's Account.

Page 3 of 7

4) Agent's Account and Customer Files. (a) The Master Agent agrees to assist Lender in the preservation of its collateral interest in Agent's Account and Customer Files. The Lender agrees that Master Agent shall not assist Lender in the preservation of any collateral other than Lender's interest in Agent's Account and Customer Files.

(b) Master Agent has executed or shall execute an Agent Agreement and Lender's Protection Addendum with Agent in the form and content attached hereto as exhibit ____.

(c) Master Agent shall code or designate Agent's Account and Customer Files in a manner which readily identifies Agent's interest in such accounts or files. Master Agent agrees not to change or transfer the designation of Agent's interest or coding for Agent's Account or Customer Files unless Lender provides prior written consent.

(d) Within five (5) business days following Master Agent's receipt of Lender's written notice that Agent is in default and has not cured the default on its obligation to Lender, Master Agent shall transfer Customer File information to the Lender.

(e) The parties agree that the Master Agent shall charge or debit Agent's Account, before and after notice to the Master Agent that Agent is in default and has not cured the default, for any amounts that may be due to Companies, customers, vendors, or suppliers by Master Agent for Policies sold through Agent at any time before or after default and that payment of all such amounts to the Master Agent shall be an obligation that is prior to any obligation that is due to Lender and Master Agent may set off any such amounts against Agent's Account.

(f) Although the Master Agent is not under any obligation to do so, the parties acknowledge that the Master Agent may make unsecured advances to the Agent from time to time to pay Agent's business expenses, for which a charge or debit is made to Agent's Account. Upon Lender's written request to Master Agent, Master Agent agrees not to thereafter make any unsecured advances to Agent; however, the payment of all such amounts prior to Lender's request shall be an obligation that is prior to any obligation that is due to Lender and Master Agent may set off any such amounts against Agent's Account.

(g) The Lender agrees that Master Agent shall not be required to take any legal action on behalf of Lender or others to enforce Lender's collateral interest or preserve Lender's collateral value.

5) Errors and Omissions Insurance. The Master Agent agrees to maintain a professional errors and omissions insurance policy. If requested by Lender in writing and subject to the approval of the issuing insurance company, the Master Agent shall name the Lender as an additional insured on said policy.

6) Waivers, Amendments and Enforcement of Agent Agreement. (a) The Master Agent agrees that it shall not amend or waive any term, condition or provision of the Agent Agreement or addenda thereto (including but not limited to the Lender's Protection Addendum) which may have a materially adverse effect on Lender or Lender's security interest without Lender's prior written approval. Master Agent agrees to enforce those terms, conditions and provisions of the Agent Agreement and addenda thereto for which a lack of enforcement may have a materially adverse effect on Lender or Lender's collateral interest.

(b) If an event occurs which may result in termination of the Agent Agreement by the Master Agent, then the Master Agent shall notify Lender at the same time and in the same manner that notification is provided by the Master Agent to the Agent.

7) Trust Agreement (a) The parties acknowledge that the Master Agent is not required to obtain Lender's approval to remove a trustee and appoint a successor trustee pursuant to the Trust Agreement, although Master Agent agrees to notify Lender of any such change.

(b) Except for the appointment of trustee as provided above and changes to the fees charged by trustee pursuant to the Trust Agreement, the Master Agent shall obtain the Lender's written consent prior to terminating or making any material changes to the Trust Agreement. However, in the event that Master Agent has entered into Collateral Preservation Agreements with other parties that are similar to this Agreement, then Master Agent and Lender agree that the Master Agent shall determine the outstanding balances of all loans for which the Master Agent has agreed to preserve collateral and Master Agent shall be entitled to make material changes to the Trust Agreement upon obtaining the prior written consent of those parties to Collateral Preservation Agreements representing 51% of all such loan balances. Upon Master Agent's request, Lender agrees to provide information to Master Agent sufficient to determine the outstanding loan balances of all loans for which the Master Agent has agreed to preserve collateral.

(c) By the close of the first business day following Master Agent's receipt of Lender's written notice that Agent is in default and has not cured the default on its obligation to Lender, Master Agent shall instruct the trustee of the Trust Agreement not to make any electronic deposits or other payments to Agent and to make payment directly to Lender of any amount which, but for default, would be due to Agent as recorded on the Agent Statement.

8) Notice of Default. (a) Lender agrees to provide Master Agent with a copy of any notice to Agent of default and right to cure that is delivered to the Agent. Such copy shall be sent to Master Agent on the same day it is sent to Agent.

(b) Lender agrees to provide Master Agent with a copy of any notice to Agent that Agent's default has not been cured. The parties agree that copy of this notice to Agent shall constitute Lender's notice to Master Agent that Agent is in default and has not cured the default of its obligation to Lender. Such copy shall be sent to Master Agent on the same day it is sent to Agent.

(c) The parties agrees that Lender, at its sole discretion shall determine when Agent is in default and has not cured its default and the Master Agent shall have no obligation or liability in this regard. Master Agent is entitled to rely exclusively upon Lender's determination.

9) Lender's Possession, Acquisition and/or Assumption. (a) Upon written request from Lender, the Master Agent agrees to assist Lender in the operation of Agent's business after Lender's possession, acquisition and/or assumption of Agent's business for the lesser period of: i) Twelve months from date of Lender's possession, acquisition and/or assumption; ii) upon Lender's sale or divestiture of possession or Lender's cessation of operations; iii) upon termination of the Agent Agreement for any reason; iv) or, Lender notifies Master Agent in writing that its services relating to the operation of Agent's business are not required. Nothing in this subparagraph shall be interpreted to give Lender any greater rights than Agent to terminate or assign the Agent Agreement.

(b) The parties agree that Master Agent's assistance to Lender in the operation of Agent's business shall be limited to providing personnel for management and staffing. As such, i) the management and staff shall be employees of Master Agent; ii) the management and staff shall be supervised by Master Agent; iii) Master Agent shall be responsible for the payment of salaries, wages and benefits of management and staff; iv) Master Agent shall be solely responsible for the selection of management and staff; and, v) Master Agent shall be solely responsible for determining proper staffing levels.

(c) The Lender agrees that it is responsible for all other operations, including without limitation, leasing office premises, purchasing office supplies, providing office equipment and paying for other typical office expenses. The Lender further agrees that Agent's business shall be operated in accordance with the Master Agent's rules and procedures.

(d) The parties agree that if Lender requests Master Agent's assistance as provided in above, then Lender shall pay a service fee in an amount equal to 25% of Sales Commissions for Policies associated with the Agent's business, in addition to any amounts that may be owed (whether based upon Sales Commissions or other) to Master Agent pursuant to the Agent Agreement between Master Agent and Lender, as Agent's successor.

(e) The parties agree that if Lender requests Master Agent's assistance in the marketing of Agent's business after Lender acquires the rights, title and interests therein, Master Agent will assist Lender in the marketing of Agent's business pursuant to a brokerage agreement the terms of which (including without limitation, payment terms) shall be negotiated by Master Agent and Lender on an agency by agency basis. Master Agent shall not be required to provide assistance if the laws of the jurisdiction require Master Agent to obtain additional licenses or regulatory approvals to perform such marketing or brokerage services.

10) Notice of Loan Pay-Off. Lender shall provide to Master Agent written notice of Agent's payment in full of the loan obligations to Lender within thirty (30) days of said payment in full.

MISCELLANEOUS

11) Amendments. This Agreement may not be modified, revised, altered, added to, or extended in any manner, or superseded other than by an instrument in writing signed by all of the parties hereto.

12) Additional Documents. Master Agent agrees to sign, acknowledge, deliver and/or file any additional documents that Lender may consider necessary to carry out the intent of this Agreement.

13) Indemnification; Hold Harmless. (a) Master Agent and Lender agree jointly and severally to indemnify and hold harmless the trustee under the Trust Agreement and its directors, officers, agents, partners, independent contractors and employees (collectively the "Trust Parties") against any and all claims, damages, losses, liabilities or expenses (including, but not limited to, reasonable attorneys' fees, court costs and costs of investigation) of any kind or nature whatsoever arising out of or in connection with this Agreement or the Trust Agreement or Trust Parties' performance of its obligations pursuant thereto; provided, however, that this shall not relieve trustee from liability for its breach of any of its agreements under the Trust Agreement or for its own willful misconduct, recklessness, bad faith or gross negligence, nor for the gross negligence, recklessness, bad faith or willful misconduct of its officers, directors, independent contractors or employees. The provisions of this paragraph shall survive the resignation or removal of the trustee or any successor trustee and the termination of this Agreement and the Trust Agreement. If requested by the trustee, Lender agrees to sign a separate document (to which the trustee may be a party) releasing and indemnifying and holding harmless trustee.

(b) Lender agrees to indemnify and hold harmless the Master Agent and its directors, officers, agents, partners, independent contractors and employees (collectively the "Master Agent Parties") against any and all claims, damages, losses, liabilities or expenses (including, but not limited to, reasonable attorneys' fees, court costs and costs of investigation) of any kind or nature whatsoever arising out of or in connection with this Agreement or Master Agent Parties' performance of its obligations pursuant thereto; provided, however, that this shall not relieve Master Agent from liability for its breach of any of its agreements under this Agreement or for its own willful misconduct, recklessness, bad faith or gross negligence, nor for the gross negligence, recklessness, bad faith or willful misconduct of its officers, directors, independent contractors, or employees. The provisions of this paragraph shall survive the termination of this Agreement.

14) Notices. Any notices required hereunder shall be deemed effective if in writing, and delivered by hand or mailed by United States Mail, postage prepaid, or mailed by certified mail, with return receipt requested or mailed by express courier with confirmed deliver date. The effective date of notice shall be the day of delivery by hand, and if mailed by regular mail, four days following the mailing thereof, and if by certified mail or express courier, the date of receipt thereof. For purposes of notification, a business day shall be deemed any day on which the United States Postal Service shall have regular mail deliveries to the address to which the notice is mailed. Unless otherwise directed in writing, notices shall be sent to the following addresses:

Master Agent

_____
_____
_____

Lender

_____
_____
_____

15) Execution in duplicate. This Agreement may be executed in duplicate, each of which shall be deemed an original, but all of which together shall constitute one and the same instrument representing the agreement of the parties hereto.

16) Enforceability, severability. The failure by any party to enforce any provision of this Agreement shall not be in any way construed as a waiver of any such provision nor prevent that party thereafter from enforcing each and every other provision of this Agreement. The invalidity or nonenforceability of any particular provision of this Agreement shall not affect the other provisions hereof, and this Agreement shall be construed in all respects as if such invalid or unenforceable provision were omitted.

17) Binding effect. This Agreement shall be binding upon and inure to the benefit of the parties hereto and their heirs, administrators, successors, assigns and legal representatives, but the rights and property interests hereunder shall not be assignable by any party except as set out herein. The use of the masculine shall include the feminine, and the use of the singular shall include the plural.

18) Entire Agreement. This Agreement contains the entire agreement between the parties hereto and shall supersede and take precedence over any and all prior agreements, arrangements or understanding between the parties relating to the subject matter hereof. No oral understanding, oral statements, oral promises or oral inducements exist. No representations, warranties, covenants or conditions, express or implied, whether by statue or otherwise, other than as set forth herein, have been made by the parties hereto.

19) Termination and Survival. Master Agent and Lender agree that the provisions of this Agreement shall remain in force until Agent's loan from Lender has been paid in full, at which time it shall terminate.   Provisions of this Agreement shall survive termination of this Agreement if specifically stated herein.

20) Governing law. This Agreement shall be construed and governed by the laws of the State of _____.
At the option of _____, jurisdiction and venue for any dispute arising under or in relation to this Agreement will lie only in _____-with the _____ County District Court, _____, _____, or the U.S. District Court with jurisdiction over_____. In the event a lawsuit or litigation is brought with respect to this Agreement, the prevailing party shall be entitled to be reimbursed for and/or have judgment for all of their costs and expenses, including reasonable attorney's fees and legal expenses.

21) Timeliness. Timeliness and punctuality are essential elements of this Agreement.

Executed on the date above written.

MASTER AGENT: **LENDER:**

_____   _____
By: By:
Its: Its:

C H A P T E R

Applications

The following are Master Agent applications and disclosures used by Brooke Corporation. These forms have been successfully used by Brooke Corporation to fully disclose and qualify agents when implementing the Master Agent standards discussed in the preceding chapters.

Contrary to the Brooke Corporation agreements provided in the previous chapter, the following forms are revised regularly and are not proprietary. As such, these applications may be used without permission or license from Brooke Corporation although they may not be suitable for use by others.

Agreement	Description
Franchise Disclosures to Agent	Disclosure to agent by Master Agent (Brooke Corporation) using a franchise disclosure format. Exhibits referenced in disclosure are not included.
Agent Application	Application from prospective agent to Master Agent (Brooke Corporation) to become an agent.

Subagent Application	Application from prospective subagent to agent (Brooke Corporation Agent) to become a subagent.
Broker Agent Application	Application from agent to Master Agent (The American Agency, Inc.) to become a broker.
Licensing Application	Application from agent to Master Agent to license an owner, director, officer, employee or independent contractor with state or federal regulators.
Seller Survey	Survey completed by agency seller to provide preliminary information to agency buyer.
Credit Application	Application from agent to lender (Brooke Credit Corporation).

Franchise Offering Circular

Brooke Corporation
2nd Floor, 205 F Street
Phillipsburg, Kansas 67661
(785) 543-3199

The franchise agent will sell insurance services, credit services, banking and investment services. The initial franchise fee is $1,000. (The estimated initial investment required ranges from $1,900 to $22,100.)

THE FRANCHISE AGREEMENT PERMITS THE FRANCHISE AGENT TO SUE BROOKE CORPORATION ONLY IN KANSAS. OUT OF STATE LITIGATION MAY FORCE YOU TO ACCEPT A LESS FAVORABLE SETTLEMENT FOR DISPUTES. IT MAY ALSO COST MORE TO SUE BROOKE CORPORATION IN KANSAS THAN IN YOUR HOME STATE.

Information comparing franchisers is available. Call the state administrators listed in Exhibit U or your public library for sources of information.

Registration of this franchise by a state does not mean that the state recommends it or has verified the information in this offering circular. If you learn that anything in the offering circular is untrue, contact the Federal Trade Commission and the State Attorney General.

Effective Date: March 27, 2000

TABLE OF CONTENTS

Item

Exhibits

1. THE FRANCHISOR, ITS PREDECESSORS, & AFFILIATES:

To simplify the language in this offering circular, "Brooke" means Brooke Corporation, the franchisor. "You" means the person or entity who buys the franchise.

Brooke was incorporated in Kansas on January 17, 1986, with the name of Brooke Financial Services, Inc. The name was changed on May 19, 1987, to Brooke Corporation.

Brooke does business as "Brooke Financial Services" and "Brooke Insurance and Financial Services". Our principal business address is Processing Center, 2nd Floor, 205 F Street, Phillipsburg, Kansas 67661.

Brooke's agent for service of process is disclosed in Exhibit T.

Brooke offers franchises for the start-up of new agencies and conversion to franchises of existing agencies. Brooke also owns and operates insurance agencies that are available for sale to franchise agents.

The primary financial service offered by most franchise agents is property and casualty insurance; however, franchise agents may also offer life and health insurance services, investment services, banking services, and credit services.

Many of the services sold by you are required by consumers in order to conduct normal everyday activities. For instance, insurance services are generally required to legally operate automobiles, credit services are often required for consumer purchases, and investment services are required to save for retirement. As such, the market for insurance and financial services in the United States is expected to grow along with the country's population and standard of living.

Insurance services are primarily regulated by individual states and you must be licensed to sell insurance. Credit services are regulated by individual states and, in some instances, the federal government. You may have to be licensed to sell credit services. Sale of investment services is regulated by individual states and the federal government. You must be licensed to sell investments. Banking services are regulated by individual states and the federal government. You may be restricted as to the sale of banking services and/or may need to be licensed to sell credit services.

Your competition for sales of property and casualty insurance and life and health insurance includes commercial banks, insurance companies, independent insurance agents, captive insurance agents, Internet solicitation and direct mail solicitation. Your competition for sales of credit, banking and investment services includes commercial banks, securities firms, savings banks, automobile companies, finance companies, insurance companies, credit unions, mortgage brokers, Internet solicitation, and direct mail solicitation.

The current franchise relationship has evolved from a supplier affiliation to a more comprehensive affiliation that gradually acquired some of the characteristics of franchising. To ensure adequate disclosure and regulatory compliance, Brooke has elected to disclose its affiliations as franchises and the affiliation agreement has been relabeled as the franchise agreement.

Brooke sells insurance "targeted market" programs and surplus lines insurance through The American Agency, Inc. and The American Heritage, Inc., which are brokerage agencies and Brooke subsidiaries. Brooke sells life and health insurance through Brooke Life and Health, Inc., another brokerage agency subsidiary. Brooke's brokerage agency subsidiaries make their services available to Brooke franchise agents and to agents that are not Brooke franchise agents.

Through Brooke Credit Corporation, a finance company Brooke subsidiary, Brooke originates loans to franchise agents and others.

Brooke has offered franchises (affiliations) since June 1988. Brooke has operated one or more company-owned insurance agencies since May 1986.

Brooke has not offered franchises in other lines of business.

2. BUSINESS EXPERIENCE:

Chairman and Chief Executive Officer: Robert D. Orr

From Brooke's inception in May 1986, Robert D. Orr has been Chief Executive Officer of Brooke. Robert D. Orr concurrently served as Chairman of Brooke State Bank in Jewell, Kansas, from December 1991 to December 1994 and Chief Executive Officer of Farmers State Bank in Phillipsburg, Kansas, from January 1992 to December 1995.

Secretary/Treasurer and Chief Financial Officer: Leland G. Orr, CPA

From Brooke's inception in May 1986, Leland G. Orr has been Secretary/Treasurer. Leland G. Orr concurrently served as President of Brooke State Bank in Jewell, Kansas, from December 1991 to December 1994.

President and National Sales Manager: Michael S. Hess

From March 1989 to March 1996, Michael S. Hess was Vice President and Sales Officer of Brooke. In March 1996, Michael Hess was promoted to President and National Sales Manager of Brooke.

3. LITIGATION:

There is no pending or threatened litigation between Brooke and any present or former franchise agent.

4. BANKRUPTCY:

No person previously identified in Items 1 or 2 of this offering circular has been involved as a debtor in proceedings under the U.S. Bankruptcy Code required to be disclosed in this item.

5. INITIAL FRANCHISE FEE:

Franchise agents may pay a non-refundable $1,000 lump sum franchise fee when they sign the franchise agreement. We are willing to finance up to $1,000 of the franchise fee (see item 10).

6. OTHER FEES AND OBLIGATIONS:

Name of Fee	Amount	Due Date	Remarks
Commissions Retained from Franchise Agents (note 1)	15% of total commissions subject to monthly minimum fee of $250.00	Payable monthly on the 20th day of the next month	Total Commissions includes all commissions from insurance, investment, banking, or credit services.
Net Premium Reimbursement (note 2)	Reimbursement of actual net premium	Payable monthly on the 20th day of the next month	Franchise agents reimburse Brooke for the actual net premium paid by Brooke to insurance companies for insurance policies that are billed through the franchise agent. Net premium is the total premium less any sales commissions.
Return Commissions Reimbursement (note 2)	Reimbursement of actual return commissions	Payable monthly on the 20th day of the next month	Franchise agents reimburse Brooke for the actual return commissions paid by Brooke to insurance companies for commission reductions on policies that are billed through the insurance company. Return commissions result from policy premium reductions or policy cancellations.

6. <u>OTHER FEES AND OBLIGATIONS Continued</u>:

Postage Reimbursement (note 2)	Reimbursement of actual postage expenses	Payable monthly on the 20th day of the next month	Franchise agents reimburse Brooke for the actual postage expense incurred by Brooke for mailings to franchise agent or franchise agent's customer.
Vendor Payments made on behalf of Franchise Agents (note 2)	Reimbursement of actual payments made to vendors	Payable monthly on the 20th day of the next month	Franchise agents reimburse Brooke for the actual payments made to vendors, employees, & others by Brooke on their behalf.
Advertising Reimbursement (note 2)	Reimbursement of 50% of actual advertising expenses	Payable monthly on the 20th day of the next month	Franchise agents reimburse Brooke for 50% of the actual payments made to others by Brooke for advertising expenses pre-approved by the Franchise agent.
Errors & Omissions Insurance Reimbursement (note 2)	Reimbursement of a pro-rata share of errors & omissions insurance policy premium expense subject to a minimum annual premium and adjustment for an agent deductible fund	Payable annually on the 20th day of August	Franchise agents reimburse Brooke for a pro-rata share of the premium payments made by Brooke to an insurance company or its agent. Franchise agent's pro-rata share is calculated by dividing franchise agent's estimated annual commissions by Brooke's total estimated annual commissions. Franchise agent's pro-rata share is subject to a minimum premium and adjustment for an agent deductible fund.
Errors & Omissions Insurance Claims (note 2)	Reimbursement of actual defense and other claims expenses up to $2,500 per incident	Payable monthly on the 20th day of the next month	Franchise agents reimburse Brooke for the actual defense and other claims incurred by Brooke as result of franchise agent's actions or lack of actions up to $2,500 per incident.
Third Party Fees Reimbursement	Reimbursement of actual fee expenses	Payable monthly on the 20th day of the next month	Franchise agents reimburse Brooke for the actual expense incurred by Brooke on behalf of franchise agent or franchise agent's customers for fees such as motor vehicle reports, licensing fees, clue reports, etc.

Note 1:   Brooke may indirectly retain additional sales commissions for "targeted market" insurance program policies, surplus lines policies, life/health policies, credit services, banking services, and investment services sold through Brooke's brokerage subsidiaries because services are provided by the brokerage subsidiaries which are in addition to the services provided by Brooke.

Note 2: All fees and reimbursements are payable to Brooke and are non-refundable except as noted below.

7. INITIAL INVESTMENT:

	Amounts	Method of Payment	When Due	To Whom Payment Is To Be Made
Initial Franchise Fee	$1,000	Lump Sum	At Signing of Franchise Agreement	Brooke Corporation
Travel & Living Expenses While Training	$150 to $800	As Incurred	During Training	Transportation Provider, Hotels, & Restaurants
Real Estate & Improvements	(Note 1)	(Note 1)	(Note 1)	(Note 1)
Equipment	$400 to $7,500 (Note 2)	Lump Sum	Prior to Opening	Vendors
Signs	$200 to $800	Lump Sum	Prior to Opening	Vendors
Miscellaneous Opening Costs	$0 - $1,000 (Note 3)	Lump Sum	Prior to Opening	Utilities, Vendors, etc.
Opening Inventory	(Note 4)	(Note 4)	(Note 4)	(Note 4)
Advertising Fee- 3 months	$150 - $1,000 (Note 5)	As Incurred	As Incurred	Advertisers (Note 5)
Additional Funds- 3 months	$0 to $10,000 (Note 6)	As Incurred	As Incurred	Employees, Vendors, etc. (Note 6)
Total	$1,900 to $22,100 (Note 7)			

Note: 1: If you do not own suitable office facilities, you may lease office facilities for the Brooke Financial Services agency. Typical locations are retail areas, strip malls, and office buildings. The typical Brooke Financial Services agency has 1,000 - 2,000 square feet. Rent is estimated to be between $4,500 - $14,500 per year depending on factors such as size, condition, and location of the leased premises.

Note 2: Equipment costs are estimates. Your actual costs will depend on the number and quality of computer stations, desks, chairs, etc.

Note 3: Miscellaneous Opening Costs include security deposits, utility costs, beginning cash on hand. If you are converting an existing agency to a Brooke Financial Services agency, then these expenses will probably not reoccur.

Note 4: Brooke Financial Services agencies do not typically require any inventory.

Note 5: Brooke will pay for 50% of advertising that is pre-approved by Brooke. Brooke is reimbursed by franchise agents for payments made to advertisers on behalf of franchise agents.

Note 6: This estimates your initial start-up expenses and includes payroll costs. These figures are estimates and Brooke cannot guarantee that you will not have additional expenses starting the business. Your costs will depend on factors such as: your management skill, experience, and business acumen; local economic conditions; the local market for insurance and financial services; the prevailing wage rate; competition; and the sales level reached during the initial period. Brooke is reimbursed for payments made to employees, vendors, etc. on behalf of franchise agent for initial start-up expenses. If you are converting an existing agency to a Brooke Financial Services agency, then existing revenues may offset these expenses.

Note 7: This total does not include real estate costs. Brooke relied on its experience in the insurance and financial services business to compile these estimates. You should review these figures carefully with a business advisor before making any decision to purchase the franchise.

Note 8: Brooke offers financing for 100% of the initial franchise fee and 90% of the cost of equipment purchases.

8. RESTRICTIONS ON SOURCES OF PRODUCTS AND SERVICES:

Franchise agents must purchase all property and casualty insurance polices through Brooke. Additionally, life and health insurance policies, credit services, banking services, and investment services must be purchased through Brooke unless prior written approval is obtained from Brooke or Brooke does not provide such services at the time.

With regards to the sale of "targeted market" insurance program policies, surplus lines policies, life/health policies, credit services, banking services, and investment services, franchise agents may be required to use the facilities of one of Brooke's brokerage agency subsidiaries for which Brooke indirectly receives extra sales commissions.

Franchise agents are generally restricted to the sale of policies through suppliers that bill premiums directly to policyholders.

We shall not pay to you a share of any advertising allowances, prizes, override commissions, profit sharing commissions, bonus commissions, or similar payments made by suppliers to us.

Although Brooke may represent numerous suppliers of insurance policies, credit services, banking services, and investment services, you are restricted to using a list of suppliers approved by Brooke. (We sometimes refer to our suppliers as "companies" and your list of approved suppliers as a "company list".) A list of approved suppliers will be provided to you at least five business days before you sign a franchise agreement.

We may change your list of approved suppliers at any time for any reason, such as: (1) to accommodate our suppliers; (2) to reduce suppliers' risk concentration; (3) to match suppliers with the types and volumes of purchases that you make; (4) because Brooke may discontinue doing business with a supplier; (5) because a Brooke brokerage subsidiary offers the same service.

Your list of approved suppliers or company list will include guidelines that we have developed for contacting suppliers, obligating suppliers, and distributing supplier's manuals or materials.

You must purchase from us all advertising items or office supplies with Brooke's logo, such as stationery, business cards, signage, and envelopes. Your cost for purchasing any advertising items or office supplies with Brooke's logo shall be 50% of the estimated cost of production which shall be adjusted at least once each year.

9. FRANCHISE AGENT'S OBLIGATIONS:

Obligation	Section in Agreement	Item in Offering Circular
Site selection & acquisition/lease	6.2(j), 6.2(k)	11
Pre-opening purchases/leases	None	11
Site development & other pre-opening requirements	None	11
Initial & ongoing training	3.11	11

9. FRANCHISE AGENT'S OBLIGATIONS Continued:

Opening	None	None
Fees	2.4, 2.7, 3.9	5,6,7
Compliance with standards/operating manual	3.12	11
Trademarks & proprietary information	3.15, 3.16	8,11
Restrictions on products/services offered	3.3, 3.4, 3.5, 3.13, 3.14	8
Warranty & customer service requirements	None	None
Territorial development & sales quotas	None	None
Ongoing product/service purchases	3.4	8
Maintenance, appearance, and remodeling requirements	3.12	11
Insurance	2.5, 3.9, 3.17, 3.18, 6.2(b), 6.2(n)	11
Advertising	2.6, 2.13, 3.15, 3.16	6,7,8,11
Indemnification	4.5,4.7	None
Owner's participation/management/ staffing	3.2,6.2(c), 6.2(d), 6.2(e), 6.2(f), 6.2(g), 6.2(h)	15
Records/reports	3.11, 3.20	None
Inspections/audits	None	None
Transfer	6.2(i),6.12	17
Renewal	6.1,6.2	17
Post-termination obligations	6.5, 6.6, 6.7, 6.8, 6.9, 6.10, 6.11	17
Non-competition covenants	None	None
Dispute resolution	8.10	17

Although not required, if you wish to use Brooke's proprietary Document Manager system, you will be required to purchase at least one personal computer with sufficient resources to run Microsoft NT Server and Microsoft SQL Server. You will be responsible for purchasing, licensing, installing, and maintaining NT Server, SQL Server, and all other computer software and equipment that you own.

You are licensed to use Brooke's proprietary Document Manager system if used in accordance with Brooke's rules and procedures. You may not sell, lease, license, copy, or authorize the use of the Document Manager programs or documentation. You may not configure, reconfigure, program, reprogram, or change any Document Manager programs. If you install computer programs that conflict with Brooke's proprietary Document Manager, then it may not work properly.

You must obtain our written approval before relocating your agency from the address you provided in the Franchise Agreement. If you have told us that this address is a temporary location, then you must move to a permanent location within a reasonable period of time and must obtain our prior written approval of the permanent location. We also prohibit the location or relocation of your agency to any area or facility that does not have a professional appearance or which would not be acceptable to the general business community.

You must obtain written approval of any agreement to purchase additional agency assets.

Copies of insurance applications and all other documents processed by you and related to insurance, credit, banking or investment sales must be provided to Brooke on a timely basis.

10. <u>FINANCING</u>:

Item Financed	Amount Financed	Down Payment	Term (Yrs.)	APR %	Monthly Payment	Prepay Penalty	Security Required	Liability Upon Default	Loss of Legal Right on Default
Initial Fee (Note 1)	$1,000	None	2	Varies		None	Agency Assets	Unpaid Amount; Attorney Fees; Court Costs; Post & Pre-judgment Interest	Loss of Agency Assets
Land-Construct	None								
Leased Space	None								
Equipment Lease	None								
Equipment Purchase (Note 2)	$360 to $6,750	$40 to $750 (10%)	5	Varies		None	Equipment & Agency Assets	Unpaid Amount; Attorney Fees; Court Costs; Post & Pre-judgment Interest	Loss of Equip-ment & Agency Assets
Opening Inventory	None								
Other Financing	(Note 3)	(Note 3)	10	Varies		None	Agency Assets & Personal Guarantee	Unpaid Amount, Attorney Fees, Court Costs, Post & Pre-judgment Interest	Loss of Equip-ment & Agency Assets & Any Other Assets Pledged & Non Exempt Property After Judgment

Note 1: We are willing to finance 100% of the initial franchise fee over a two-year period at an APR generally 3.50% above the New York Bank's prime interest rate, using the standard note form as shown in Exhibit M and the agreement for loan advancement as shown in Exhibit M.

Note 2: We are willing to finance up to 90% of the cost of equipment purchased to open a Brooke Financial Services agency over a five-year period using the standard note form as shown in Exhibit M and the agreement for loan advancement as shown in Exhibit M.

Note 3: In some circumstances, we are willing to finance or refinance agency assets if the loan balance does not exceed 90% of the estimated fair market value of the agency assets offered as collateral. The personal guarantee of franchise agent's primary owner or owners is required as additional collateral. Agency loans may be amortized over a ten-year period with an APR at a rate that generally varies on December 31st of each year to 3.50% above the New York Bank's prime interest rate. The standard note form shown as Exhibit M and the agreement for loan advancement shown as Exhibit M are used.

Note 4: Brooke does not typically arrange financing from other sources. Although Brooke does not typically guarantee your obligations to third parties, in some instances Brooke will guarantee a franchise agent's payments to agency sellers.

Note 5: Brooke may sell or assign franchise agent's note to other lenders or investors. Accordingly, Brooke may distribute credit and other information provided by franchise agent to potential lenders or investors.

Note 6: Brooke may offer financing that requires you to waive notice, confess judgment, or waive a defense against Brooke or the lender.

11. FRANCHISOR'S OBLIGATIONS:

Except as listed below, Brooke need not provide any assistance to you.

Before you open your agency, Brooke will:

1) Acquire and deliver to you advertising items or office supplies that carry Brooke's logo. (Franchise Agreement paragraphs 2.13) Brooke shall pay for 50% of the estimated cost of acquiring these items.

2) Acquire and install for you signs that carry Brooke's logo. (Franchise Agreement paragraphs 2.6 & 2.13) Brooke shall pay for 50% of the estimated cost of acquiring and installing signs.

3) Endorse Brooke's insurance policy to provide errors and omissions insurance coverage for you. (Franchise Agreement paragraph 2.5)

During the operation of your agency, Brooke will:

1) Account for and process the insurance policies, credit services, banking services, and investment services that you sell to your customers. (Franchise Agreement paragraphs 2.1, 2.2, 2.3, 2.4 and Addendums)

2) Calculate and charge your account with Brooke commission fees and costs for any other supplies, services, and benefits provided to you by Brooke. (Franchise Agreement paragraphs 2.4, 2.5, 2.6,2.7 and Addendums)

3) Provide you with an accounting of your balance with Brooke each month. (Franchise Agreement paragraph 2.8)

4) Electronically credit your checking account if we owe you money or electronically debit your checking account if you owe us money each month. (Franchise Agreement paragraph 2.9)

5) Loan you a copy of our Rules and Procedures Manual that we also refer to as an Agency Manual. (Franchise Agreement paragraph 2.10) This manual is confidential and is owned by Brooke. We will distribute new Agency Manuals when revisions are made and you will be expected to destroy all previous versions. You may not reproduce or copy the Agency Manual without our written permission.

6) Update your list of approved suppliers by adding or removing suppliers or companies when Brooke determines it is appropriate. (Franchise Agreement paragraph 2.11)

7) Update your list of approved suppliers by providing written guidelines that restrict your authority to obligate our suppliers or companies. (Franchise Agreement paragraph 2.12)

8) Update your list of approved suppliers by providing written guidelines that restrict the level of contact that you may have with our suppliers or companies.

Brooke may hold regular meetings to discuss sales, operations, accounting, promotions, and other related issues. There is no fee to attend these meetings, but you must pay all of your travel and living expenses. These meetings are not mandatory.

Brooke will provide some advertising and promotional materials to you. You may also develop advertising materials for your own use, at your own cost. Brooke must approve the advertising materials in advance and in writing.

Franchise agents typically open their agencies one to three months after signing a franchise agreement. The factors that may affect this time period are equipment installation, sign installation, licensing requirements, and office space availability.

During the months before and after you are open, we will provide at least eight hours of training and set-up assistance. Training in the use of advice forms, request forms, mail flow, work flow, deposits, and money handling is required for all franchise agent personnel.

We do not provide training which may be required to meet continuing education or licensing requirements although this education is required. This training may be obtained from industry groups and others.

12. TERRITORY:

You will not receive an exclusive territory. Brooke may establish other franchised or company-owned outlets that may compete with your location.

13. TRADEMARKS:

Advantage Franchises shall do business under the trademark and name of Brooke Financial Services or Brooke Insurance and Financial Services, and shall prominently display the trademark symbol in all advertising, correspondence, and signs. Standard Franchises may do business under the trade name Brooke Financial Services or Brooke Insurance and Financial Services. Franchise agents may also use our other current or future trademarks to operate their agency. By trademark, Brooke means trade names, trademarks, service marks, and logos used to identify your agency. Brooke registered the below trademark on the United States Patent and Trademark Office principal register on March 20, 1990:

You must follow our rules when you use these marks. You can not use a name or mark as part of a corporate name or with modifying words, designs, or symbols except for those which Brooke licenses to you. You may not use Brooke's registered name in connection with the sale of an unauthorized product or service or in a manner not authorized in writing by Brooke.

No agreements limit Brooke's right to use or license the use of Brooke's trademarks.

You must notify Brooke immediately when you learn about an infringement of or challenge to your use of our trademark. Brooke will take the action we think is appropriate. While Brooke is not required to defend you against a claim against your use of our trademark, Brooke will reimburse you for your liability and reasonable costs in connection with defending Brooke's trademark. To receive reimbursement, you must have notified Brooke immediately when you learned about the infringement or challenge.

You must modify or discontinue the use of a trademark if Brooke modifies or discontinues it. If this happens, Brooke will reimburse you for your tangible costs of compliance (for example, changing signs). You must not directly or indirectly contest our right to our trademarks, trade secrets, or business techniques that are part of our business.

Brooke does not know of any infringing uses that could materially affect your use of Brooke's trademark.

14. PATENTS, COPYRIGHTS, AND PROPRIETARY INFORMATION:

You do not receive the right to use an item covered by a patent or copyright, but you can use the proprietary information in Brooke's Rules and Procedures Manual. The Rules and Procedures Manual is sometimes referred to as an "Agents Manual". Although Brooke has not filed an application for a copyright registration for the Agents Manual, it claims a copyright and the information is proprietary. Item 11 describes the limitations on the use of this manual by you and your employees. You must also promptly tell us when you learn about unauthorized use of this proprietary information. Brooke is not obligated to take any action but will respond to this information as we think appropriate.

15. OBLIGATION TO PARTICIPATE IN THE ACTUAL OPERATION OF THE FRANCHISE BUSINESS:

Brooke does not require that you personally supervise the franchised business; however, you must ensure that all of your employees respect the proprietary nature of the Agency Manual, comply with software licensing agreements, and comply with the terms of the franchise agreement. The manager need not have an ownership interest in a corporate or partnership franchise agent.

16. RESTRICTIONS ON WHAT THE FRANCHISE AGENT MAY SELL:

Brooke does not restrict the type of goods or services that you may offer using trade names other than Brooke's trade name. However, you must sell only the products and services offered by Brooke when using the Brooke trade name and when insurance, investments, banking, or credit services.

17. RENEWAL, TERMINATION, TRANSFER, AND DISPUTE RESOLUTION:

This table lists certain important provisions of the franchise and related agreements. You should read these provisions in the agreements attached to this offering circular.

Provision	Section in Franchise Agreement	Summary
a. Term of the franchise	6.1	Term is five years
b. Renewal or extension of the term	6.1	If you are in good standing you can renew for an additional five years
c. Requirements for you to renew or extend		Sign new agreement
d. Termination by you	6.4	You may terminate for any reason and at any time by giving us 30 days notice
e. Termination by Brooke without cause	None	
f. Termination by Brooke with cause	6.2	Brooke may terminate or not renew for any of the reasons listed in section 6.2
g. "Cause" defined - defaults which can be cured	None	
h. "Cause" defined - defaults which cannot be cured	6.2	Brooke does not have to provide you with an opportunity to cure a default caused by the reasons listed in section 6.2
I. Your obligations on termination/non-renewal	3.16, 6.5, 6.8, 6.9, 6.10, 6.11	Your obligations include complete de-identification, transfer of your customer accounts and payment of amounts due
j. Assignment of contract by Brooke	None	
k. "Transfer" by you - definition	6.2(i)	Includes sale or transfer of franchise or your customer accounts
l. Brooke's approval of transfer by franchise agent	6.2(i)	Transfers may result in termination by Brooke. All new franchise agents must be approved by Brooke
m. Conditions for Brooke approval of transfer	6.2(i), 6.12	New franchise agents must meet Brooke's qualifications, initial fee paid, and new franchise agreements signed

17. RENEWAL, TERMINATION, TRANSFER, AND DISPUTE RESOLUTION:

n. Brooke's right of first refusal to acquire your business	6.12	Brooke has right to match any offer for the franchise agent's agency assets
o. Brooke's option to purchase your business	None	
p. Your death or disability	None	
q. Non-competition covenants during the term of the franchise	None	
r. Non-competition covenants after the franchise is terminated or expires	None	
s. Modification of the agreement	2.10, 3.12	No modifications generally but Agency Manual subject to change
t. Integration/merger clause/ Entire agreement	8.8	
u. Dispute resolution by arbitration or mediation	None	
v. Choice of forum	8.10	Litigation must be in Phillips County District Court, Phillipsburg, Kansas, a U.S. District Court with jurisdiction over Phillips County, Kansas
w. Choice of law	8.10	Kansas law applies

These states have statutes which may supersede the franchise agreement in your relationship with the franchisor including the areas of termination and renewal of your franchise: ARKANSAS [Stat. Section 70-807], CALIFORNIA [Bus. & Prof. Code Sections 20000-20043], Connecticut [Gen. Stat.. Section 42-133e et seq], DELAWARE [Code, tit.], HAWAII [Rev. Stat. Section 482E-1], ILLINOIS [Rev. Stat. Chapter 121 ? par 1719-1720], INDIANA [Stat. Section 23-2-2.7], IOWA [Code Sections 523H.1-523H.17]. MICHIGAN [Stat. Section 19.854(27)], MINNESOTA [Stat. Section 80C.14], MISSISSIPPI [Code Section 75-24-51], MISSOURI [Stat. Section 407.400], NEBRASKA [Rev. Stat. Section 87-401], NEW JERSEY [Stat. Section 56:10-1], SOUTH DAKOTA [Codified Laws Section 37-5A-51], VIRGINIA [Code 13.1-557-574-13.1-564], WASHINGTON [Code Section 19.100.180], WISCONSIN [Stat. Section 135.03]. These and other states may have court decisions which may supersede the franchise agreement in your relationship with the franchisor including the areas of termination and renewal of your franchise.

18. PUBLIC FIGURES:

Brooke does not use any public figure to promote its franchise.

19. EARNINGS CLAIMS:

Brooke does not furnish or authorize its salespersons to furnish any oral or written information concerning the actual or potential sales, costs, income, or profits of a Brooke Financial Services agency. Actual results vary from unit to unit and Brooke cannot estimate the results of any particular franchise.

20. LIST OF OUTLETS:

Franchised Agency Status Summary
for Years 1999/1998/1997

State	Transfers	Canceled or Terminated	Reacquired by Franchisor	Ceased doing Business	Total (note #2)	Franchisees Operating at Year End
Arkansas	0/0/0	0/0/0	0/0/0	0/0/0	0/0/0	0/0/0
Colorado	0/0/0	0/0/0	0/0/0	0/0/0	0/0/0	4/0/0
Kansas	0/3/0	3/3/3	0/0/0	0/0/0	2/6/3	50/51/44
Missouri	0/0/0	1/0/1	0/1/0	0/0/0	1/0/2	15/8/1
Nebraska	0/0/1	0/1/1	1/0/0	0/0/0	1/1/1	6/6/4
Oklahoma	0/0/0	0/0/0	0/0/0	0/0/0	0/0/0	4/0/0
Tennessee	0/0/0	0/0/0	0/0/0	0/0/0	0/0/0	0/0/0
Texas	0/0/0	0/0/0	0/0/0	0/0/0	0/0/0	0/0/0
Total	0/3/1	4/4/5	1/1/0	0/0/0	4/7/6	79/65/49

Note 1: All numbers are as of December 31 for each year.

Note 2: The numbers in the "Total" column may exceed the number of agencies affected because several events may have affected the same store. For example, the same agency may have terminated their franchise agreement and been reacquired by the Franchisor.

Projected Openings
as of December 31, 1999

State	Franchise Agr. Signed but agency not opened	Projected New Franchises next year	Projected New Company Owned Agencies next year
Arkansas	0	4	0
Colorado	0	4	0
Kansas	0	4	0
Missouri	0	4	0
Nebraska	0	4	0
Oklahoma	0	4	0
Tennessee	0	2	0
Texas	0	4	0
Totals	0	30	0

Status of Company Owned Agencies for Years 1999/1998/1997

State	Agencies Closed During Year	Agencies Opened During Year	Total Agencies Operating at Year End
Arkansas	0/0/0	0/0/0	0/0/0
Colorado	0/0/0	0/0/0	0/0/0
Kansas	0/0/0	0/0/0	0/1/1
Missouri	0/0/0	0/0/0	0/0/0
Nebraska	0/0/0	0/0/0	0/0/0
Oklahoma	0/0/0	0/0/0	0/0/0
Tennessee	0/0/0	0/0/0	0/0/0
Texas	0/0/0	0/0/0	0/0/0
Totals	0/0/0	0/0/0	0/1/1

Names of All Franchise Agents, Addresses and Telephone Numbers of All of Their Outlets

Business Name	Primary Contact	Address	City, State, Zip	Telephone Number
Ross Olson Ins. Inc. dba/Brooke Financial Services	Dane Devlin and Ross Olson	1409 Lincoln P.O. Box 657	Concordia, Ks 66901-0657	785-243-3182
Ashton Ins dba Brooke Financial Services	Craig Ashton	2205 Main Street P.O. Box 69	Belleville, Ks 66935-0069	785-527-5951
Sunflower Ins Services Inc.	Galen Haas	103 W Parallel P.O. Box 100	Clifton, Ks 66937	785-455-3463
Palco Ins Services	Leo VonFeldt	402 Main Drawer 9	Palco, Ks 67657	785-737-2325
SBB Inc dba Brooke Financial Services	Brett Biggs	110 W State P.O. Box 386	Phillipsburg,Ks 67661-0386	785-543-5254
Alden State Agency	Charles P. Rowland	201 N Pioneer P.O. Box 185	Alden, Ks 67512	785-534-2135
Kent Lambert Inc dba Brooke Financial Services	Kent Lambert	2310 Planet	Salina, Ks 67401	785-825-2112
Lenora Ins Agency Inc	Bradley A. Danielson	105 S. Main P.O. Box 128	Lenora, Ks 67645	785-567-4286
Citizens Ins Agency of Hiawatha Inc dba Brooke Financial Services	Cathy Henson	610 Oregon P.O. Box 360	Hiawatha, Ks 66434	785-742-2102
First National Ins Agency	Philip H. Gosling	200 Stahl Ave P.O. Box 37	Goff, Ks 66428	785-939-2150

Business Name	Primary Contact	Address	City, State, Zip	Telephone Number
First Insurance Inc	John R. Ballhorst	133 S Main P.O. Box 346	Smith Center, Ks 66967	785-282-6641
First National Insurance Agency	J.P. Kennedy	124 N Kansas P.O. Box 186	Frankfort, Ks 66427	785-292-4433
Suburban West Insurance Agency	George Hubbard	701 N Goddard Rd Ste D P.O. Box 34	Goddard, Ks 67052	316-794-2511
The People's State Bank	John W Powell	304 Rawlins Avenue P.O. Box 106	McDonald, Ks 67745	785-538-2233
The Sylvan Agency Inc	Robert E Sorem	102 N Main P.O. Box 338	Sylvan Grove, Ks 67481	785-526-7155
Hamilton Ins Agency	Linda Snyder	32 E Main P.O. Box 127	Hamilton, Ks 66853	316-678-3417
Northeast Kansas Insurance Agency	Rosalind Jackson	520 Main Street P.O. Box 328	Nortonville, Ks 66060	785-886-2121
Donald Robertson dba Brooke Financial Services	Donald Robertson	502 N 7th Street P.O. Box 833	Garden City, Ks 67846	316-275-7134
GI Agency Inc dba Brooke Financial Services	Dave Keeling	3022 Old Potash Hwy P.O. Box 4909	Grand Island, Ne 68802-0409	308-382-8400
Citizens State Bank dba T.A. Dudley Ins Agency	Neal R. Gillispie	600 South Main P.O. Box 728	Hugoton, Ks 67951	316-544-4314
Heinze & Associates Insurance Inc	Gregory Heinze	102 Main P.O. Box 278	Luray, Ks 67649-0278	785-698-2272
Harkness Ins Inc	Keith L Harkness	119 B S Penn Ave P.O. Box 547	Ness City, Ks 67560	785-798-2245
ASB Insurance Services Inc	Mick Haugen	511 N Andover Rd P.O. Box 278	Andover, Ks 67002	316-733-0819
Bank of Whitewater Insurance Agency Inc	Donald Patry	126 S Main P.O. Box 69	Whitewater, Ks 67154	316-799-2137
Brooke Financial Services	George Anshutz	138 W Oak P.O. Box 7	Harveyville, Ks 66431	785-589-2503
Sherri Linton dba Brooke Financial Services	Sherri Linton	120 N Mill P.O. Box 422	Beloit, Ks 67420-3235	785-738-5128
Fairview Insurance Agency	Gregory Jackson	412 W Commercial P.O. Box 8	Fairview, Ks 66425	785-467-3560
Cushing Ins Agency Inc	Alan Feist	800 Morgan P.O. Box 186	Downs, Ks 67437	785-454-3315
Daniels L Heinze Jr dba Brooke Financial Services	Dan Heinze Jr	200 W Douglas Ste 101 P.O. Box 87	Wichita, Ks 67201	316-744-7815
Marshall County Ins Agency	Edwin Nutt	722 Main P.O. Box 49	Beattie, Ks 66406	785-353-2298
First Agency Inc	Lloyd Culbertson	225 State Street P.O. Box 627	Phillipsburg, Ks 67661	785-543-6511

Business Name	Primary Contact	Address	City, State, Zip	Telephone Number
Home Insurance Agency	Leroy Deines	201 E Main P.O. Box 383	Norton, Ks 67654	785-877-3313
Brooke Financial Services	Jim Steider	211 N Burlington P.O. Box 1065	Hastings, Ne 68902	402-463-3121
People's Ins Agency	Linda Crowe	101 East Main P.O. Box 727	Coldwater, Ks 67029	316-582-2166
Hamm & Associates dba Brooke Financial Services	Bill Hamm	423 SE 10th P.O. Box 627	Newton, Ks 67114	316-283-5870
Brooke Financial Services	Jim Steider	246 S Columbia P.O. Box 96	Seward, Ne 68434	402-643-2909
Freeman Jones Agency dba Brooke Financial Services	Freeman Jones	412 N Washington P.O. Box 1214	Liberal, Ks 67905	316-626-7468
Dwight Ins Agency	Jan Oleen	160 Main P.O. Box 8	Dwight, Ks 66849	785-482-3229
Hier Insurance Services	Nancy L Hier	301 Main P.O. Box 250	Maple Hill, Ks 66507	785-256-4600
Young, Inc.	David Young	102 N Highland P.O. Box 494	Conway Springs, Ks 67031	316-456-2346
Brooke Financial Services	Richard Connally	302 N Douglas P.O. Box 105	Ellsworth, Ks 67439-0105	785-472-3911
Newhouse & Company dba Brooke Financial Services	Joe Newhouse	11414 W Center Rd Ste 341	Omaha, Ne 68144	402-330-5141
Arensberg Insurance dba Brooke Financial Services	Tom Arensberg	600 Lawrence Ave	Lawrence, Ks 66049	785-865-0077
Brooke Financial Services	James Vader	10895 Grandview Dr Bldg 24 Ste 250	Overland Park, Ks 66210	913-661-0123
Brooke Financial Services	Steve Frazier	1014 Poyntz Ste B	Manhattan, Ks 66502	785-776-2211
Brooke Financial Services	Geoff Gobble	10895 Grandview Dr Bldg 24 Ste 250	Overland Park,Ks 66210	913-661-0123
Brooke Financial Services	Jason Winter	2025 N Commerical	Harrisonville, Mo 64701	816-380-5222
Brooke Financial Services	Clarence A Martin and John J Coyne	6900 Mexico Road	St Peters, Mo 63376	314-970-2696
Brooke Financial Services	Wayne Kellner	100 Center Drive P.O. Box 44	Silver Lake, Ks 66539	785-582-5430
Brooke Financial Services	Charles R Bowman	330 Broadway P.O. Box 369	Fullerton, Ne 68638	308-536-2113
Brooke Financial Services	Andrew Arensberg	10895 Grandview Dr Bldg 24 Ste 250	Overland Park, Ks 66210	913-661-0123
Brooke Financial Services	Scott Uehling	401 W 1st	Ogallala, Ne 69153	308-284-3755
Brooke Financial Services	Don Lowry	2421 10th Street PO Box 889	Great Bend, Ks 67530-0889	316-792-3611
Brooke Financial Services	Jack Cassell	800 E 1st Ste 200	Wichita, Ks 67202	316-269-1001
Brooke Financial Services	Robert Culver	504 ½ N Ash PO Box 628	Cimarron, Ks 67835	316-855-2422

Business Name	Primary Contact	Address	City, State, Zip	Telephone Number
Brooke Financial Services	Elaine Downing	10895 Grandview Dr Bldg 24 Ste 250	Overland Park, Ks 66210	913-661-0123
Brooke Financial Services	Ken Viers	10895 Grandview Dr Bldg 24 Ste 250	Overland Park, Ks 66210	913-661-0123
Brooke Financial Services	Don Howell	114 W 8th Street P.O. Box 368 104 W Walnut P.O. Box 128	Ashland, Ks 67831 Protection, Ks 67127	316-635-2297 316-622-4501
Brooke Financial Services	John Haupt	P.O. Box 587	Troy, Ks 66087	785-985-2131
Brooke Financial Services	Brad Noll	224 M ain P.O. Box 12	Cheney, Ks 67025	316-540-0123
Brooke Financial Services	Judy Anweiler	215 W 4th P.O. Box 7	Holton, Ks 66436	785-364-3366
Brooke Financial Services	Bill Hudson, Jr	200 W Douglas Ste 101 P.O. Box 87	Wichita, Ks 67201	316-733-1081
Brooke Financial Services	Karen Johnson	119 N Main P.O. Box 511	Fayette, Mo 65248	660-248-3322
Brooke Financial Services	Don Griggs (Hugo) Krystal Weeks (Idabel)	P.O. Box 609 14 N Central	Hugo, Ok 74743 Idabel, Ok 74745	580-326-3354 580-286-3348
Brooke Financial Services	Tyler Kemp	907 N Main P.O. Box 2177	Noble, Ok 73068	405-872-3636
Brooke Financial Services	Russell French	1111 Mansion Mall Drive P.O. Box 249	Poplar Bluff, Mo 63901	573-686-5001
Brooke Financial Services	Seann Howe	103 Walnut P.O. Box 50	Greenville, Mo 63944	573-224-3344
Brooke Financial Services	Bruce Jordan	P.O. Box 1125	McAlester, Ok 74502	918-423-4045
Brooke Financial Services	Karen Dunn	510 S Park Dr Ste B	Broken Bow, Ok 74728	5805849304
Brooke Financial Services	Anthony Taylor	564 US Highway 60 E P.O. Box 454	Republic, Mo 65738	417-732-2345
Brooke Financial Services	Larry Bilke	1049 Cherokee Street P.O. Box 190	Seneca, Mo 64865	417-776-8707
Brooke Financial Services	Donald Newton	124 E Center P.O. Box 945	Sikeston, Mo 63801	573-472-1111
Brooke Financial Services	Stephen Twiss	517 SE 2nd Street P.O. Box 1860	Lee's Summit, Mo 64063	8165259848
Brooke Financial Services	Warren Dale	11115 W Highway 24 Ste 2D-1 P.O. Box 808	Divide, Co 80814	719-687-3500
Brooke Financial Services	Christopher Prall	2575 Youngfield St Unit E	Golden, Co 80401-1541	303-237-1220
Brooke Financial Services	Harold Krabbe	1100 E Main P.O. Box 88	Montrose, Co 81402	970-249-3286
Brooke Financial Services	K.L. Pattison	10559 W 44th Avenue	Wheatridge, Co 8003	303-425-3210
Brooke Financial Services	Kent Lambert	116 W 2nd Street P.O. Box 192	Minneapolis, Ks 67467	785-392-3073
Brooke Financial Services	Tom Fellers	203 N Fowler P.O. Box M	Meade, Ks 67864	316-873-2099

Who has had an Outlet Terminated, Canceled, Not Renewed or Otherwise
Left the System during 1999

Name	Address	City &State, Zip	Telephone Number
Insurance Office of America, Inc. Ins Services dba/Brooke Financial Svcs	Randy Dodge	10895 Grandview Dr Bldg 24 Ste 250 Overland Park, Ks 66210	913-661-0123
Palmer Ins Agency	Donald K. Heitman	104 E 2nd St P.O. Box 90 Palmer, Ks 66962	785-692-4511
Hardtner Insurance Inc	Michael Platt	515 N Main P.O. Box 468 Kiowa, Ks 67070	316-825-4035
Security Ins Services	Wayne Newell	1741 N Washington P.O. Box 119 Auburn, Ks 66402	785-256-2000

21. FINANCIAL STATEMENTS:

See Exhibit A for Financial Statements.

22. CONTRACTS:

See Exhibits B through N for a copy of those contracts or agreements typically required by Brooke.

23. RECEIPT:

THIS OFFERING CIRCULAR SUMMARIZES PROVISIONS OF THE FRANCHISE AGREEMENT AND OTHER INFORMATION IN PLAIN LANGUAGE. READ THIS OFFERING CIRCULAR AND ALL AGREEMENTS CAREFULLY.

IF BROOKE OFFERS YOU A FRANCHISE, BROOKE MUST PROVIDE THIS OFFERING CIRCULAR TO YOU BY THE EARLIEST OF:

(1) THE FIRST PERSONAL MEETING TO DISCUSS OUR FRANCHISE; OR

(2) TEN BUSINESS DAYS BEFORE SIGNING OF A BINDING AGREEMENT; OR

(3) TEN BUSINESS DAYS BEFORE ANY PAYMENT TO BROOKE.

YOU MUST ALSO RECEIVE A FRANCHISE AGREEMENT CONTAINING ALL MATERIAL TERMS AT LEAST FIVE BUSINESS DAYS BEFORE YOU SIGN ANY FRANCHISE AGREEMENT.

IF BROOKE DOES NOT DELIVER THIS OFFERING CIRCULAR ON TIME OR IF IT CONTAINS A FALSE OR MISLEADING STATEMENT, OR A MATERIAL OMISSION, A VIOLATION OF FEDERAL AND STATE LAW MAY HAVE OCCURRED AND SHOULD BE REPORTED TO THE FEDERAL TRADE COMMISSION, WASHINGTON, D.C. 20580 AND THE APPROPRIATE STATE AGENCY LISTED IN EXHIBIT U.

I have received a Franchise Offering Circular dated March 27, 2000. This offering circular included the following exhibits:

A.   Financial Statements
B.   Franchise Agreement
C.   Franchise Agreement Addendum for 2000 Bonus Plan
D.   Franchise Agreement Addendum to Purchase Service Center Option
E.   Franchise Agreement Addendum to Purchase Standard Option
F.   Franchise Agreement Addendum Regarding Lender Protection
G.   Office Space Agreement
H.   Franchise Agent Authorization for Pre-Authorized Collection
I.   Agreement For Sale of Insurance Agency Assets from Brooke to Franchise Agent
    a)   Bill of Sale
    b)   Listing of Office Equipment and Other Personal Property
    c)   Listing of Obligations Assumed by Purchaser
J.   Assignment of Interest in Purchase Agreement from Brooke to Franchise Agent
K.   Agreement For Purchase of Insurance Agency Assets
    a)   Bill of Sale
    b)   Transfer Letter
    c)   Listing of Office Equipment and Other Personal Property
    d)   Affidavit
    e)   Listing of Agreements
    f)   Listing of Trade Names, Etc.
    g)   Listing of Obligations Assumed by Purchaser
    h)   Confidentiality Agreement
    i)   Seller Survey
L.   Agency Finder Agreement
M.   Agreement for Advancement of Loan
    a)   Promissory Note Form
    b)   Security Agreement Form
    c)   Security Agreement Addendum
    d)   UCC-1 Financing Statement Form
    e)   Guaranty Form
    f)   Borrower's Attorney Opinion Form
    g)   Borrower's Affidavit Regarding Financial Status And Other Material Facts
    h)   Borrower's Authorization to Release Information
    i)   Agent Agreement Addendum Regarding Lender Protection
    j)   Borrower's Settlement Statement Form
    k)   Borrower's Signature Acknowledgement
N.   Borrower Authorization for Pre-Authorized Collection
O.   Franchise Agent Application
P.   Credit Application
Q.   Licening Application
R.   E&O Application/Questionnaire
S.   Insurance Company Notification Letter
T.   Uniform Consent to Service of Process
U.   State Administrators

_____   _____
Date   Franchise agent

FRANCHISE AGENT APPLICATION TO BROOKE CORPORATION

(Use Attachments If Required To Fully Respond)

Agency/Corporation Name _____

Agency/Corporation Street Address _____

GENERAL INFORMATION

Mailing Address _____

Agency Phone _____   Agency Fax _____

Internet E-Mail Address _____   Tax I.D. # _____

Corporation ☐   Partnership ☐   Sole Proprietor ☐   Proposed Effective Date _____

PERSONNEL

Officers, Partners, or Owners	DOB	Social Security #	Home Address

Has Agency or any officers, partners or owners of Agency declared bankruptcy or been convicted of a felony? _____   If yes, explain,
_____

List of Employees
(excluding Officers, Partners, Owners)   Job Description

OTHER

E&O Carrier _____ Policy Number _____ Limits _____
Describe Any Losses _____
_____

Agency License # _____   Licensed in which State(s) _____

Trade References _____   _____
_____

PREMIUM & LOSS HISTORY

Company Name (Five Largest by Annual Premiums)	Annual Premium Volume	1st Prior Year Loss Ratio	2nd Prior Year Loss Ratio	3rd Prior Year Loss Ratio	Annual Personal Premium	Annual Commercial Premium

SIGNATURES - I certify that I have received and read the Franchise Disclosure and related exhibits. I further certify that everything I have stated in this application and on any attachments is correct. You may keep this application whether or not it is approved. Permission is granted Brooke Corporation to investigate my business history, employment history, credit history, education and background, and solicit statements or information from any person or companies.

_____   _____   _____   _____
Applicant   Date   Applicant   Date

SUBAGENT APPLICATION TO FRANCHISE AGENT

(Use Attachments If Required To Fully Respond)

Subagent/Corporation Name _____

Subagency/Corporation Street Address _____

GENERAL INFORMATION

Mailing Address _____

Agency Phone _____   Agency Fax _____

Internet E-Mail Address _____   Tax I.D. # _____

Corporation ☐   Partnership ☐   Sole Proprietor ☐   Proposed Effective Date _____

PERSONNEL

Officers, Partners, or Owners   DOB   Social Security #   Home Address

_____   _____   _____   _____

_____   _____   _____   _____

_____   _____   _____   _____

Has Agency or any officers, partners or owners of Agency declared bankruptcy or been convicted of a felony? _____ If yes, explain, _____

List of Employees
(excluding Officers, Partners, Owners)   Job Description

_____   _____

_____   _____

_____   _____

OTHER

E&O Carrier _____ Policy Number _____ Limits _____
Describe Any Losses _____

_____

Agency License # _____ Licensed in which State(s) _____

Trade References _____   _____

_____   _____

PREMIUM & LOSS HISTORY

Company Name (Five Largest by Annual Premiums)	Annual Premium Volume	1st Prior Year Loss Ratio	2nd Prior Year Loss Ratio	3rd Prior Year Loss Ratio	Annual Personal Premium	Annual Commercial Premium

SIGNATURES - I certify that I have received and read Brooke Corporation's Franchise Disclosure and related exhibits. I understand that I was given the Franchise Disclosure for informational purposes and that it gives me no rights or remedies against Brooke Corporation. I further certify that everything I have stated in this application and on any attachments is correct. Brooke Corporation and its agents may keep this application whether or not it is approved. Permission is granted Brooke Corporation and its agents to investigate my business history, employment history, credit history, education and background, and solicit statements or information from any person or companies.

_____   _____   _____   _____
Applicant   Date   Applicant   Date

BROKER AGENT APPLICATION TO THE AMERICAN AGENCY, INC.

(Use Attachments If Required To Fully Respond)

Broker/Corporation Name _____

Broker/Corporation Street Address _____

GENERAL INFORMATION (Not Required if Brooke Agent)

Mailing Address _____

Agency Phone _____ Agency Fax _____

Internet E-Mail Address _____ Tax I.D. # _____

Corporation ☐   Partnership ☐   Sole Proprietor ☐   Proposed Effective Date _____

PERSONNEL (Not Required if Brooke Agent)

Officers, Partners, or Owners	DOB	Social Security #	Home Address

Has Agency or any officers, partners or owners of Agency declared bankruptcy or been convicted of a felony? _____ If yes, explain, _____

List of Employees
(excluding Officers, Partners, Owners)   Job Description

OTHER (Not Required if Brooke Agent)

E&O Carrier _____ Policy Number _____ Limits _____
Describe Any Losses _____

Agency License # _____ Licensed in which State(s) _____

Trade References _____

PREMIUM & LOSS HISTORY

Company Name	Annual Premium Volume	1st Prior Year Loss Ratio	2nd Prior Year Loss Ratio	3rd Prior Year Loss Ratio

Number of accounts currently written _____

Premium size of typical account $ _____

List the size of the five largest accounts $ _____

SIGNATURES - Permission is granted The American Agency, Inc., to investigate my business history, employment history, credit history, education and background, and solicit statements or information from any person or companies. I certify that everything I have stated in this application is correct. PLEASE COMPLETE THE REVERSE SIDE of this page because it is an important part of this application.

Applicant Signature _____   Date _____

PROGRAM - Fully describe proposed insurance program or other brokerage business (class of business, typical risk, individual or group program, history and nature of class of business relationship, association sponsorships, existing or new program, potential of program, coverage offered, etc)

MARKETING - Fully describe marketing plans (who will produce, brokers role in underwriting/servicing, what states market in, company contracts in place and needed, commission rates, etc)

EXPERIENCE - Fully describe brokers qualifications for administration of the proposed programs or other brokerage business:

LICENSING APPLICATION
(Use Attachments If Required To Fully Respond)

Franchise Agent # _____

Licensee Name _____

GENERAL INFORMATION

Home Address _____

Home Phone # _____

Social Security # _____

Internet Address _____

PERSONAL INFORMATION

Martial Status _____   Date of Birth _____

Previous Employer: Company Name _____

Company Address _____

Describe Insurance and Securities work experience: _____

_____

Have you been censured or any other way disciplined by any State Insurance Department or Security Regulator? If yes, provide explanation:

_____

Have you been involved in any litigation of an agent's E&O related incident? If yes, provide full explanation:

_____

Have you been declared bankrupt in the last 10 years? If yes, where and when: _____

_____

Have you ever been convicted of a felony? If yes, give particulars: _____

_____

LICENSING

Insurance License # _____

Licensed by which state(s)? _____

Licensed in what lines? _____

Life & Health ☐   Property & Allied Lines ☐   Casualty & Allied Lines ☐   Title ☐   Variable Contracts ☐   Crop ☐   Securities ☐

Please Attach Copy of All Licenses

SIGNATURES - I certify that everything I have stated in this application and on any attachments is correct. You may keep this application whether or not it is approved. Permission is granted Brooke Corporation to investigate my business history, employment history, credit history, education and background, and solicit statements or information from any person or companies.

_____   _____
Licensee Signature   Date

SELLER SURVEY

(Use Attachments If Required To Fully Respond)

Agency/Corporation Name

Agency/Corporation Street Address

GENERAL INFORMATION
Mailing Address

Agency Phone _____ Agency Fax _____

Internet E-Mail Address _____ Tax I.D. # _____

Corporation ☐   Partnership ☐   Sole Proprietor ☐   Proposed Effective Date _____

COMMISSION TOTALS
Most Recent 12 Mo. _____ Previous 12 Mo. _____ Projected Next 12 Mo. _____

COMMISSIONS by CATEGORY for most recent 12 months

P&C _____ Direct Billed

L&H _____ Agent Billed _____

Commercial Lines _____ Standard Carrier

Personal Lines _____ E&S, Brokered & Non-Standard Carrier _____

Contingency _____ Consulting Policy Fees _____

COMMISSIONS by ACCOUNT SIZE for most recent 12 Months
Comm on Accts > $2,500 in Annual Comm _____ Comm on Accts > $5,000 in Annual Comm _____

PERSONNEL
List Producers and Length of Time with Agency

List Staff (other than producers) and Length of Time with Agency

Written Producer/Employment Agreements with Non-Solicitation Covenants? If no, then explain

Producer Ownership or Vesting? If yes, then explain.

OTHER
E&O Carrier _____ Limits _____

Describe Any Losses

Agency License # _____ Licensed in which State(s) _____

PREMIUM & LOSS HISTORY from company production reports

Company Name (Five Largest by Annual Premiums)	Annual Premium Volume	1st Prior Year Loss Ratio	2nd Prior Year Loss Ratio	3rd Prior Year Loss Ratio

Companies (not listed above) with > $50,000 in Annual Premiums

Signature _____ Date _____

CREDIT APPLICATION TO BROOKE CREDIT CORPORATION
(Use Attachments To Provide Requested Information)

Borrower/Corporation Name _____

Borrower/Corporation Street Address _____

GENERAL INFORMATION

Mailing Address _____

Agency Phone _____   Agency Fax _____

Internet E-Mail Address _____   Tax I.D. # _____

Corporation ☐   Partnership ☐   Sole Proprietor ☐   Requested Loan Amount _____

FINANCIAL OR NET WORTH INFORMATION

Provide Agency's financial statements (corporate or partnership).

Provide agency owner's financial statements (owning more than 25%).

Provide agency income tax returns or income statements for last three years.

Provide agency owner's income tax returns or income statements for last three years.

AGENCY COLLATERAL

Describe any assets other than agency assets offered as collateral.

Are any agency assets encumbered or secured by lender? If yes, then explain.

Are any agency producers vested in ownership of a portion of agency assets? If yes, then explain.

DOWN PAYMENT

If down payment is cash payment, then identify the source of cash. If cash down payment is borrowed, then explain repayment terms and collateral requirements.

If down payment in form of additional collateral, then explain.

MANAGEMENT AND OWNERSHIP

Provide copy of articles of incorporation or partnership.

Identify each agency owner and percentage of agency ownership and provide biographical information.

Identify employees responsible for agency management and provide biographical information.

PLANS

Provide cash flow projections.

Briefly describe business and marketing plans.

Describe plans for owner's compensation

OTHER

Describe current and proposed life insurance on agency owners.

List credit or bank references (names, addresses and phone numbers)

List trade references (names, addresses and phone numbers)

Attach copy of agency purchase agreement or provide explanation of loan purpose.

SIGNATURES: I certify that everything I have stated in this application and on any attachments is correct. I understand that Brooke Credit Corporation will keep this application and all attachments whether or not it is approved. Brooke Credit Corporation is authorized to check my personal credit history, employment history, education and background. Brooke Credit Corporation is also authorized to check the agency's credit history, business history and solicit statements or information from any person or companies.

Date: _____   Applicant: _____